THE JOURNALS OF
A WHITE SEA WOLF

Mariusz Wilk

THE JOURNALS OF
A WHITE SEA WOLF

Translated from the Polish by
Danusia Stok
Photographs by Tomasz Kizny

THE HARVILL PRESS
LONDON

First published as *Wilczy Notes*
By słowo/obraz terytoria in 1998

2 4 6 8 10 9 7 5 3 1

Copyright © Mariusz Wilk, 1998 and © słowo/obraz terytoria, 1998
English translation copyright © Danusia Stok, 2003

Maps drawn by Reginald Piggott

Mariusz Wilk has asserted his right under the Copyright, Designs
and Patents Act 1988 to be identified as the author of this work

First published in Great Britain in 2003 by
The Harvill Press
Random House, 20 Vauxhall Bridge Road,
London SW1V 2SA

Random House Australia (Pty) Limited
20 Alfred Street, Milsons Point, Sydney,
New South Wales 2061, Australia

Random House New Zealand Limited
18 Poland Road, Glenfield,
Auckland 10, New Zealand

Random House South Africa (Pty) Limited
Endulini, 5A Jubilee Road, Parktown 2193, South Africa

The Random House Group Limited Reg. No. 954009
www.randomhouse.co.uk

A CIP catalogue record for this book
is available from the British Library

This translation is supported by the
Foundation for International Initiatives, Poland

ISBN 1 84343047 9

Papers used by Random House are natural,
recyclable products made from wood grown in sustainable forests;
the manufacturing processes conform to the environmental
regulations of the country of origin

Designed and typeset in Walbaum by Palimpsest Book Production Ltd

Printed and bound in Great Britain
by Biddles Ltd, Guildford & King's Lynn

To Veronica

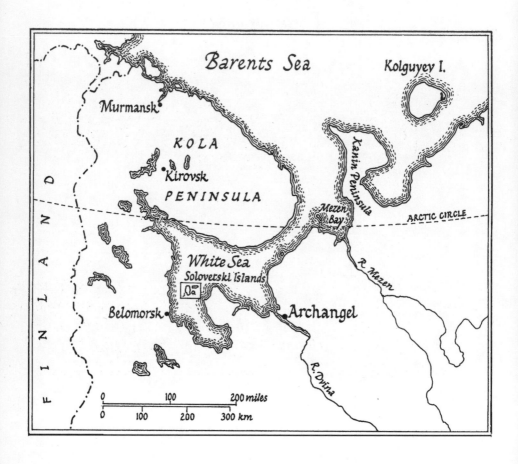

Barents Sea

Kolguyev I.

Murmansk

KOLA

Kirovsk

PENINSULA

Kanin Peninsula

Mezen
Bay

ARCTIC CIRCLE

R. Mezen

White Sea

Solovetski Islands

Belomorsk

Archangel

FINLAND

R. Dvina

0   100   200 miles

0   100   200   300 km

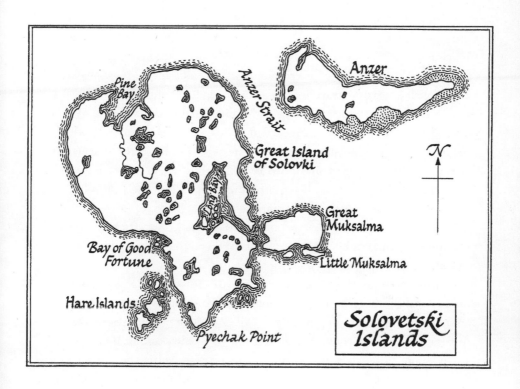

Pine Bay

Anzer

Anzer Strait

Great Island
of Solovki

Long Bay

Great
Muksalma

Little Muksalma

Bay of Good
Fortune

Hare Islands

Pyechak Point

N

Solovetski
Islands

Translator's Note

The original Polish title, *Wilczy Notes* – A Wolf's Notebook – is a play on words. The author's name, Wilk, literally translated, means Wolf, a name fitting for a man who, like a wolf, has made the desolate Far North his habitat.

Mariusz Wilk, accredited correspondent in Russia for *Kultura*, a Paris-based Polish magazine, travelled the country widely before settling on the Solovetsky archipelago, the group of islands in the White Sea. Wilk's experience and reflections are recorded in his White Sea Journals, which are not so much a travelogue as an attempt to touch on the essence of Russia – not the Russia with an historical beginning and a chronology of events, but of Holy Russia, the soul of the land and of the peasantry.

The text has been difficult to translate not least because the Polish language is so close to the Russian. So much so that many Russian words, with merely a small modification, practically read like Polish words, while others have become accepted, if not integrated, in the Polish language. The author has played on this aspect by both "Russianizing" some words and including others in the original Russian. Where he has kept the Russian word, he has done so for good reason. The original word carries within it a wealth of connotations and images, which cannot be rendered by any single English equivalent. Most of these words the author has explained in the copious Glossary, those he has omitted (to a large extent because they are comprehensible to the Polish reader), I have briefly explained either in a footnote or within square brackets. I have also left the original Russian names of certain species of flora and fauna, which are specific to the North Russian climate and to the tundra. The list of mushrooms is such an example. (Mushrooms – in their various forms - are a staple of the Russian diet while the English have no names for them.)

I would very much like to thank Robert Chandler for his guidance over the many Russian words and place names.

D.S.

Russia cannot be embraced by reason
Nor measured on our scale.
Russia is a different dimension
Russia needs to be experienced.
(Parody of Tyutchev)

NOTES FROM SOLOVKY
(1996–1998)

Take some small rectangular pieces of iron, perforated, so that threaded on string, they can easily be submerged and pulled out. If you haven't got any to hand, take some old locks, keys, chains. You can use uncorroded iron, rust-free, although some people prefer, on the contrary, rusty scrap-metal, or even waste from under the blacksmith's hammer. Place the iron and some coarsely ground marble galls in a vessel, where a so-called "ink nest" will form, which you will be able to use for eight to ten years. Marble galls are knars found on oak trees and are made by insects. Choose them carefully as some can be hard, green and perforated, pale. Crush them, cover them with water and kvass (or cabbage soup made from pickled cabbage) and set aside in a dark place or immediately lower the iron into the solution. Then add a decoction of oak, alder or ash bark to the nest. Strip the bark in spring, as soon as it is seeped with juice, dry it — dry bark yields more black pigment. Boil it in a copper vessel until the water evaporates. Cover it with more of the liquid and keep on a low heat until it thickens. Pass it through a riddle and wring out. Then pass it through a sieve and wring out. Then pass it through cloth and wring out again. Pour it into the nest. In order to obtain iron salts, add honey, barley beer, or wine, preferably red. Stand the vessel containing the black *chernilo* in a dark place and stir several times a day. The process is long: from twelve to forty days. To ease stirring, add a decoction of hops, thus also preventing mould from forming. If the *chernilo* permeates the paper, add some cherry glue so as to make it harder

and to enable it to come off the pen more easily, add some
cloves and ginger . . .

This recipe for *chernilo* (ink) is taken from a 16th-century recipe book
from Solovky. Scribes from Eastern monasteries were not allowed to
take pen in hand unless they had prepared the *chernilo* themselves.

I

He who discovers Russia from books cannot understand it.
Within it are concealed oddities, which I would willingly
study in the provinces . . . if only I spoke the language.

Joseph de Maistre

1

The reader may ask why I chose Solovky. What made me settle on
the Islands, as if on a watchtower, and observe Russia and the world
from here? I'll try to answer, although it is difficult to exhaust the
subject in a few chapters: the most you can do is give an "outline",
as they used to say. Because Solovky reminds you of a precious stone:
however long you look at it, it keeps on changing . . . breaking up
the light . . . playing with the way it is cut. You only have to alter
the story a little, change the accents, rearrange the plots, and the
whole immediately takes on different meanings – sparkles differently.
So it is impossible to expand on the reasons, to pick out single threads
from the structure, to analyse and discuss them: you have to look at
them as a whole, one through the other. In other words, you have to
put aside linear principles of language and look at the subject from
a distance. Then move yourself, step by step, and change the angle
from which you look.

2

Seven years ago, I arrived in Moscow as a correspondent for one of the Polish newspapers. During the March referendum of the same year, the nations that made up the territories of the Soviet Empire spoke out in favour of the Union. Half a year later, the Union ceased to exist. The twilight of the Soviets followed. I decided to stay: I wanted to see what would become of all this. I saw many new things, some incomprehensible, some irritating, but what annoyed me most was Tyutchev [the 19th-century lyric poet], whose words my Russian acquaintances used in order to silence my questions:

> *Umom Rossiyu ne ponyat'*
> *Arshinom obshchim ne izmerit':*
> *U ney osobennaya stat' —*
> *V Rossiyu mozhno tolko vyerit'.*[*]

In this quatrain I sensed the arrogance typical of most believers who patronisingly look down from the height of their community on to the quests and doubts of the individual. This quatrain, like a *koan*, took hold of me and inflamed me. Until I found a solution! For Tyutchev's last word — "to believe" — I substituted my own — "to experience". I had to experience Russia for myself.

3

From the very earliest times there have been two Russias, according to Rozanov: the Russia of visible appearances (in the original: *vidimost'*

---

[*]Russia cannot be embraced by reason / Nor measured on our scale / Russia is a different dimension / Russia needs to be believed.

— both visibility and appearance), that is, the Empire whose shape has been stamped in external forms and whose history has been written by events with a definite beginning and a clear end; and Holy Rus or Matushka,* with incomprehensible rules, unclear forms, undetermined tendencies — the Rus of living blood and unblemished faith. You can read Karamzin about the former, writes the author of *Fallen Leaves*, and hear about the latter in the *skit*s of the old faith. People in Moscow or St Petersburg talk loudly about the Empire, but Matushka is only whispered about in the depths of the country. Foreigners were rarely allowed into the depths of Russia, to wander at large. That is why the image of the Empire — that is, a Russia of visible appearances, to use Rozanov's words — prevailed in the accounts of travellers and in the despatches of correspondents and agents. Very few had any idea of Rus Matushka. In my opinion, the situation still remains to this day.

Because today, too, both Russias exist: both the Empire, on shaky legs, and Matushka, wallowing in the ditch. I sampled the former at press conferences and in the Caucasian wars, in diplomatic salons and at Moscow coup d'états, at receptions held by "new Russians" and in old Stalinists' dachas, at festivals, presentations and secret meetings; and the latter, at village revelries and in Siberian wildernesses, in Arkhangel mud and Ural *zona*s, at the tables of former *zeka*s and in the refectories of Orthodox monks, at weddings, wakes and secret-penitential rituals. I lived in *chuma*s** with nomads on the Yamal, in fishermen's huts on the White Sea, with shepherds in the Altay mountains, with huntsmen on the banks of the Yenisey, in the home of a history professor in Grozny, an Abkhazian minister in Sukhumi and the godfather of the mafia in Rostov-on-Don . . . I bought a house on a kolkhoz not far from the Kargopol *zona*s where Herling-Grudzinski had once been imprisioned, and I took part in the "show" at the

---

*Little Mother. *Tr*.
**Tents made of reindeer skins. *Tr*.

opening of the tax-free zone in Kaliningrad. I smoked marijuana with rock musicians from Leningrad and drank vodka with the heroes of Varlam Shalamov's tales from Kolyma. I saw drunken experts from Poland during the exhumation of the remains of Polish officers at Kharkov and listened to Russian *chastushka*s[*] sung by drunken Soviet officers at a reception held at the Polish consulate in St Petersburg on the anniversary of the Polish Constitution of 3 May. I'd meet up with the Georgian president Zvyad Gamsahurdya and General Dzhohar Dudayev, the leader of fighting Ichkyerya – both no longer alive. I talked to the Chechen warlord, Shamil Basayev, and his fighters, many of whom were *vor v zakone*.[**] I feasted with the Mayor of Petersburg, Anatoly Sobchak, with the Metropolitan of St Petersburg and Ladoga, His Holiness Yoann, and with the *bomzh*s from Petersburg. I heard many tell of their lives – pilgrims on their travels, *bich*s in the forest, rogues in *kabak*s, *muzhik*s on deep sea fishing boats, as well as the grandsons of Pasternak, Florensky, Shpet . . .

I drew from both Russias as from a bucket. But the picture refused to come together. Maybe there were too many threads, or the expanse I was exploring was too vast? The more I got to know it, the more I doubted that I would ever grasp it all. At each turning, a new perspective would open; at each meeting, a different point of view. Finally, as a vagrant, I understood the meaning of Eurasia, or "one sixth of the world". Yes, yes, as a "vagrant", because it is a matter of experiencing Russia, that is, recounting journeys and not collecting a tourist's impressions. And so I came across the Islands.

---

[*] Two- or four-line folk verse, usually humorous and topical. *Tr.*
[**] See Glossary.

On Solovky, you can see Russia like the sea in a drop of water. Because the Solovetsky Islands are, at once, the essence and the anticipation of Russia. For centuries, they have been the heart of the Orthodox Church and a powerful focus of Russian statehood in the North. Here, in the Solovetsky monastery, in its cells for monks and prisoners, the history of Russia has been written over hundreds of years: on the parchment of chronicles and pages of history, changing the face of the country and crushing the characters of those who thought differently, adapting plants to polar conditions and people to work in confinement. Here, new technologies were tested and new social utopias put into practice. The first hydraulic power station in Russia was built here and a monumental stone wall, thicker than the walls of the Kremlin in Moscow. It is no accident that before beginning his fundamental work, *The Course of Russian History*, about colonization – the driving force of Russian history – Vasyaley Kluchevsky first defended his thesis, *The Lives of Saints as an Historical Source*, in which he showed the importance of the Solovetsky monastery in the colonisation of north-eastern Rus. And it is here, in the *skit* on Anzer, that the schism of the Russian Orthodox Church, the event which Solzhenitsyn claims influenced the destiny of Russia more than the Bolshevik Revolution, had its beginnings. To this day, old Orthodox believers make a pilgrimage to Solovky as Muslims do to Mecca. Finally, it is here, in the dungeons of the monastery, that the oldest political prison in Rus was situated and then, after the Revolution, SLON (Solovetsky Lager Osobovo Naznachenia), the first labour camp in the Soviet Union, emerged – the testing ground for the GULAG. And even now, for many, the Islands remain a prison since the economic reforms of recent years have made it impossible for people to earn enough money to buy a ticket and escape.

On Solovky, both Russias would repeatedly meet; here, the Empire would sit together with Matushka at the same table or in the same cell. Here, tsars, princes, Muscovite boyars, Decembrists, castrates and merchants would come and stay. Here, writers, painters and usurpers, travellers, scholars and rogues would come and visit. And lastly, all sorts of rabble, scum and human dregs would be washed up from the furthest corners of the "one sixth of the world". Lomonosov, Maksimov, Nemirovich-Danchenko, Prishvin, Gorky, Kazakov and Kublanovsky wrote about Solovky. Vereshchagin, Borisov, Nesterov, Bazhenov, Krestovskaya, Petrov-Spiridonov and Chorny painted it. The great men of this world brought gifts to the Solovetsky monastery: Peter the Great founded the Orthodox church on Hare Islands, Solzhenitsyn donated dollars for a ship to transport pilgrims, and Gryebyenshchikov, the leader of the rock group Akvarium, donated an Orthodox icon, then himself converted to Buddhism. His Imperial Highness the Grand Duke Georgy Mikhailovich, Heir to the Imperial Crown of Russia, with his mother, Her Imperial Highness the Grand Duchess Maria Vladimirovna, and his grandmother, Her Imperial Highness the Grand Duchess-Widow, Leonida Georgieevna, the Minister of External Affairs of Russia, four ambassadors, two consuls, the commander of the Northern Fleet, several big shots from the arms trade, one metropolitan, one archbishop and a dozen Orthodox priests, a few television crews, including a French one, a few film units, including a Polish one, a few heads of the Russian mafia, a blues group from Odessa, a Krishna sect from Vologda, several descendants of Solovetsky *zeka*s from "Memorial", a hippy commune from Omsk, participants of the international jazz festival in Arkhangel, satanists from Kuibyshev, the community of the Virgin Mary from Kiev, a banker from Tel-Aviv, a photographer from the Polish newspaper *Polityka*, a priest-professor from KUL (Catholic University of Lublin), as well as thousands of pilgrims, nutters, neophytes and tourists, passed through Solovky last year.

6

The Solovetsky Islands are not very large, none being more than a day's journey on foot. It is as if they had been created for someone who didn't want to use any form of transport other than his own pair of legs. And just the right number of people live here for you to be able to meet them all over a couple of winters. It is an excellent place for the contemplation of nature, history, people, events. Here, your eyes can embrace processes which over there, in Russia, take place over vast expanses and are, therefore, difficult to grasp. On Solovky, you can see Russia in miniature, as if on the palm of your hand: there are local authorities and the Orthodox Church, culture in the museum, a small business and a local mafia; there is a hospital and a school of music, a bull farm and privately owned cattle, a forest industry and a small agar-agar factory; there is a militia and a detention cell; only the tribunal sits rarely, flying in from time to time. Solovky has its own newspaper, *Solovetsky Vestnik* [Solovetsky Messenger], whose editor is the great granddaughter of Eugeniusz Przegodzki, a Polish deportee to the Urals. It has a local radio station, which is run by an old pal of Vladimir Vysotsky,* as well as three hotels, a youth club and a bar with a disco every Saturday. Only public services are vanishing. Poaching, on the other hand, has made good progress. Finally, passion between the two sexes boils over, political squabbles carry on in the *banya*, while legendary Russian drunkenness has taken on apocalyptic dimensions. So, you need only sit on your doorstep, lean your back against the timber wall warm from the spring sunshine, let go

---

* A well-known singer and songwriter in the 1970s.

of your thoughts – they can go and frown on their own – and watch and listen and remain silent.

7

Opposite my doorstep – on the other side of the Bay of Good Fortune – stands the Orthodox monastery: its Cyclopean walls – the stones dripping, but covered with ice in the shade – gleam. As soon as they ring for the morning service, the sun rises behind the monastery, etches the black outline of towers, domes, crosses in the sky and then, at lunchtime, casts lateral light from the side on to the mass of the building, captures the texture of the stones, spreads light and shadow, and, in the evening, while the brothers are bowing their goodnights, it sets behind Babya Luda, bathing the façade in pink, crimson or gold, depending on the weather and the wind.

There! The bells are ringing and the paschal procession emerges from the monastery; they are bearing banners and icons, they sing. The wind bears the scent of *ladan*, tousles the tails of the monks' coats, ruffles their beards, spatters holy water. Among the tiny figures against the stone wall, I recognize some about whom separate tales could be spun, for each deserves his own story; but here I will weave them all into one sentence because they are all following the same procession: Father Superior Yosif at the head; behind him *starets* German, confessor to the brothers (he once told me not to read too many philosophers otherwise I'd go bald, and that true philosophy consists of contemplating death); next comes Father Zoshima, a couple of years ago a taxi-driver, today the monastery's steward, and the young Savvaty, Solovky's first novice; behind him go *inok* Filip, Yelisey, Naum and Longin, formerly a Moscow journalist, now editor at the monastery's publishing house, Andrey and Yov, an agricultural engineer in secular life, in monastic life responsible for the community's cows, then Yoann, and Brat,[*] who used to be an architect and designed the House of the Soviets in Kishinyov and now, on Solovky, carves crosses for prostration, renewing an old coastal craft; behind him come Pyetya, Mikhail and Dmitry, until recently a fanatical anarchist and already a mystic and fervent ascetic; shuffling along at the side is Kushma, once a champion footballer who represented his country, later a cripple and a madman; beside him are Boris and Gleb, who both create icons; and finally, the pilgrims, the enlightened, the local womenfolk and visiting guests.

They have walked past. The bells have stopped ringing. The sun burns more fiercely, and beneath the monastery wall sways Vova, drunk. Vova was born on Solovky; here he grew up, and here he took to drink. And only once did they take him away from here – to the army to serve in Legnica. There, in faraway Poland, for the first and last time in his life, he saw apples growing on a tree. He told me himself how they had picked them, still green, and how all the troops had devoured them as if they were potatoes, and how this had purged them . . . Vova doesn't get purged now, he only suffers. He has fallen over. Varvara has picked him up, the good woman. She's the daughter of a *zeka* who, following her father's tracks, found her way to Solovky a few years ago. Here her papa's tracks stopped short, but Varvara stayed on. They gave her a room with a kitchen in an old SLON barrack. Vova wanted to take Varvara for his wife, but then the whole thing fell apart and they remained friends thanks to the bottle. With faltering steps, holding each other up, they have disappeared from my field of vision. You could say that they have left this chapter unsteadily . . .

---

[*] Brat – Brother. *Tr.*

13

II

Avoid fame, isolate yourself from the world, and stay in your cell, as if you were wandering through foreign lands.

Anthony the Great

He brought me the epigraph himself, when he heard that I was writing about him. And he asked that I enclose him within a chapter, as if in a cell.

"A chapter's just long enough, Mar, to tell about a man, although, in actual fact, you'll lie anyway because about man you should remain silent."

He has a gaunt face, as if etched in hard wood, and it is hidden by a beard incrusted with grey. His shiny black hair falls to his waist and is tied with a scarlet ribbon. He is a Bulgarian from Moldavia. He is married with two children: three-year-old Nikita and a seventeen-year-old stepdaughter, Yelena. They live on Herring Point, in the house next door to ours, in what used to be a biology centre. We're friends. He wears a black *podryasnika* so that many visitors, as well as locals, take him for a monk, which irritates the Fathers, especially Zoshima, who often snarls:

"Some kind of monk — living with a woman!"

In reality, this is the second year that Brat is living with his wife "like brother and sister", just like St Yoann from Kronstadt. He underwent major heart surgery recently. The Lord granted that he survived. He doesn't trust people and says that the local drunks are rabble sold to the devil and damned. He also looks down on the monastic community, which is "directed by dark Moldavians". The oldest monks of Solovky, German and Zoshima, come from Kishinyov, (Ukraine) which annoys the Russians who make pilgrimages to the Islands. Although he grew up in Moldavia, Brat considers himself a Bulgarian and makes the point that it is they, the Bulgarians, who brought enlightenment to Rus! He claims that the brothers only live in the monastery physically and that their hearts are out there in the world, whereas he lives outside the monastic walls while his heart dwells within. All this kindles the conflict between Brat and Fathers Zoshima and German, who are in charge of the monastery during the absence of the Father Superior, who spends most of his time in Moscow. In the winter, the Fathers wanted to denounce Brat to his confessor, the elder Yoann from the Orthodox Pskov-Pecherska Lavra,[*] as "a brigand and one who leads the brothers into temptation" but the Father Superior didn't give his blessing. So they restricted themselves to publicly slandering Brat from the pulpit, without actually naming him, it's true, but pointing at him – "here, here is one who comes here and preaches to the brothers while he, himself, is no more than a proud, fraudulent monk. . . ." Well, true penitents were often persecuted in Orthodox monasteries, suffice it to mention the story of Nil Sora, whom Brat takes as a model. That is why he dreams of his own *skit*, in Filip's Hermitage, maybe, or on Hare Islands. And, in the meantime, he carves crosses. Because a cross is the whole world; even more – it is the way to eternity. He began with crosses of veneration. First, he erected one at the foot of Sekirna Mountain, where they used to throw prisoners, tied to logs, down steps. Then, on the isle of Anzer at the foot of Mount Golgotha, which flowed with blood during the days of the gulag. Finally, he carved the largest cross, which was to stand at the Harbour of Good Fortune, opposite the Holy Gates, in the water. But it didn't! Right at the beginning, there were some

---

[*] A Lavra is a complex of monasteries. *Tr.*

dogmatic disputes, contentions and intrigues, then the matter died down, silence fell and, to this day, the cross lies flat instead of standing erect. It has been lying in pieces now for two years, the pedestal growing dirty, in the rain, beneath the snow. The same thing happened to the iconostas for the Church of St Nikolay. It was barely begun when rumours began to spread: whole excursions came to see it − traders, tourists, sponsors. Even roubles − and dollars − flowed. Then it all died down, just like with the cross. The Holy Gates stand in the workshop; funds ran out for finishing the rest of the altar. Nor is it clear as to what will happen next. The Father Superior spends less and less time on the Islands. The Fathers have forbidden the monks to visit Brat. They have withheld materials and there is no word about any money. It is a good thing that at least Nadezhda brings in an income. Brat's wife works in the museum. And he, himself, together with *poslushnik* Nikola, a young wood-engraver from Moscow, has begun carving crosses according to the old patterns from the North − Kargopol, Shenkur, Vyelsk, Yarnya, Solvichegod. They are, like an obsession, extraordinary labyrinths of prayer. This is thinking in shapes, geometry, construction. No faces, limbs or images. Only symbols, signs, letters. The texts of prayers form the ornaments. Language reduced to decoration. The death of language. Crucifixion of the Word! There it is − the Byzantium of the 21st century. Or modern . . . *hesychasm.*[*] They leave an impression. There are large, small and tiny ones, crosses to take on journeys, crosses made for cells, altar crosses and crosses to wear around the neck, crosses that can be opened and ones that can be folded up, crosses to hold relics, crosses to do penance with, crosses to inscribe, crosses for pilgrimages, Lent, cemeteries, crosses for sea (in the shape of anchors) and for meditation, inverted crosses and ones with four arms. More than a hundred all in all. And not a single one is repeated! Brat and his *poslushnik* carved all through Lent, in complete isolation. For seven weeks they

---

[*] See Glossary.

didn't even go to the *banya*. They lived by prayer and fasting. In a cell.

"Because the cell is the most important element. It's a creative principle. It's only in the cell that you can see what is superfluous and should be removed. The creative process is nothing more than limiting yourself — like in asceticism — to what is necessary. True creation takes its beginnings from Light. And you can only find Light in silence, in solitude — within yourself. Others will always draw you out, drag you out of yourself, into darkness. That's why you have to lock yourself up in what you're doing, like in a cell, and travel without leaving the spot. Sometimes, chiselling a psalm out in cedarwood, I feel sand from the Egyptian desert under my feet. At other times, following the grain of a larch, I'll suddenly find myself in the marketplace in Jerusalem or at the foot of Golgotha. Do you like them? Zoshima says they're Old Orthodox designs but what can an elderly semi-literate *muzhik* from Moldavia know about the true 'art of the cross'? Yes, yes, because it is an art to carve out your own cell, the rest of the world and the whole of eternity in a cross, isn't it?"

III

I regret not having the words to do justice to some of the landscapes of the North, especially to the effects of light. A few strokes of the brush would show you the extraordinary originality of this sad and singular country better than entire volumes full of descriptions.

Astolphe de Custine

1

First of all, the water seeps through under the ice as if it were soured milk. The ice becomes spongy, slushy and treacherous. In some places it grows yellow, in others grey . . . in a dirty streak. Far away, on the horizon, a band of living water appears, like a thread of light. It is the sea approaching. And birds come with it. Lapwings arrive first. Then the ice turns black and cracks, like burnt earth. Slashed with crevices, shattered, it still banks up and creaks here and there, while, in places, it already sinks into the depths. The band of living water on the horizon grows, sparkles, shimmers. The wind brings with it the scent of the sea and the cry of birds. Cranes, swans, geese arrive . . . Finally, the first storm of spring shatters the ice with a thud. Waves crumble the ice-floes. Water grinds the brash-ice. The sea is very near. And the birds are in turmoil. They scream, gurgle, beat their wings, dive, chatter, mate. Oyster-catchers, loons, puffins, mergansers, eiders, crested tomtits, terns, scoters, fulmars, guillemots, wild duck . . . We open the windows. In the wink of an eye, the house is full of the birds' uproar, the smell of bitumen, and *mat* . . . It is the *muzhik*s patching and pitching their boats. And, on the last ice-floe, slowly drifting out towards the open sea, float four fat seals, bellies up.

2

The windows of our house give out on to the Bay of Good Fortune; the sea is an extension of the table on which I write. In winter, my sheets of paper merge with the whiteness of the ice beyond the window-pane, and the traces of *chernilo* turn into the *tropa* left by skis so quickly that I often don't know whether I am still sitting at my table or am being lifted over the sea. In winter, the winds sculpt the snow, every day differently, and cover up the tracks. While in summer water laps the edge of the green table-top and, for hours on end, I can watch the tide going out and coming in, the changing images drawn by the waves on sand and by the salt on stones. In summer, too, I can drown (my sight) in the depths of the sea without getting up from my chair. And perhaps it is right here, where the sea meets the table – where elements meet objects – that it is easier to understand my intention to try and grasp reality, give it form, imprint it in words. For Russian reality, especially in the North, has no form: expanses here are endless, mud is bottomless, settlements are shapeless. It is a sort of "pea jelly" (to use Dostoyevsky's expression) from which various objects protrude: here, an Orthodox cross; next to it, some barbed wire; there, a Saam tumulus and the fragment of a human skull with a bullet hole in it; somewhere else, a piece of rocket or submarine. To put it briefly, the landscape in the North is reminiscent of a panel on which successive generations of "splash artists" have diligently immortalized their god, smearing on thick layers of paint so as to cover images of their predecessors, and then some acid, toxic and corrosive rain has washed it off — although not entirely — leaving fragments of a drawing, vestiges of colour. Can they be restored?

3

I believe it is Berdyaev who observed that the landscape which a nation inhabits is a symbol of its soul, and the flat boundlessness of the northern plains makes it difficult for people to define themselves. The muddy slush (Rus's fifth element), which the Russian *muzhik* kneads with his feet every day, and the distances to be conquered use up all his energy and he has no strength left for culture (form). On the other hand, the magma of the North has, since time immemorial, instilled anxiety in newcomers, invited the need to tame the expanse and to make themselves at home in it. All the more so in that Russians believed that the pagan tribes, the Samoyeds, the Karels, the Lopars, who inhabited the northern boundaries of the Empire, had at their disposal impure powers which could deform space. Lopar shamans were accused of casting spells whereby "eyes were turned away" — that is, of possessing the art to turn the world inside out. Then, as the new lands became colonized, so the geography became sacred — the regions were subjected to Orthodox order. Pagan sanctuaries were destroyed, sacred forests cleared, idols and totems were burnt and *skit*s, chapels and temples built in their places; lakes and mountains were given biblical names (Tabor, Golgotha, Jordan), directions were divided into the sacred (east) and the impure (west), and crosses were erected in such a way that their lower, diagonal arm always pointed north. Slowly, from out of the topographical chaos of the North, the sacred cosmos of Holy Rus emerged and Russians began to feel at home. Then came the Revolution, and traces of the Orthodox religion were assiduously wiped out just as those of paganism had been previously: names, maps, appropriations were changed. People were imprisoned in the temples, horses were kept in the *skit*s, Holy Lake was named Workers Lake. Later still, the Revolution was declared an historical mistake and some people set about destroying the traces once more, while others moved back in time to resurrect past times, and still others designed everything anew and are trying to build America in Russia. The world returned to chaos, this time semiotic chaos. The landscape has become blurred; all around is stagnation and entropy. Continuing Berdyaev's and Dostoevsky's line of thought, you could say that today the Russian landscape of the North is the symbol of the "pea jelly" in people's heads.

4

People on the Islands live together with animals, about 1,100 inhabitants all in all, not counting visitors: vagrants, tourists, pilgrims, seasonal gatherers of sea-grasses and all sorts of artists, *osolovely** for a period of time or for good. The dominant décor of a Solovetsky *posyolok*** is barbed wire, which is used to fence their gardens here. The *posyolok* itself, like a carbuncle, has grown around the kremlin and, from a distance, you can see that it is a sickly growth. Barracks from the labour camp protrude among damp houses made of hollow clay bricks, monuments of monastic architecture, looted for bricks to make stoves (the old monastic bricks are more durable and fire-resistant), show their age, roads are full of holes and footbridges rotten; wherever you look rubble is scattered about, scrap metal and broken

---

* See Glossary.
** A Russian hamlet. *Tr.*

glass. All around, there are sheds, wood-houses, barns and pigsties, askew and rotten, put up higgledy-piggledy, any old how. A lack of decent sanitation means that the sewers run into the sea and, in summer, when the tide is out, the Harbour of Good Fortune stinks like a cesspool and the shores are covered with a thick layer of slime. Against this backdrop drift drunk people and emaciated animals: dogs drag scraps out from *pomoikas*,[*] cows and goats graze everywhere, on the streets and between the houses, while pigs root wherever they can, especially by the kremlin wall. And, at first glance, the Solovetsky *posyolok* reminds anyone who is not from this land yet has somehow found himself here, of a monstrous kitsch in the *informel* style, where nonsense and chance rule. You need time – and concentration – to get used to this picture and to discern the work of individual authors: the monks (from the beginning of the 15th century to 1920), the Chekists (1923–1939), the military (1939–1957), the museum management (1967–1991) and today's anarchy. Let us try and take a stroll, at our leisure, through the streets of the *posyolok*, starting at the kremlin.

5

The Solovetsky kremlin stands on a narrow isthmus which separates the Holy Lake from the White Sea. Stone walls (the length of one verst),[**] made of enormous boulders and covered in rust-coloured lichen, surround the monastic complex which, despite its dilapidated state, is exceptionally beautiful. Once it used to be one of the richest monasteries in Rus, and the Empire's most powerful fortress in the North. Two cathedrals, five churches, as many gates, seven towers,

---

[*] See Glossary.
[**] 1 verst is approximately equal to 1 kilometre.

a belfry, three palaces, living and farming quarters, an enormous refectory (the largest single-columned hall in Ancient Rus!), cloisters, passage-ways, cells and casemates. You only have to look at pre-Revolution photographs to see how far Russia has gone in devastating her cultural landscape. Even the trees were slaughtered and, where flowers once grew, there is now earth and clay. In the days of the labour camp, this used to be a *zona, zeka*s were imprisoned in the temples and a star was erected on the belfry in place of the cross. In the cathedral, where the altar used to be, they made a privy, in the refectory a theatre and in one of the churches, an exhibition of atheism. After the labour camp, the military took over the kremlin. There are still bullet marks on the bells. Then the site was given over to Administration and transformed into a state museum: the monastic buildings were used to house exhibitions, collection storerooms and a hostel for excursion groups, a workers' hostel, a youth club and a shop selling vodka. Work on restoration was begun: the star fell from the belfry, excrement was scraped from the cathedral, together with 19th-century frescoes, in order to restore to the temple its somewhat older appearance. As the rubble was removed, monastic graves were dug up, crosses, rings and rosaries were pulled off the corpses. At night, in the cloisters, tourists and local *shpana* – that is, adolescent whores and underage rogues – would run wild. Five years ago, monks arrived on Solovky. Some of the farm buildings and two temples were given over to them. The monks are not counting on getting any more for the time being because there are only a few of them and the monumental complex of buildings requires enormous sums to maintain and repair. The shop and club have gone. At the moment, negotiations are under way to remove the hotel from monastic territory. The bakery in the Church of the Dormition (Uspensky) is also a big problem. The *shpanas* continue to run wild in the galleries during summer, tempting the *poslushnik*s with moonshine vodka and loose girls. Father Superior Yosif intends to bring in a squad of Cossacks to defend the brothers.

North of the kremlin, on a small square next to Constantine chapel, stands a boulder commemorating sea cadets killed in action; it is a place where annual mass meetings are held to celebrate *Den Pobedi* (Victory Day). After the meetings, cows devour the wreaths. Further north from the stone, in the direction of the tourist steamboat harbour, runs Severnaya (Northern) Street. In high season, there is roaring music there, discos on deck, hordes of drunken tourists, a chance of local girls, and opportunities for brawls. On the way, there are barracks from the days of the labour camp, where people live. Beyond the harbour, just by the sea, lies a monstrous pile of fuel barrels; the beach is saturated with crude oil and petrol. On a level with Filip's chapel, turning right from Severnaya Street, an unnamed street branches off: there you find the social services office, a machine plant, a stone *banya* dating from 1717, warehouses, stores, sawmills, a listed wood-distillery, the management of Leskhoz,* and an enormous cement hall with no roof or windows, abandoned halfway through construction. A bakery for several thousand inhabitants had been planned there, but nobody knows why.

East of the kremlin, next to the stone forge dating from the end of the 17th century, Sivko Street, named after a hero of the Soviet Union and graduate of the Solovetsky school for sea cadets, makes its way towards the airport. There, in the building of what used to be a seminary for *poslushnik*s, opposite ancient barns and stables, sits Nebozhenko, the *Glava* (Head) of Administration. Next to him is a newspaper's editorial office, radio and telephone (you can even telephone through to Maison-Laffitte).** Beyond Sivko Street, in the depths of the forest, in the place of the old brickyard, a special prison was built in 1939 which nobody managed to put to use because the *zeka*s were evacuated from the Island. Today, a hotel for "new Russians" and foreigners, stands there. Between Severnaya and Sivko

---

*The Forestry Office.
**Maison-Laffitte publishes *Kultura*, where Wilk's articles appear. *Tr.*

Streets runs a street named after another hero, Kovalov; there, you find the militia, the fire brigade, three shops, a seaweed processing plant, Galavany Hotel (reasonable prices: ten dollars a night). Further along are the boiler house, coal tips, gardens and the Bread Hills, where, as word has it, they had once tried to cultivate spring grains but now, at picnics, they quaff "wheat vodka" accompanied with a sniff of bread.

South of the kremlin, on a hill where there was once a monastic cemetery and then collective graves, now stands a hospital built during the days of the labour camp: the walls, with peeling plaster, are falling away in large chunks, the roof is leaking, the ceiling is rotten. Further along is Zaozernaya Street, the Solovetsky Street of Crocodiles, where there are three shops, eight seedy cafés, Bar Maks and a deserted barrack from the days of SLON where you can have cheap (in the region of a three-dollar bottle) primitive sex with ladies aged from twelve to sixty. Along the continuation of Zaozernaya Street, beyond the confines of the *posyolok* is the cemetery on Sour Bay: *stakans** on the graves, traces of prayers for the dead beneath the fence – empty bottles, rusty tins, broken benches. From Zaozernaya Street, a dead-end street branches off, named after Florensky, a Solovetsky *zeka*, priest, philosopher and inventor, who discovered how to derive agar-agar from seaweed. A stone stands there in memory of the victims of SLON, as at Lubyanka Prison in Moscow. On the other side, on the shore of Holy Lake, rattles an old diesel power station. Spillages of mazut [fuel oil] have burnt out the surrounding forest. Completely.

West of the kremlin, stands Petersburg Hotel. Dating from the times of the monastery, it now houses the management of the Museum and the scientific library which, for thirty years, has not managed to compile a catalogue. Below, on the Harbour of Good Fortune itself, protrude the ruins of Preobrazhensky** Hotel where, before the Revolution, rich

---

* See Glossary.
** Transfiguration. *Tr.*

pilgrims and guests of the monastery used to stay. Later, it became SLON administration and a shop (R., the last warden of the *zeka*, told me about it). Later still, soldiers from a unit posted in Solovky were quartered there. The soldiers, leaving the Islands, organized a big party with fireworks and set fire to the building . . . Today, there is a boiler house there, a hangout for Solovetsky *bomzh*s and whores, whom nobody needs any more. All around, heaps of cinder smoke. Further on extends Primorskaya Street; on it are four chapels (pigs are still kept in one of them), the remains of a very old hydraulic power station, a unique monastic dock which is falling apart in front of our eyes, a building called "Shanghai" – the depths of poverty, drunkenness and despair – and then Primorskaya forks in two: left is School Bay where work on a gigantic sewage purification plant was abandoned in mid-construction, and right is Herring Point which divides the Harbour and the Bay of Good Fortune. At the end of the Point, among old, 19th-century buildings – stone holds for melting and storing seal fat, rope and barrel storage houses, wooden sheds on the water which serve to unload and repair boats, dug-out ice houses and cellars made of enormous boulders covered with turf – stands our house, where I write this "View of Solovky", as if it were a new Vermeer.

6

It is the end of May. I've just returned from fishing. I've still got the roar of the water, the cry of the birds in my ears. We were at Pine Bay, at the northern tip of the Island, near Savvatevskaya Hermitage, where, in 1429, the first monks – St German and St Savvaty – settled on Solovky and, in 1923, the first *zeka*s, anarchists and S.R.'s (Social Revolutionaries) were shot. Later, a dairy farm was set up there, then a school for sea cadets and, in the '80s, a camp for pioneers and a holiday centre for trade unions were planned. Now

Savvatevo has been returned to the monks, who exile insubordinate brothers there or send *poslushnik*s to undergo ordeals.

There was still ice near the shore of Lagoon Lake. We approached by tractor as near as possible in order not to drag the boat through the forest across softened snow. Then Maksimka lugged it along by himself: at first, for some 100–150 metres, he pushed it along the ice, then, when the ice became brittle, he climbed inside and pushed himself along with a birch pole until the ice cracked as if a pane of glass had shattered, and the boat splashed into water. We, in the meantime, walked around the lake through marshes covered with dirty, soggy snow, wading, in places, up to our waists. Hazel grouse flew from under our feet. Maksimka waited by the brook which joins the lake with the sea and where, without going far, you can fish both fresh and salt water fish. It turned out that the monks had arrived before us. Their nets were already set. We threw ours out next to theirs. Father Naum, from Moldavia, emerged from the forest. He did not look like an *inok*,[*] more like . . . a bandit. Stocky, broad-shouldered, with raven-black, plaited hair, he wore a short pelisse embroidered with silver thread, green army trousers, a huge knife tucked into his belt, and muddy waders up to his hips. With him was a *poslushnik* from Savvatevo, who did not appear quite normal. We greeted each other. The sun was setting between the islands of Pine Bay. Ice by the shore − the so-called "*pripay*" − tinted a deep shade of ultramarine, was shimmering mysteriously against the forest. Dried grass glowed rusty on the illuminated slopes. Higher up − leafless birches and a wine-coloured thicket with white smudges of trunks. And above them, the harsh green of fir trees and the luminous blue of a spring sky, quilted, at the edges, with pure gold. The cry of birds, the roar of water. I am left alone. Maksimka and Smirny are setting the nets in the sea; Father Naum and the *poslushnik* have gone to check theirs. I prepare a fire. The forest is damp; there is little dry wood. There is a scent of wet moss.

---

[*] See Glossary.

Somewhere far away, a wood grouse toots. Through the sharp, piercing chirping of thrushes, the *mat* of *muzhik*s resonates from the water. The thrushes don't give up and scream to the heavens. It is as if I were hearing: "Clear out, you vandals, you don't belong here, ravagers; you've broken young birches that had barely let out shoots with your tractors; you're frightening birds with your *mat*; you're fishing during the spawning season, and leaving behind burnt-out earth, empty bottles, tins and yellow traces of urine in the snow . . ." The nets are set. The fire is crackling. We squat on the wet earth. Cold rises from the ice. The sun has disappeared; everything has turned pale. Neither light, nor dark. White night has turned grey. On a tree stump – vodka, pork fat, rye bread, an onion. We are waiting for daybreak. Naum has emerged from the forest again. He must have smelt the "Russian"[*] – he likes a drink apparently. We pour the Father a generous *stakan*. Rumours about Naum circulate in the *posyolok*, that he was sent to the hermitage by the Father Superior because of his drunkenness . . . Suddenly, the *muzhik*s jump up; the incoming tide has brought ice floes in on the net. They have run up to the boats. I try to make the most of the moment and ask Naum about his past. We have another *stakan*, then another, and another. The Father murders language, mutilates the sentences, sometimes goes off at a tangent. Semi-literate, infantile, good. He grew up in a Moldavian kolkhoz, without parents or schooling, then there was the army, where they trained him as a driver, broke his ribs and jaw and dislocated his spine, which allowed him to be discharged from service ahead of time. When he recounted his story on the train back to his family kolkhoz, one of the passengers muttered that this was God's work and that he ought to thank God. So he made a round of the monasteries; from Kiev, through the Lavra of the Holy Trinity, to Solovky. He decided to stay on the Islands: he was happy here – forests all around, water, not many people.

"But the most important thing is that they do your thinking for

---

[*] Vodka. *Tr.*

you, they feed you and give you work. There's hunger and unemployment in the *posyolok*, like everywhere else, but here there's plenty of work, we eat three times a day until we're full . . ."

Maksimka and Smirny have returned. They've brought back some flounder. We prepare *ukha.** The *mat* doesn't subside; the *muzhik*s aren't embarrassed by the monk. Sometimes this sounds grotesque. For example: "Why the sh— set the nets, Father? Dynamite's enough to get them to come the f— out themselves." The fish soup is delicious. It is dawning. The sun rises above New Pine Forest, outlining the stone dike built in the '30s by the *zeka*s, the railway embankment leading to nowhere and the remains of monastic fishing quarters from the 19th century. In summer, *bich*s and seasonal gatherers of sea grass camp there. Father Naum disappears in the brightness. We pull in the ice-covered nets. Our hands grow numb. In the sea-nets are enormous, fat herrings, cod and *stunka*, strange fish smelling of fresh cucumbers, whereas in the freshwater nets there are a number of roach, perch, a few pike, burbot and one silvery lavaret. We pack our spoils on to the tractor. The sun is already quite hot although it is barely four o'clock. Then – what's that? A long, drawn-out sound from the sea. Neither siren, nor cry. It grows louder, fills the forest. It makes the air vibrate, sends shivers down our spines. The light fluctuates, a hard lump grows in my throat. Finally, they are here, flying in from the sea. Cranes with their clangour. Piercing, through and through. To the core. And there, growing silent. They have flown past. Silence . . . as if our eardrums had burst.

We gather ourselves for our journey in silence. We are stuck, for a while, in the mud mixed with snow. The engine roars, oil drips, there is a stench of fumes. We budge. Across glazed mud to Savvatevo, then right, towards Sekirna where, under the sky itself, glistens the chapel of the Lord's Ascension – they sat *zeka*s on poles there, like chickens – and then straight on to the *posyolok*. On both sides of the road, the forest is knee-deep in water, dark and still.

---

*Fish soup. *Tr.*

29

IV

There, totally distracted by all that surrounded me, I was
suddenly gripped with admiration at the sight of one of those
effects of the light which you are only privileged to see in
the North, and during the magical clarity of polar nights.

Astolphe de Custine

1

White nights on Solovky quietly smoulder to lilac: from tints of pale violet in the foreground, at the very shore, to amaranth congealing in the distance, on the line of the horizon, where the sun sinks into the sea for a split second. Water, sky, clouds and stones are all various shades of pink, even the mists and sea foam look like cranberry mousse. During white nights, the White Sea is calm: not a quiver, or ripple. Like an enormous, darkened mirror in which you can see both islands and people. And yourself. People are sitting in boats, black against the light, as if they were not there – dark holes in the purple background. They are hungry and motionless. They are waiting for herring, for many here the only source of protein. And the herring, also famished after winter, take empty hooks. It is enough to have a small stick, some line, two pieces of tin can to imitate a fish, and six or seven hooks between them. If the herring are moving in schools, there is not even enough time to pull them off the hooks, several take the lure at once.

Then the picture comes to life, people move, the rods sway; with each motion, a herring flashes, here, there. Sometimes you hear laughter across the water but usually it's *mat*. The days, during this period, tend to be blue, from pale indigo to lacquered lapis lazuli, or transparent like . . . *shilo.** Young foliage appears on the trees, fluffy and delicate like the velvet of a stag's antlers; from the earth, fat and saturated, grass emerges, insects, and sometimes also a human bone, if you dig deep enough. The beginning of June on Solovky is the season for gardens: the time to sow potatoes, repair greenhouses, twist barbed wire around stakes and gather stones from the earth, which the frost squeezes out like blackheads, each spring. Long ago, during the late Neolithic period, the Saams built labyrinths of stones, and today people curse succinctly, because their hands ache from the stones:

"*Blyad*".**

2

On a photograph of Solovky, taken from a sputnik (from an altitude of 260 versts), you can see the extraordinary muddle of lakes, inlets, spits, lagoons, canals, headlands and dikes, which together form an enormous labyrinth of water mirrors, bringing to mind the stone constructions of the ancient Saams. *Tropas* run between the lakes: ranging from monastic tracks, comfortable, no doubt, at one time, because designed for horse-drawn wagonettes but today bumpy, potholed, broken up by lorries and tractors, to rotten footbridges thrown across marshes, and faint human tracks, imprinted in the heather. Some lead into the depths of the island, others into the depths of time; some wind along the seashore etched out by the waves, like

---

* See Glossary
** Cunt. *Tr.*

Russian lace, others cut across mud, or someone's memory. Sometimes a track rises and falls, repeating the rhythm of the moraine hills, at others, it weaves like the threads of a story, avoiding treacherous places. You can read the Solovky *tropa*s endlessly, you can wander along them, look for the truth (where is it?), go for a walk, play the philosopher, gather herbs, stones or birch withes for the *banya*. You can also pray, walking along them, like Father Ilarion, a *zeka*, who, before his death, marked out versts with his legs, as if they were rosary beads, or you can get lost in the muddle of paths and lakes, in the tangle of time present, past or actual, in the reflections, echoes and echolalia. And so I shall try — although I cannot guarantee its accuracy — to sketch out a plan (a sort of travel guide) in order to make it easier for the reader to find his orientation in this world which I have written myself.

3

Solovetsky Archipelago lies in the southern part of the White Sea, on the edge of Onega Bay, 160 versts from the Arctic Circle. It is made up of six large islands and dozens of small ones. The largest one, the Great Island of Solovky, is twenty-five versts long and sixteen wide, making it larger than Malta. Anzer, ten times smaller, is the most northern of the islands. The two Muksalmas jut out eastwards, the two Hare Islands westwards. And all around reefs, shoals, boulders, skerries, scars, shelves protrude — various forms of rock projections: from bare boulders patched with lichen to small bars covered with copses of stunted sallow and birch trees, and with names like Woman, Dog, Crow, Priest, Filip . . . In other words, Solovetsky Archipelago is a pile of stones brought down by a glacier, covered with a layer of earth, mud and sand, and overgrown with lush forests of all sorts: dry pine forest, and wet taiga, and tundra. The forests on the Islands are as if from a fairytale and it is not by accident that Ivan Bilibin illustrated Russian stories with landscapes from Solovetsky woods. Here grow pine, spruce, birch, aspen and alder, rowan and willow, as well as cedar, planted by man, fir trees, maple, poplar, larch, hagberries and lilac. The air is scented with iodine and sap. A sea climate prevails — temperate, much warmer than on the mainland. A multitude of lakes and brooks guarantees fresh water, an abundance of fish, berries and mushrooms — nourishment. Perhaps that is why in both monastic and lay descriptions of Solovky, the metaphor "oases in the desert of the North" appears.

The main island of the Archipelago is the Great Island of Solovky, almost 250 square versts in area. Here is the kremlin, the *posyolok* and our house; here are most of the monastic *skit*s, traces of SLON and thousands of other peculiarities; here the history of the monastery begins, the chronicle of Rus in the North and my story. On the aforementioned photograph taken from space, the Great Island of Solovky reminds one of a human skull, its empty eye sockets turned towards the east. The intricate outline of the shore, curved like a Byzantine ornament, is 200 versts long, although the perimeter is barely 100 versts. The difference disappears in the multitude of bays, harbours and headlands, inundated by the incoming tide. From the west, protected on all sides from winds and ideal for a harbour, the Bay of Good Fortune carves into the Great Island of Solovky. Here, steamboats of tourists, goods barges and fishing boats moor. Here, the *zeka*s disembarked . . . To the north, Pine Bay opens out; there, the fattest herring are wont to go, which is why the monastery had its deep-sea fisheries there; these were then used for fishing by SLON and today by *muzhik*s. While from the east, Long Bay comes right up to the *posyolok*. It is strewn with masses of small islands where, in the days of the labour camp, there were farms of fur-bearing animals, which were fed better than Solovetsky *zeka*s, because people were given slops, while foxes got meat and fresh fish, and sables even got nuts and honey. No wonder — after all, their fur was worn in Paris. To the south, the Great Island of Solovky narrows down to Pechak Point, which has a triangular tower on the top of the *sopka*,[*] visible from far out at sea. The island's relief, repeating the path of the glacier, is made up of a chain of moraine hills stretching from the north-west to the south-east: Bread, Valday, Thundering, Wolf. The highest elevation, Sekirna Mountain, is ninety-five and a half metres high. A significant part of the Great Island of Solovky is taken up by peat-bogs of extraordinary beauty. In 1925, extraction of peat began from one of these, the Filimonov Bog. Those who survive recall the hell: digging ditches in the bogs, clearing dead tree trunks, mosquitoes, small, biting midges, hallucinations. In 1929, the narrow railway track was extended there so as to link Filimonov Bog with the Bay of Good Fortune. The embankment remains to this day – a beautiful path for taking a walk among the lakes. And there are masses of lakes on the island, over 500. In the days of Igumen Filip (Ivan IV's time), many of them were linked up by canals, at the same time elevating the level of water in Holy Lake, which enabled waterworks to be constructed in the monastery and a mill to be built. In the days of SLON, the canals were used to raft the timber, and trees were destroyed without any qualms. Today, tourists are transported by boat along the canals, as if on gondolas; then there is no end of laughter, and drunken shrieks are sometimes heard. In June, the tourist season begins.

Anzer is the second largest island of the Archipelago and has the long shape of a horse's lower jaw, stretching from west to east for sixteen versts. It is separated from the Great Island of Solovky by a *salma* – that is, straits – five versts in breadth, where the sea boils with such force that even in winter it rarely freezes over and cuts Anzer off from people for many months. Maybe that is why you can still come across reindeer living in the wild there. Anzer is a singular island in the Solovetsky Archipelago, an island with a special mission. Discipline, in its *skit*s, was stricter than in others; meat and fish

---

[*] A hillock with sparse vegetation. *Tr.*

34

weren't eaten there; female pilgrims weren't allowed in and even the ritual of worship was different: only *panikhidy* — Masses for the dead — were celebrated. In the days of SLON, they took "wet nurses" to Anzer, that is, women with children born in the labour camp, syphilitics and clergy of various denominations, including a group of Polish Catholic priests (their case-files, so-called *delo*s, can be found in the KGB archives in Arkhangel). Nobody returned from there. At present, Anzer is also under special protection: without written permission, entry is strictly forbidden. Even the inhabitants of the Islands go there faint-heartedly, in passing. Whereas tourists, travelling across the White Sea, can only look at Anzer from a distance. And they will immediately notice Golgotha, the highest point on Solovky (200 metres above sea level). This is the peak of the island, in the geographical sense as well as mystical. On the summit, sparkle the remains of the Temple of the Lord's Crucifixion; white walls as if eaten away by salt, empty hollows of windows where the wind now lives. Next to it are the stumps of the *skit*, remnants of cells overgrown with *ivan-chay*,* ceilings caved in . . . the remains of visitors from another world. At least, not from the world which stretches out below, at the foot of Golgotha. A forest of tall trees grows there, forever green; in it are windows of lakes (over eighty) in which you can see the sky; here and there graze herds of wild reindeer; further off is the roar of the sea. And, on the horizon, in the grey mist, looms Tabor mountain on the island of Muksalma.

Muksalma is oval in shape, grassy and muddy. It covers an area of nearly seventeen square versts, over half of which is made up of lush meadows, which, from early times, were used as pasture for the monks' cows. Mention of cattle and horses on Muksalma can be found in the first *Description* of the monastery dating from 1514. In the 19th century, Muksalma was linked with the Great Island of Solovky by a famous *damba* — a stone dyke the length of 300 toises. At the same

---

* A kind of willow-herb. *Tr.*

35

time, a significant surface of the mud on Muksalma was drained, extending the area of pastureland. On the western shore of the island, the monks built a cattle farm, stables and henhouse as well as lodgings for shepherds, monks' cells, an inn for pilgrims and the temple of Sergey Radonezhsky. In the days of SLON, a *selkhoz* was organized in which Ukrainian women transported to Solovky for cannibalism worked, while the *zona* itself looked like a "small, cosy village set in the remote countryside", as the labour camp magazine *Solovetskye Ostrova* described it in 1929. In the 1930s, Muksalma was a model centre of animal husbandry and a base for the entire Soviet North; young animals were taken from here. Now the pastures are overgrown with nettles and thistles, the houses are rotting and decaying, and bars on the windows are eaten away by rust. The western part of the island, on the other hand, is covered with extensive mud, rising in terraces to Tabor's ridge. This is my favourite spot on Solovky: in spring, there is a smell of marsh herbs, in summer cloudberries ripen like cornfields of amber, and, in autumn, the mud turns orange-crimson and blazes like rotten wood. The ground falls beneath your feet, then swells, and it feels as if you were walking across a blister of earth filled with thick serum. Further on, Tabor breaks off, abruptly, towards the sea. At its foot are waves, sea spray and Little Muksalma in plaits of foam and, on the island, a small colony of seasonal gatherers of sea-grass.

On the opposite side of the Great Island of Solovky, two and a half versts to the west, lie Hare Islands. There is no mud there, no lakes and no forests. Only scree on the slopes of low *sopka*s, piles of grey boulders between which blueberry shrubs and "dancing" birches grow. In this seemingly disordered rubble you can find traces of Neolithic man if you look closely enough: fourteen labyrinths, over 600 tumuli, two dolmens and a number of other stone constructions. The Hare Islands were once a sacred site for the Saams. Later, the Orthodox monks left their own hallmarks: crosses, chapels and cells. In 1702, the Emperor of Russia, Peter the Great, in memory of his visit to Solovky, lay the first wreath of the chapel of St Andrew with his own hands. The chapel stands to this day. In 1854–1855, during the siege of the Solovetsky monastery by the British, invaders landed on Hare Islands in order to catch the monks' goats. In the days of SLON, a penal isolation unit for "loose" women was set up on the islands and, according to some witnesses, sectarians were starved to death. "The educational significance of the Punishment Cell on Hare Islands cannot be underestimated," the newspaper *Novye Solovky* said in 1925. "Whoever has found himself there, will never return." And it is difficult to say any more because there are no reports from there, only rumours, suppositions. Nowadays, Hare Islands are a point of interest for tourist excursions, an archaeological camp location for students and, for the people of Solovky, a place for drinking binges. Rumours circulate in the *posyolok* that, during full moon, naked harlots gambol about there.

4

And now, I would like to invite you on an excursion. There are many paths on Solovky and it is impossible to cover (let alone describe) them all, so let's follow at least one together. I suggest the old monastic road, which makes the round of the main *skit*s of the Great Island of Solovky, known, among local guides, as "the great circle".

We leave the *posyolok* by Severnaya Street, watching out for drunken motorcyclists; we pass the harbour, the fuel depot and enter the forest. The smell of mazut disappears after a while. On our left opens out a view on the sea bay which is cut off by a stone dike built in the 16th century at the initiative of Igumen Filip (Kolichev), thus creating an enclosed reservoir of salt water which enabled the monks to always have fresh cod on their tables, regardless of the weather at sea. Today the Filip ponds are covered over with weeds.

Two versts further on, a branch to the right leads to Makarev Hermitage. There, in the deep valley, sheltered on all sides from the wind, stands "the archimandrite's dacha" — the residence of the priors of Solovetsky monastery, built at the beginning of the 19th century. The singular microclimate allowed the monks to grow pumpkins, watermelons and roses here. In the days of SLON, Eichmans, the commandant of the labour camp, lived in the dacha. The German Communist, Karl Albrecht, who visited Eichmans in 1928, remembered the precious tapestries, Persian carpets and period furniture for many years. The commandant had a superb time: every day he had women fresh from the female *zona*, cocaine, alcohol. And all around there were slaves bent over the beds of plants, vegetables and flowers. In Eichmans' day, the hermitage was called "Gorky's farmstead" and that is how it has remained to this day. At present, it is a botanical garden, a museum department. The caretaker, crazy Grisha, the son of a KGB agent from Murmansk, lives here. He read Solzhenitsyn a few years ago and came to Solovky to see for himself how it compared to his father's stories. And when he felt the earth slipping away from under his feet, he began to believe in God and took to drink. Sometimes, when he's drunk, he'll talk to Eichmans or even call himself Eichmans.

We move on. The road falls and rises, emulating the breathing of the glacier, and, in places, times gone by or somebody's story. On both sides, there are forests, lakes quivering among the trees. At the fifth verst, there is Korzhino: luminous water, a boat harbour, a summerhouse. In the bushes, there are traces of picnics, empty bottles, crushed tins, burnt-out grass. There used to be a chapel here, but it was dismantled in the days of SLON for its bricks. In the 1930s, the *zeka*s rafted timber from here, for the distillation of tar. Two versts beyond Korzhino there is a fork: to the right is the road to Isakovo, but we go left, to Sekirna Mountain. From a distance, you can see the white patch of the chapel of the Ascension at its summit as if caught in the frame of the *tropa*. In the drum of the chapel, built in 1860, is the beacon, serviced, in the days of the labour camp, by the monk Flavyan. Close by is a large wooden house with a glazed balcony. The watchman, Feliks, and his wife live here. There are rumours in the *posyolok* that Feliks and his wife vanished from sight so as to hide a murky past. Opposite the house is a stable, below that, a stone *banya* and a granary. Ever since the beginnings of SLON, there have been strict discipline punishment cells there. Nobody survived a long sentence on Sekirna. Corpses were buried on the slopes, among blueberry bushes. To this day, the blueberries which grow there are exquisite. On the summit — a panoramic view, benches, rubbish bins. Below — a landscape: sheets of lakes surrounded by forests, extensive marshy meadows, brooks, the chain of the Wolf Hills, and all around is the sea, which glows in the sun here, glimmers in the mist there. Every time I am here, I wonder whether it would have been easier or harder to die with such a view in front of you. We descend by the steps down which *zeka*s, tied to ice-covered beams, used to be dropped. At the foot of the mountain stands a cross. Every year, at the beginning of spring, on the Orthodox Radonitsa,* when the snow is still obstructive but the birds are beginning to screech, the Solovetsky monks celebrate a *panikhida* here for the victims of SLON, burning incense of spruce sap, freshly oozing from the trees. The smoke is bitter, making the head spin.

A couple of versts further is Savvatevo, a former *skit*. Not much of it remains today: a body of stone cells without a roof, the wreck of a church, the remains of a wooden house, foundations, rubble. They once thought of opening a boarding-house here, a holiday centre or a camp for pioneers. But times have changed and "new Russians" prefer to invest in Majorca. So Savvatevo was handed over to the monks. The brothers tidied the place up and, under the south wall of the chapel where the sun is hottest, dug up a patch of earth to make into cabbage, rape and turnip beds. They installed hotbeds for cucumbers, glasshouses for tomatoes. Kostek oversees them. He was a student of international law and Arabic philology at Moscow

---

* All Souls' Day. *Tr*.

University until recently and is now the monastery's gardener. Here, in the seclusion of the hermitage, he is slowly pulling himself together after his head burst from a surplus of knowledge. Kostek has grown unaccustomed to people and does not invite us in, yet it is time for tea; after all, we have covered fifteen versts. Not far from Savvatevo, on the road to Isakovo, lies the small lake Kupalneye. On its shore stands a wooden cabin, some benches, a fire. You can sit, have a rest, a snack and take a dip. And, in clear weather, you can still see the remains of the submerged barrack at the bottom of the lake: a door with a Judas-hole and a feeding hatch, the shadows of plank-beds. These traces of SLON are sometimes so distinct that you find yourself looking around to see if it's not a reflection.

After a short rest, we move on. The road leads through a high, thick forest, where the sun seeps in, like an effluence, in thin streaks. Suddenly, on the left, the sheet of Red Lake splits the forest and opens up the sky under our feet. It is here that Nesterov painted his famous *Silence*: two boats in the foreground, in each a monk with a fishing rod, both gazing into the depths as if they were repeating the litany of clouds sung by the water, Sekirna Mountain in the background, the chapel of the Ascension . . . In the past, before the Revolution, Red Lake used to be called White. On one of its islands is a tiny lake, and on it a very tiny island. We approach Isakovo. A wide meadow runs down to the lake; on the shore stands an enormous stone house, next to it another, subsiding into burdock, further on, a plywood pavilion, neither camping hut nor workers' canteen, above it, in a cluster of trees, a half dilapidated wooden barn, overgrown with raspberries. At the beginning of the 19th century, a small *skit* was built here for the brothers who did the fishing and haymaking. In the days of SLON, the *skit* expanded into a fairly large *posyolok*, with a telephone, a club and a school for *likbyez* (that is: the liquidation, abolition, of illiteracy). There was also a dairy farm, a centre for the forestry industry, labour camp gardens and greenhouses, which Yevdokya Yakovlevna, the wife of the last Solovetsky *zeka* warden told me about. Then Isakovo became deserted and derelict. Some of the buildings were looted, some burned down and the rest were bought by "Avtokombinat" from Arkhangel, who set up a rest home in the old *skit*. *Chinovniks*[*] of all ranks used to come here, from *apparatchik*s of the lowest rank to first secretaries, generals and ministers. Today, Isakovo is again derelict because it turned out that the Arkhangel "Avtokombinat" did not have the right to buy the historical building and Solovetsky museum does not have the money to maintain it. And so, the remains of Isakovo *skit* are used by local authorities for all sorts of drinking bouts *à la russe*.

Further along, the roads meet and we return to the *posyolok* along the same wide road by which we left. And so, we have traced a circle, like the June sun above the horizon, or like the story about forking paths. Because Solovky has neither a beginning, nor an end . . .

5

And one more thing: you should be careful! The hundreds of lakes on Solovky reflect the world bent over their waters, and optical illusions — frequent in the North — make these reflections sometimes seem more real than reality and the boundary between them disappears. I heard about a drunken pilgrim who fell into the water and drowned because he mistook the reflection of the monastery in the Bay of Good Fortune for the real Holy Gates . . . I was also told about Yulka M., the local poet, who became confused by these multiple images and hanged herself so as to return to unity. On the bark of a birch, she left this couplet:

> *To come to You, I go —*
> *It's on my way, you know.*

---

[*] State officials. *Tr.*

V

Most of what has been written about Russia abroad does not have much to do with reality.

Joseph de Maistre

1

The first foreigners, the English sailors, Thomas Southem and John Spark, landed on the Solovetsky Islands in 1566. We read in their notes: "29th June, we left Zhizhgin, on an easterly wind, at five in the afternoon. Steering south-west, at a distance of 30 miles from Zhizhgin, we passed the island of Anzer. 15 miles further on, following this course, we arrived at the headland of (Solovky) Avdon island." We don't know where the Englishmen got the name of Avdon. The name doesn't appear in any other sources. Whereas in Dyachenko's *Comprehensive Dictionary of Orthodox Church-Slav*, "avdon" means *rabsky*, which is "slave".

2

The first "notes" made by foreigners about Muscovy (the beginnings of this literary genre), correspond to the birth of the Russian Empire.

The eastern frontiers of Europe at that time ran along the River Don, so that Moscow was in Asia, according to the notions and maps of the period. In the 16th century, Europeans discovered a new world — Muscovite Rus. The Pole, Maciej of Miechov, wrote, in his preface to *A Treatise on Two Sarmatias*: "Southern countries and the nations right up to India were discovered by the king of Portugal. May the northern countries and the nations which live on the Northern Ocean, discovered by the armies of the Polish king, be known to the world." The Miechovite's *Treatise*, according to E. Kluge, is an example of the Poles' bias when writing about Russia: "towards the end of the 16th century — to a large extent due to Polish influence — a picture of a barbarian, Asiatic and hostile Russia arises and the attitude of the West towards Russia takes on an isolationist and xenophobic character." Apart from the Miechovite, there were others who claimed to be "discoverers" of the new world: Albertus Campensis, Ioannes Fabri, Paulus Iovus. It is significant that none of them had ever been to Rus and that they copied the details of their accounts from each other. The main informants of European writers about Muscovy were the interpreters of Russian legates.

This new world, discovered with the help of interpreters, resembled the countries of Europe (there is nothing more deceptive than this apparent similarity), but not quite: the scale was not the same, and the religious rites were somewhat different, and the organization of the state was strange . . . Authors of the first accounts of Muscovy did not always fully understand what was being said to them. They often fashioned information to fit in with realities which were familiar to them and their readers. They tore facts out of context, judging them according to their own criteria, and introduced foreign concepts into their own systems of reference — which gave these concepts a different nuance or meaning. In a word, ever since Russia has been written about, apart from the problem of language, there has been the problem of transference from one cultural code to another. Furthermore, European writers, embroiled in religious and political conflicts of the period, often adapted the description of Muscovite Rus to fit in with their arguments against their opponents, giving, in effect, a desired picture rather than a true one. For example: the alleged inclination of the Russian tsar to convert to Catholicism served as an argument against the Reformation. One can also find traces of the imagination of Russian informants in 16th-century treatises about Muscovy, be it to mislead the adversary (for example, overstating the size of the tsar's army), be it as a joke, be it through lack of knowledge, especially where the confines of the Empire were concerned – like the Far North which was inhabited, according to Europeans, by babbling pygmies, by Samoyeds covered in hair down to their navels, and by people covered in fish scales. I think that even today many Europeans don't know much more about the Samoyeds . . .

Besides, Europeans who write about Russia today rarely go beyond the trivialities which had been formulated then – in the first half of the 16th century. That is why it is worth reading the old treatises in order to see how Russian stereotypes developed. For example: Russia as a prison. As long ago as 1522, Campensis wrote: "the whole of this country, irrespective of its great size, is so hermetically closed and guarded that not only slaves but also free people are unable to leave or enter without the tsar's *hramota*".* There was already talk of displacing entire nations at the tsar's whim, of exceptional drunkenness among Russians, of their laziness, cunning and distrust, and also of the loose ways of their wives (supposedly, every wife could be possessed for a small fee), and of the filth, and of the mud . . . And it was already noted at that time "that no other nation enjoyed such a bad reputation as the Russians". Why? Because no other nation was so like the Europeans without actually being them. Neither then, nor later, did Westerners go to the trouble of understanding Russian reality from within, that is, of looking at Russia through Russian eyes and only later translating this into their own language while maintaining

---

* Safe-conduct. *Tr.*

true proportions. Unfortunately, Westerners look at Russia from the outside – from a European point of view – and fashion what they have seen to fit in with their own order. The best example of this Eurocentric vision of the world is the map of Muscovy drawn up by Anthonius Wied of Gdańsk in 1544, on which the sides of our globe are shifted by ninety degrees so that we look at Rus from the west, having north to our left, while the east extends upwards, and in the place of the North Pole lies . . . Tartaria.

3

With the expansion of the Russian Empire came the development of the literary *genre* itself: foreigners' "notes" consisting both of eye-witness accounts and of accounts based on rumours heard from a third party. The afore-mentioned Miechovite, who was the precursor of Polish interest in Rus, most probably obtained information about his eastern neighbours from stories told by Russian prisoners of war taken into captivity at the Battle of Orsza. Hence the great lack of clarity and the great inventiveness in his work. Another classic author of the *genre*, Siegmund von Herberstein, who wrote *Rerum Moscoviticarum Commentarii*, did indeed visit Moscow twice – in 1517 and 1526 as a legate of the Habsburgs – but his description of Vassily III's state, although detailed and accompanied by maps, is not free from fabrication either, especially the description of places which Herberstein did not visit himself but for which he based his accounts on those of others (for example, the description of Solovky). And it is only the English sailors of the 16th century, Thomas Southem and John Spark, who really wrote about what they them-selves saw. Later, it varied. Diplomats, mercenaries, scholars and spies, travellers, writers, prisoners and exiles wrote about Russia. Among them were the Jesuit, Antonio Possevino, Priest Gregory XIII's legate, the German adventurer, Heinrich Staden, Ivan the Terrible's *oprichnik*,* the French condottiere, Jacques Margeret, the captain of Boris Godunov's bodyguards, the last king of the Poland, Stanisław August, Catherine II's unfortunate favourite, and Prince Adam Jerzy Czartoryski, Alexander I's talebearer, the King of Sardinia's legate, Joseph de Maistre – he lived in St Petersburg for fourteen years, Madame Anne Louise Germaine de Staël who escaped here from Napoleon, Astolphe de Custine, Alexander Dumas *père*, Théophile Gautier, then revolutionaries of various shades and colours, then the guests of Generalissimo Stalin, André Gide and Leon Feuchtwanger, and *zeka*s of Stalinism: Weissberg-Cybulski, Herling-Grudziński, Aleksander Wat, and finally, quite recently, the winner of the Nobel Prize for Literature, Claude Simon, invited by Mikhail Gorbachev, and Ryszard Kapuściński, author of *Imperium*. Of course, not all of them wrote about what they themselves saw; some preferred to repeat what they had been shown, others couldn't see what they really wanted to; and yet others saw what was not there at all, but did not notice what everyone else saw. "That's why the notes foreigners made about Russia should be read discriminately and carefully," stresses Kluchevsky, "for, apart from a few exceptions, foreigners generally wrote intuitively, going according to rumours and usually drawing general conclusions from chance events, while the public who read these accounts could neither verify nor question their trustworthiness. It is not without reason that, at the beginning of the 18th century, one foreign writer said that it has been the Russian nation's misfortune, over many centuries, that anyone could spread all sorts of nonsense about it across the world without risk of being ridiculed."

---

*Bodyguard. *Tr.*

46

Ryszard Kapuściński's *Imperium* is the last account written by a foreigner about the Eurasian power or, to put it more accurately, about its collapse. And so we have here not only the disintegration of the Empire but also a crisis of the literary *genre*, for ". . . the whole does not end in a higher and ultimate synthesis but, on the contrary, disintegrates and falls apart since, while the book was being written, it's main subject and theme – the great Soviet power – fell apart."

Kapuściński delves in the subject both in breadth and in depth. He travels both in time and in space. Now he returns to his own first meeting with the Empire "at the bridge which links the small town of Pinsk with the world's South" in 1939, now he ventures into Kolyma of today, now he looks into the future, repeating after Tolstoy: "We're going God knows where and God knows what's happening to us." At the same time, he emphasizes that he undertook these journeys alone – avoiding official institutions and routes – and the trajectory led from Brześć on the Bug to Magadan on the Pacific, and from Vorkut beyond the Arctic Circle to Termez on the Afghanistan border. Let us further add: Tbilisi and Baku, Erevan and Upper Karbakh, Yakutsk, Irkutsk and Ufa, and Donetsk, and Kiev and Drohobych, and Novgorod, and Minsk, and Pinsk . . . and here my first doubts appear: what was his choice founded on? Why did precisely these (and not other) points on the Empire's map draw Kapuściński's attention?

"If I can," the author of *Imperium* planned, "I'd like to travel across the whole of the Soviet Union, across its 15 federal republics . . ." The matter appears to be clarified, but not entirely. Because, planning further, among the most far-reaching points of this journey, Kapuściński mentions Vorkut or Novaya Zemlya in the North. But Vorkut and Novaya Zemlya are, after all, two different things. In the latter, one finds unremunerative mines, remnants of labour camps and unemployed miners; in the former, atomic testing grounds, nuclear waste and ecological disaster. To trust to chance while choosing an itinerary is like writing a book by throwing dice, where fate and the will of civil servants (who grant permission to visit Novaya Zemlya) – and not the logic of the case – prompt the subject matter. The intention to embrace all the Soviets, from end to end, carries within itself the risk of not really seeing anything, especially what is in the middle (*v glubinke*). Take, for example, post-Soviet rural life, which is completely absent from *Imperium*. Kapuściński's method is as simple as a tourist's voyage; a few days here, a few days there, and from every hole of a place a chapter-picture, like a souvenir slide. Of course, an excellent writer renders the pictures exquisite, but . . . what for? To produce a comic book about the Empire?

An attempt to travel across the whole of the Soviet Union and to see what is happening in Tomsk and in Omsk, impressive but super-ficial, inevitably leads to simplified diagnoses, to summaries and sym-bols into which the author crams impressions which are often not entirely clarified. In *Lapidarium III*, Kapuściński notes: "To live in a country for so long as to be able to say that I don't know it at all." Exactly! How else can one explain this tendency to draw conclusions in *Imperium* except by haste? Oh, people eat quickly in the bar – the author remarks. It is probably the spectre of hunger, coded in the col-lective memory, that has found expression . . . Or: why is there a shortage of spoons and knives? Because all the raw materials needed to manufacture them have gone into the production of barbed wire . . . I've taken the first examples that come to mind; there are many of them. Kapuściński is aware of these simplifications because: ". . . it is impossible to avoid an abstract approach. The enormous scale of the events taking place can only be presented by using a language and concepts which are general, synthesizing, indeed abstract, while being aware that, time and again, you will fall into the trap of using simplifications and easily undermined statements." Despite this, how-ever, the scale of the subject outgrew the possibilities of the literary *genre* and, instead of a synthesis, the whole thing falls apart . . . into details.

Details? The strength of documentary prose lies in detail, provided that, carefully chosen, it focuses on the problem or event like a lens. Otherwise, details are tedious and, instead of condensing, blur the picture. It is enough to compare "First meetings" from *Imperium* (1939–1967) – which have already settled in the author's memory like wasps in amber – with the chapter "From above" (1989–1991), where everything sticks, any speck of dust. In the former, the sugary deposits in a box of boiled sweets were expressive; in the latter, the author's sweat is superfluous (at Stepanakert airport, for example). For an author's attention registers every detail; at a given moment, everything seems important and only after some time, from a distance, can what is essential be sifted from what is merely rubbish. The choice of detail indicates whether the author has the upper hand over the reality which he has undertaken to describe, or whether that reality imposes its chaos, where hazard reigns . . . That can only be justified by saying that the subject described has fallen apart. (Even the choice of books quoted in *Imperium* gives the impression of randomness, as if the author cited everything that he had read while writing: Ingarden and Bruno Schulz, Leonardo and Simone Weil . . . . Sometimes the sources used speak volumes about the book, and to reach for the Marxist Ejdelman while leaving out Karamzin or Kluchevsky as a source of historical knowledge, speaks for itself.)

And, finally, the language: ". . . I am trying to use short sentences," we read in *Lapidarium III*. "They create tempo and movement. They are quick and lend clarity to prose. But while I was writing *Imperium*, I suddenly realized that, in this case, description requires longer sentences. This results from the extensity of the subject, which cannot be embraced in short sentences. Style must be appropriate to subject. Description of the infinitely broad, extensive Russian landscape requires long sentences." And so we compare: ". . . the Russian language, with wide, extensive and unending sentences, like the Russian land," – this is from *Imperium* – "where there is no Cartesian discipline, no asceticism in the aphorisms." Hey, but what about Gogol's, Akhmatova's, and Shalamov's laconism? Varlam Tikhonovich Shalamov wrote that there are two traditions in the Russian language: Tolstoy's sentence, slow and heavy, like turning soil over with a spade, and Pushkin's sentence, short and sonorous, like a slap on the cheek. If you forget about one of these, you can only get to know half of Russia, according to Miłosz's formula that everything there is to know about Russia is already in the Russian language.

5

With the evolution of mass media, a new kind of foreigner writing about Russia has emerged – the foreign correspondent. Unfortunately, in most cases, the same criticisms can be leveled against accounts written by these correspondents as Kluchevsky made against accounts written by their predecessors. I worked in Moscow for one of the Polish newspapers at the beginning of the 1990s and had the opportunity to observe the work of my fellow correspondents from close up. I remember one of them in particular – his name is irrelevant. He wrote for three newspapers at the same time and the most important event of the day for him was the afternoon edition of *Izvestia*, from which he concocted a few pieces which, in the evening, he presented as his own. Others, less indolent, would dash to every possible press conference, meeting and reception, where they diligently swallowed the *chepukha* (nonsense) served up to them. One has to admit that the Russians are expert at serving this up as many a foreigner has learnt, not least Custine. Some of the correspondents also watched Russian television and sought inspiration there. Add to this the special shop on Byegova Street, where every correspondent could supply himself with provisions which could not be bought in Moscow at the time, and the many other privileges separating us from reality like an opaque pane of glass, and you can understand that the image of Russia in foreign mass media and Russia in reality are two different things. Apart from human factors such as laziness, ignorance and lack of knowledge (the above-mentioned colleague had not read Gogol, and attributed *Chronicles of Years Gone By* to Pushkin!), equally crucial are the general shortcomings from which the media suffers: urgency (you have to meet successive deadlines), which makes it impossible to concentrate – and you need to concentrate if you are to analyse events in depth which is often more important for a correct diagnosis than for an impressive, though superficial, piece; the journalistic herd instinct, which means that the correspondents are despatched *en masse* to the location of events, be it war, a coup d'état, a press conference, and all write and comment about the same thing; the pursuit of sensation, scandal and blood, without regard for the commonplace, which holds little attraction for the mass reader; concentrating attention on major political events while leaving out that which is peripheral and provincial; all this means that a large part of what journalists write about the Russia of today fails to go beyond the trivial, or beyond stereotypes or hearsay.

6

Now here, let us take, for example, the *vyushka* – the little shutter on a Russian stove. You can read this paragraph in Rozanov's *Fallen Leaves*: "In new stoves, you turn the handle one way and the chimney is open, you turn it the other way and it is closed. This is ungodly [*neblagochestivo*, in the original] because there is no thought or care here. In the past, you would put up a tiny shutter, without inclining it either to the right or to the left and it fitted straight away and tightly. Then you would put a large shutter over the small one like a cap . . ." What foreigner can understand Vasyaley Vasyalyevich's concept of "ungodly" in this paragraph? After all, there are no Russian stoves or shutters in European houses. When I first read *Fallen Leaves*, while living in a Moscow tower block not far from Izmaylovsky Park, I did not pay attention to the subtlety of the author's speculations about shutters and godliness. I did not have enough experience, my imagination was asleep. I read the work a second time on Solovky, in the building that used to be the station for biological studies on Herring Point, sitting, on long winter evenings, by the open door of our stove. The fire crackled, the flame threw shadows on the walls, reflections flickered in the windows like a magic lantern, and, at night, I would close the chimney, first putting the tiny shutter in place, being careful not to tilt it either to the left or to the right, and then I would cover the small one with the large one like a cap. "Straight away and tightly", too, I was aware of the precision of Rozanov's thought. You could say, I tried it for myself.

VI

This country is an entirely different world and it is impossible to make any judgement about it without having lived here for some time.

Joseph de Maistre

1

Summer, on the Islands, is short and sudden, like an ejaculation. Barely has the snow seeped into the earth than greenery shoots out in the wink of an eye. Delicately at first, it drapes the trees as if with emerald foam, then it springs from every cranny, it pokes out from beneath the rocks of the monastic walls, lines the roads, covers the *pomoika*,* draws duckweed over lakes and ponds, and even stones turn green! The meadows are full of flowers, juicy grasses and herbs with a strong and pungent scent: lungwort, vetches, willow-herb, feverfew, chamomile, ox-eyed daisies, bell-flowers, fescue, pink helichrysum, called cat's paws, meadowsweet, dandelions, speedwell, violets, sweet peas, marsh willow-herb, forget-me-nots, snapdragons, clover, willow-grass, fox-tail. On the marshy meadows grow sun-dew, cloudberries, ledum and heather, ferns, peat-moss, cotton grass, bog bilberries, horsetail and cranberries. All this whirls, pollinates, multiplies and

---

* See Glossary.

53

divides, and climbs towards the sun, which, in summer, shines here for twenty hours a day like a monstrous lamp. People on the Islands, like the plants, also enjoy the light, satiate themselves with warmth and couple wildly, knowing no limits. Everybody with everybody, as it comes, united by chance or by shared vodka. And later, children are born, like clippings; they are all short of something: be it brains, a mum or a home. And they grow, just like those plants . . .

2

After a month's stay in Poland and France, I returned "home" – to Herring Point. In the meantime, the garden had grown over with stinging nettles, chickweed and wild sorrel, spiders' webs had shrouded the house, and the cats' fur had got matted and will have to be shorn. And only the sea beyond my window remains White and nothing has changed in my computer – I just have to switch on the monitor and find old traces, traces of my thoughts of a month ago. And now, as I sit once again at my writing table with my eyes staring at the blazing water (the tide has just started to come in), it feels as if I have seen Paris and Normandy, Wrocław and Kłodzko Valley in a dreamy vision and that I have invented the people I met there. Even the Maison-Laffitte building, although so real because, after all, that is where I send all my copy (it is thanks to it that I exist), sometimes appears from here as a mainland where one can touch down, at other times, as a luminous mirage on a vibrating horizon . . .

Poland from here appears small and confined, and irritated. And, in my ears, I still have that peculiar pretentious intonation which characterizes the Polish language today. After seven years of absence from my country, my attention (as a philologist) was drawn to the rhythm of my compatriots' common language – the raised tone in which some argued that both the Pope and the king of pop music chose Poland and others that everybody there is a thief. Miłosz observed that Poles who had arrived from Russia couldn't find a place for themselves in Poland. The poet's father, for example: "Russia was an expanse; you didn't have to bump into anybody with every step you took and whoever grew to like it felt ill at ease in more civilized but densely populated and confined countries. This is exactly what happened to my father. When he later lived in Poland, he kept on complaining about the lack of scale, about the smallness of everything and about the torpor."

Paris, on the other hand, smells of vanilla and food, even from here. And I can still feel the ache in my legs "because, after all, Paris is as if especially designed for walking and I don't know another city in the world where one walks so ecstatically" (Krzysztof Rutkowski). But they slowly disappear – the smells, the tones, and the aches . . . The taste of rain in the wine which we drank with Victor outside Hotel Lambert fades away as does the smell of the sea in the mussels which we ate with Agata and Wojtek in Yport. And Midsummer Night in Port de Montobello pales, and Malick Laye's drums in Café Calife become quiet, and Matty Ma's bass slowly grows silent. The colours of the *Dame à la licorne* in the Musée de Cluny fade, the stained-glass windows in Notre-Dame darken. Only the features of friends whom I met after many years become sharper with the passage of time . . .

Here, on Herring Point, thousands of versts from Paris, I look through Czapski's album, listen to Paolo Conti's record, and on my writing table lie: the last edition of *Kultura*, a few photographs, some of Ducollet's engravings and a wad of notes about the decadence of the western world – evidence that it still exists.

3

According to Gombrowicz, we shouldn't write "tomato soup is good", because that is an encroachment, whereas we are fully entitled to say

"I like tomato soup". This, according to Gombrowicz, is style. Maybe it is a question of style, but I would go further – to specifics. Because, after all, there are bad tomato soups – they might be burnt or too salty – so only saying "I like this tomato soup" makes any real sense. For example: the one I ate for lunch at Maison-Laffitte was truly delicious! It's not by chance that I recall this lunch because, from the questions which I was asked at table, I realized that, although I'd been writing about Solovky for *Kultura* for three years, nobody knows how we live on a daily basis: what we eat, how we dress, how we fill our time. And there, at Maison-Laffitte, at the table over stuffed duck, I believe, or maybe over dessert (a fantastic millefeuille!), the idea for this chapter came to me. A chapter about our daily, Solovetskian life/existence. Let me immediately point out that our existence does not, in any way, differ from the lives of other Solovetskians (apart from the *bomzh*s, of course). Conditions in the Far North impose certain forms of behaviour: at home, as on the sea. And so: it is the water, earth and forests . . . that feed us here.

"The sea is our field," say the coastal people. Wheat does not grow at these latitudes and fish often replaces bread. Various fish live in the White Sea, many of which you don't come across in the Polish language, which is why I'm calling them by the names they have here. First comes *selyodka*, or fat herring, for which Solovky was already famous in the tsar's day, and *treska* [cod], thanks to which the coastal people used to be called "*treskoyeds*" [cod-eaters]. We salt both fish in solid barrels for winter. Then there's *navaga*, tiny but delicious, *koryushka* [smelt], which smells of fresh cucumbers, and the huge *kambala* [flounder], which we catch with fishing spears. The bays of Solovky are more rarely visited by *krasnaya* [red] fish, from the Salmonidae family: *syomga, gorbusha* [hump-backed salmon], *kumsha*. Sometimes *sig* [lavaret] or a *pinagor* will find its way into the net. (Apart from salt water we also eat fresh water fish because there are countless lakes with an abundance of fish in them: there are perch, and whitefish and roach and ruff and burbot and crucian carp; often we'll catch pike, sometimes trout or carp). We catch fish using rods, nets, fishing spears and fish-pots – whichever way we know and like. In winter, on the other hand, the nets are set under the ice or we sit at an air-hole in the frozen lake with our rods, watching the sun play on the ice hummocks. The sea not only gives us fish, but it throws out driftwood for heating, and sea cabbage, rich in vitamins and iodine. It really does nourish us.

The earth in the North is difficult to cultivate. There is little fertile soil here; mostly there is sand, clay and rock. Sometimes soil for plant-beds has to be brought in from afar, then the beds are boarded so that the rain won't wash the soil away, spread with manure or *nyasha* [rotting seaweed] and only then can we sow. Nor does the climate here favour gardens: the snow lies for a long time, the earth thaws slowly, and frequent frosts nip the plants. On the other hand, we do have an abundance of sunshine – even too much at times. Take radishes, for example: growth goes into the leaves rather than the roots due to the excess of light. *Kartoshka* reigns supreme on Solovky. It is the main food produced on the Islands. *Kartoshka* is more than just food here; it is the sacred plant of post-Soviet times. Sowing it takes on the character of a ritual. At the beginning of June (before *Troitsa* – Trinity – without fail), everybody, entire families, go to their plant-beds. Turning their backsides up towards the sky as if they were bowing low, they dig for two or three days, then they bury the bulbs which they had carefully stored over the winter, and drink for a week or more, feeling that they have fulfilled their duty. The same happens with earthing up and gathering the crop. Having your own *kartoshka* on the Islands guarantees that you won't starve to death. The Solovetskians, a lazy nation, also like *kartoshka* because it doesn't require much effort – it is enough to bury it, earth it up and dig it out. There is no weeding, no watering, no bedding out. Any other form of cultivation which might require more care is rarely seen here. A few tomatoes in hothouses, some strawberries here and there, turnips and sorrel, and you can count those who grow flowers on the fingers of one hand. It is not surprising that, initially, our garden stunned the Solovetskians; later, they just brushed it aside: *inostrantsy*.* Because, apart from potatoes, strawberries, turnips and sorrel, we grow six kinds of lettuce, cauliflower, peas and broad beans, chives, dill and parsley, carrots, cabbage, beetroot and rhubarb, lemon balm and mint, horseradish and golden root and no end of flowers, and even *Cannabis indica* of quite good quality has grown here. Every time I read Miłosz's *A Hunter's Year*, I can't help but compare our gardens. There, on Bear Peak, Miłosz plants bougainvillia, beds out *fedjoe*, and reindeer eat the flowers of his heliotrope. We, here on Herring Point, plant *kartoshka*, bed out rhubarb and pink rhodiola, and the neighbours' goats nibble away at our chives.

The forests on Solovky are full of mushrooms, berries and marshes. And you have to wear gum boots when you go to the forest. We visit the forest from mid-July; before then it is empty except for mosquitoes, biting midges and gadflies. The first to appear is the *moroshka* [cloudberry], which looks like an amber-coloured raspberry and grows on low bushes on marshland. Pushkin asked for them before he died . . . Then the baneberry ripens and the bog bilberry (otherwise called "the drunkard" because it stupefies), and mushrooms start to spring up, mushroom madness — I haven't seen so many mushrooms in my life. We don't pick them all because who needs *boletus luteus* when it's hard enough to cope with all the ceps. The most valuable are the *mlechaye* and *khrushche*, lacteous mushrooms which we salt for the winter so as to eat them in February with potatoes . . . finger-licking good. We dry red and ordinary *kozlarze* and, of course, ceps, which they call *belye* [white ones], here. Others — chanterelles, meadow mushrooms, *lactarus deliciosus* (Imperial mushrooms), morels — we sometimes put into soups as a spice and no more. Some people marinate toadstools to make an infusion as medicine. Apparently, the Samoyed shamans foretold the future after taking them. Autumn is the season for blueberries, rowanberries and cranberries. We gather

---

* See Glossary.

the last two after first frost. We make preserves from the berries or steam them in huge jars. And Vasyalich makes such moonshine from them that tears roll down your cheeks after one glass.

The rest, we buy. Milk — both cow's and goat's — from which we make soft cheese and butter, we buy from our neighbours, and bread, salt, oil, matches, tea and vodka in the shop. Sometimes eggs. And flour for *bliny*. While Vasha brings us meat once a year, in late autumn.

Venison rump, haunch of elk, bears' paws . . .

4

Jerzy Pomianowski complains, in *Kultura* (1–2/1997), that the image of Russia which emerges from the accounts of Polish correspondents "reminds one of a film made up of snapshots, assembled rushes before editing". Because: "Few people, and then only rarely, allow themselves a general view, let alone a prognosis." And so: "As a result, we look at the trees, not seeing the woods." As to the comparison with film, I agree: the image of Russia in Polish (and not only Polish) accounts does, indeed, remind you of assembled rushes before editing, but the reasons for this state of affairs, I see differently. You can only see the woods from a distance or from above. From the air, for example. I don't dispute the fact that such a perspective does have its advantages (even its prerogatives because it allows you to dispense with hard facts), but it is often misleading and you can mistake the smoke of a fire for a mist. In order to understand what threatens the woods, you have to look at the trees, their barks, diseases, parasites, roots and the lichen on their leaves. The same applies to Russia. Those who write about it generally look at it either from a distance — through the telescope of television and newspapers — or from high above — from the summits of Kremlin intrigues. And so they compose a collage from other people's conceptions or arrange a puzzle with chess-like end games: who will checkmate whom and in how many moves? There are also those who fly over the woods in an aeroplane or cross them in an express train and then present us with an album of slides or a tourist guidebook. Russia is so huge that not only is it impossible to understand it by reason alone (Tyutchev), but life is too short to experience it in its entirety. Hence all efforts at generalization are feeble, and prognoses miss the target. The most competent experts on Soviet Russia foretold the future from the tea leaves of politics but none of them foresaw the coup d'état or the fall of the Soviet Union. So I'd rather not expect prognoses (of the sort: "Will Russia still be here in 2000?") and generalizations, but facts and close-ups. Not fortuitous facts, of course, or any old close-ups, but that is another subject — that is a craft. Gogol could portray the whole of Russia in one district.

5

Let us take the Russian *banya*,* for example; it is a detail, but how symbolic and rich in meaning. The first allusion to the *banya*s in Russian writing is already typical because it is associated with . . . a foreigner's account! In *Chronicles of Years Gone By*, you can find a description of the apostle Andrew's journey along the Dnieper to Kiev and further north, to Novgorod, or rather the place where Novgorod was later built. (Let us not forget that this refers to the beginning of our era.) There, in the North, St Andrew met Slavonic tribes, got to know their customs, and was very struck by the way they washed and how they slapped themselves with birch twigs. The fact that, on his return to Rome, he spoke of nothing but the *banya* of the northern countries is proof of how surprised he was: "I saw amazing things among the Slavs on my way here. I saw wooden *banya*, red hot, and

---

* See Glossary.

people in them, naked, who were pouring tanning acid over themselves, raising young twigs above their heads and thrashing themselves to the point that they could only walk out with difficulty, barely able to breathe. They then poured cold water over themselves and only in this way revived. And they did this every day, without anybody forcing them, and they tormented themselves, saying that it wasn't torture, only their ablutions." If we accept that St Andrew was the first foreigner in Rus, then we can take his story about the Russian *banya* to be a precursor of the literary genre. (Let us not be troubled by the fact that the apostle's wanderings to the North belong to myth − literature was born of myth.) In other words, the chapter in *Chronicles of Years Gone By* about the *banya* can be seen as a prototype of all foreign accounts of Rus. And the *banya* itself − a metaphor of Rus?

6

There is sometimes so much steam in the Russian *banya* that it is difficult to make anything out − things emerge unexpectedly from the coils of dampness: a face, a backside, somebody's pelvis . . . A friend of mine from Poland once visited the Islands. A press-photographer. He only stayed a short while, barely a week (but he snapped a great deal!), and once managed to try out the *banya*, because the Solovetskian *banya* takes place once a week: on Fridays for women, Saturdays for men. My friend returned from the *banya* greatly impressed and, as soon as he stepped through the door, started to tell me what he imagined he had seen there, and he could have imagined seeing many things, because I remember my "first time", when steam and *mat* condensed the field of vision, and the tinkle of glasses in the clouds of the steam room took on the proportions of a banquet. For a long time, my friend could not forgive himself for not having taken a camera in with him because it seems that he suddenly understood why

Svidrigailov described eternity as a country *banya* with spiders in the corners. Unfortunately, the Polish journalist in the *banya* on the Islands only caught glimpses of things — amusing characters, pieces of some world, details, which he was utterly unable to put together into a whole in order to see the reality, and, at the same time, himself within it.

Over one thousand people live on Solovky, all with different biographies — as if they had sprung up from different worlds or different stories. But, in the *banya*, they all wash together; here, their destinies cross — in one steam room. Here, *muzhik*s come from the deep seas so as to drink to fresh fish; and young *poslushnik*s dawdle away their time, slipping away from under the eyes of the watchful monk. Here come advocates of reform and supporters of the iron fist, and Orthodox believers, and leftists and absolute non-believers; and, on one shelf, lie both thieves and *volnonayomnye* [civilian, volunteer workers] and former *zeka*s and their wardens, and guardians of order and violators of the same, and all of them naked. Some slap themselves with birch twigs, others with juniper branches, and old Dontsov with bunches of stinging nettles, which helps his rheumatism. Here you can spin fresh gossip and grumble about Yeltsin, chat about fish and about women, and about diseases and about idlers. Because the *banya* on the Islands serves as club, café, pulpit and speaker's platform. Here they spread propaganda, declaim and plot, and drink and nibble. Sasha Pinagorsky, for example, incites the people against Nebozhenko and, the summer before last, the false monk Dionizy incited people on the subject of monastic shenanigans, until it turned out that he was a schismatic and madman. News spreads in the *banya* like steam and, like steam, clouds the eyes. Here it is enough to open one's ears in order to hear Russia: its hum and *mat* and pain.

"The *banya* is a second mother," goes a Russian proverb.

The Solovetsky *banya* was built in 1717. You can recognize the monastic masters' hand from afar: a stone structure of immense dimensions, it reminds you more of a granary than a bath-house. Inside, there are two spacious rooms, rows of benches, piles of wooden buckets, taps by the wall and wooden boards on the floor. Further along is the steam room: the smell of birch twigs, three tiers of shelves – it is difficult to last out on the top one – a stone ceiling, condensed steam dripping on to rocks in the corner, blasts of heat. Next to it is a more recent extension where the changing room is located – hangers, stale air. The *banya* was built for pilgrims and *trudnik*s;[*] the monks had their own *banya* in the monastery. Then, in the days of SLON, the *zeka*s used it once a week. Today, it is listed architecture protected by the state – as the plaque above the door says – and we all wash here: from the *Glava* [Head] to the last, flea-infested *bomzh*, and the monks with us. Everyone has his time and place on the shelf: some like to come at two o'clock, as soon as the *banya* opens (especially the monks and the elderly), some a bit later, when steam curls your ears (youth, state officials, museum employees), yet others come towards evening when they return from fishing (*muzhiks, bichs*). So you have to spend some time on the Island and visit the *banya* at different times in order to find your bearings, more or less. Washing in the *banya* is a ceremony – with its own ritual, accessories, sayings. And you can immediately pick out strangers, those who don't know their way around. For example: my friends from Poland, who sometimes try the *banya* out of curiosity but have only just enough courage to go inside, and then, undressed and clearly embarrassed, wash quickly – rarely making use of the steam room, even more rarely using birch twigs – and, without cooling off, sneak out. Yet, later on, they recount fantastic stories. Like that press-photographer.

7

18 July

"Russia and Solovky" is the subject of the conference organized on the Island by the German foundation Friedrich-Naumann-Stiftung

---

[*] Volunteer helpers at the monastery. *Tr.*

and the Russian "Memorial". The main participants in the discussion were to be students from Moscow University belonging to the *stroiotryad* of Solovky, that is, from a volunteer corps of workers, and the employees of the local museum. The latter didn't turn up. The guests who took part in the meeting were: Professor Karl Schlegel from Germany, Andrey Blinushov and Yulya Sereda from *Karta* of Ryazan, Dietrich Studemann, the attaché at the German embassy, the journalist Sonya Margolina and Yury Brodsky, photographer. The discussion took place in the workers' corps' room, in the monastery. A holiday atmosphere prevailed and there was a smell of young sweat and bonfire smoke. On the tables were imported fruit juices, chocolate, bananas and apples. Solovetsky children's mouths would water, I thought, because they don't eat such things. The Germans, irreproachably punctual, sat at the side, the golden frames of their spectacles glistening, the scent of expensive eau-de-colognes as are not drunk here, emanating all around. The young people gathered lazily; you could hear the buzz at the door as they pushed their way through. They were joking, laughing. Slim, with attractive faces, they were unlike their peers from Solovky, who are primitive and feeble-minded from vodka. A programme and questions for discussion were distributed to the participants of the meeting:

"Who is guilty? What shall we do? Can the past be a lesson for the future?"

The Germans, unaccustomed to a lack of respect for time, gradually grew annoyed. Finally, Blinushov began the meeting. As an introduction, he presented the rules of discussion, introduced the meeting's guests and handed over to Professor Schlegel to open the discussion. The professor said that the silence – the conspiracy of silence – which accompanied the deeds of the Nazis in Germany, was giving him no peace and that he had come to the Islands to find out what young Russians here, among the remains of SLON, think about their grandfathers and fathers. As an historian, he was interested in the influence of the recent past on the reality of today. Next, he passed the

Dictaphone around the room so that everybody could introduce themselves and explain their motive for coming to Solovky. There was a commotion, the students played the fool, showing off in front of each other, some openly mocking. You could see that they were not prepared to open up and would answer the organizers' pathos with jokes. A beautiful, flaxen-haired student of philology hummed one of Vysotsky's songs: *"No i ptitsy letyat na syevyer, yesly im nadoyest tyeplo"* ["Well, and birds fly north if they get bored by the warmth"]. And then she added that, as a humanist, she didn't like drinking alcohol collectively and prefered to drink alone, and here, on the Islands, it was easy to isolate yourself. Laughter broke out, and applause. They had come on holiday and not to discuss their fathers' sins. Editor Blinushov, somewhat embarrassed by the light-heartedness of Russian youth, decided to set an example and described his road to "Memorial". He spoke about his grandfather, the commandant of a Soviet labour camp and how, at home, the truth used to be concealed from little Andrey; and when he would ask about the emaciated people behind barbed wire on the photographs in his family album, he was told that they were soldiers. Andrey himself worked for the Ryazan militia for a couple of years until they began beating up people who were in the right. Then he resigned.

"And if those people hadn't been right, then you would have beat them up?" a spotty boy, who looked like the Artful Dodger, asked from the back. More applause; this time the guests applauded, too. Andrey was disconcerted.

As the discussion evolved, emotions started to show and masks fell from the youngsters. Convictions, sometimes even beliefs, appeared through the laughter. The gulf between organizers and students grew increasingly wider. The bone of contention was the question: "Can one speak of Russia's spiritual rebirth without the sincere repentance of the entire nation?" In contrast to the moral conceitedness of the "Memorial" members and their categorical imperative of general repentance for their fathers' and grandfathers' sins, the young Russians argued that each life should be made to account for itself.

"If you want penance, go to a monastery, pray or hang yourself," said the same spotty youth who had a moment ago won applause. "But let others live as they want. You can't make people pay for their predecessors' sins because that leads to collective responsibility and washes away personal guilt. History is written by some at one time, by others at another time. People from different camps, holding opposing positions. What are merits to some might be mistakes to others, and nobody can guarantee that tomorrow you won't do time for what might have earned you medals today. That's why you can't justify yourself by textbooks which somebody else has written, but have to write your own life and sign it legibly."

"But doesn't such disregard for history, making it so relative, threaten SLON's return?" Blinushov asked . . .

. . . I left, interested in neither answer nor conclusions. What talk could there be of SLON's return when the spirit of that beast was still present on Solovky? And, not just here. Not long ago, when in Moscow I said that I had arrived from Solovky, I was asked what I was serving time for. For many Russians, the labour camp on the Islands still exists. And it is true; it is enough to look a little more carefully, to tear your eyes away at least for a moment from the razzle and dazzle and money granted by the West, in order to see barbed wire all around. Real, solid wire with which adults fence their gardens here, and which children use to wrap around themselves when they play at prison. Last winter, a couple of dogs were eaten on Solovky. Out of hunger! My friend's dream is the privatization of the room with a kitchen in a former labour camp barrack where she has been living for the past twenty years. Unfortunately, according to the last inventory of habitable quarters in the *posyolok*, this barrack does not exist. Sasha Kh. hung himself because he lost his concubine at cards and I've often heard the saying here: "*ne poiman, ne vor*" ["not caught, not a thief"], which describes SLON's morality. You can see traces of SLON on the Islands at every step, in the landscape as well as in people's heads. Obviously, it is difficult for someone who is living in the most expensive Solovetsky hotel and is organizing meetings with youngsters, who themselves have come here only on holiday, to understand what I was thinking about on my way home.

19 July

On 28 March, 1959, Miłosz wrote to Merton: "Geoffrey Gorer maintains that there was only one society based on the principle of sin — in opposition to western society, which is based on the principle of guilt; namely, tsarist Russia. I feel he has hit the nail on the head here. Guilt is individual; it is *my* guilt. Sin is universal — it is not I who am guilty, but society, and I can be redeemed not through any effort of my own (grace given to me) but by the community. That is why they are always searching for the Kingdom of God; one which is located in time, substituting Communism in its place and, perhaps, in the future, a different kind of eschatology. While individual responsibility is washed away; in 1945, I witnessed murders committed by Russian soldiers with a deep sense of sin but without any sense of personal guilt." After this quotation, let us return, for a moment, to yesterday's discussion at Solovetsky monastery. Members of "Memorial" ask whether the spiritual rebirth of society is possible without the sincere repentance of the entire nation. But repentance, after all, is atonement for one's sins and so the question included in yesterday's discussion programme bears out Gorer's intuition — it holds true to Russian society. Well yes, someone might say, but, on the other hand, there are students from the corps of volunteer workers, who stick, so stubbornly, to their opinion. They want to live normal lives like their peers in the West, and they don't intend to repent collectively for the sins of their predecessors. Perhaps young Russians will finally break away from the centuries' old tradition of "society based on the principle of sin", will stop searching for the Kingdom of God on earth and will start assuming individual responsibility for their actions? Unfortunately, I fear that this question is just as academic as the entire discussion at the Laundry Corps, because reality outside does not give a darn either about those who want to repent or about those who want to live for themselves.

8

The end of summer on Solovky reminds one of a dream: the horizon emerges from the mists like the thread of a story interrupted in mid-sentence, the sky is ashen grey, the sea, pearly grey, and, in the air, gossamers float. Here and there, birches already start to blaze, grasses turn yellow, a scent of moss hangs in the air. A grey vapour covers the earth, meadows and marshy fields sleep in it, and the lakes appear to slumber, dreaming of trees and of people bending over them. And people grow melancholy because summer is coming to an end, and they drink so as to prolong this dream. And only among birds is there an uproar before their journey: ducks teach their little ones to swim, lapwings chirrup for flight, eiders get agitated and loons scheme. Suddenly autumn comes. Days either dazzle with sunshine or lash with rain. The sea storms and rages, white with foam. The forests are an orgy of colours: birch trees, like candles, burn yellow against the dark green of spruce, aspens turn crimson, blueberry bushes red, and marshes glow in shades of orange. The earth slowly cools. Morning ground-frosts nip flowers in the garden. In the house there is the smell of dried mushrooms, the bubbling of simmering berries; bunches of herbs, parsley and dill hang everywhere. We pit potatoes, beetroots, carrots and swedes. We salt herrings and *khrushche*. Nights on the Islands lengthen as if they were shadows of the day, and they grow black as ink. Only sometimes, unexpectedly, can you glimpse a splash of light in the sky, as if it were seeping in from that other world. It is the *syevyernoye siyanie*, the Northern lights, the aureola borealis . . .

VII

... and I hope that my writing will not only amuse, but will also provoke thought.

Joseph de Maistre

1

4 September

Nina Mikhailovna has sent me, from Moscow, the first three volumes of the *Library of Ancient Russian Literature*, compiled by the Department of Ancient Russian Literature of the Russian Academy of Science, under the direction of Likhachov (a former SLON *zeka*). And one can confidently say that this is an event in the history of Russian culture – an event which cannot be overestimated. For the first time in the history of its writings, the entire output of Ancient Russian literature is made available (with a simultaneous translation into contemporary Russian), collected in twenty volumes: from the *Sermon on Law and Grace* by Ilarion right up to the 20th-century correspondence of Orthodox believers (included in the *Library* because of the conservative nature of the linguistics of the text). Alongside well-known works such as *The Tale of Igor's Regiment* or *The Life of Avvakum*, things which previously had been accessible only to specialists were also included: for example, excellent monuments of the *raskolnichaya*, the old believers' literary school of Vyga,

69

notes made on birch bark dating from the 12th century and apocryphal works of the Khlysts recently found near Novgorod . . . However, it is impossible to mention them all. Only mere scraps of Ancient Russian literature have reached us, but, thanks to the *Library* in which these fragments have been brought together, we can have some idea of its vast size and the image it reflects. The academician Likhachov writes, in his *Memoirs*, that he chose the faculty of Ancient Russian literature because "it recorded the traits of our national character during its maturation".

Library gives Russia back seven centuries of literature – it is like restoring memory to an amnesiac. The question is whether this sick man will want to make use of it, having grown accustomed to all sorts of pulp literature or to not reading anything at all. Many of my friends here, not in the least bit stupid, are astonished to learn that the written word in Rus has a rich tradition reaching back to the 11th century, and that medieval Russian documentary prose has no equivalent anywhere in the world. (Incidentally, let me remind some of my compatriots who like to talk of the cultural backwardness of Russians that the oldest recorded Polish sentence dates from the thirteenth century, while Gallus Anonymus's chronicles, our first vestiges in Latin, date from a century later than Ilarion's *Sermon*. So it's possible that the "fore-image" of the nation's spiritual life, retained in *Library*, will help Russians in their cultural self-identification, after dozens of years of self-destruction.

The first volumes of *Library* embrace works from the 11th to 12th centuries and include *Sermon on Law and Grace*, *Chronicle of Years Gone By*, *The Tale of Boris and Gleb*, *The Life of Theodosy*, *Teachings and Sermons* by Cyril Turovsky, the tales of *The Killing of Andrey Bogulubsky* and *Miracles of the Vladimir Icon of the Virgin*, *The Kiev-Pecherska Paterikon* . . . all of them written by monks in their *kelya*.

Let us, for example, open *The Life of Theodosy of Piechera* and peep into the old man's cell: ". . . there, sits the great Nikon writing books while Father Theodosy, huddled up at the edge of his seat, is spinning thread in order to sew them together." Or: ". . . worthy Ilarion, master among scribes, recounted how, day and night, he would transcribe manuscripts in Father Theodosy's cell while the latter hummed psalms and spun." This took place at the dawning of the Russian state, under the reign of Yaroslav the Wise, who ". . . loved monks greatly and endlessly read their books. And he gathered scribes to translate Greek into Slavonic and put it into writing. So they transcribed and collected a multitude of books designed to teach the faithful and to praise God's word. Just as with land — one ploughs it, another sows, others reap and eat — so here, Vladimir loosened the soil and enlightened through Baptism, Yaroslav sowed the words of books in people's hearts, and we nourish ourselves with them." By comparing the writing of books to the cultivation of land, the chronicler reveals the main task facing monasteries at the time when the Russian state was starting to be formed: the cultivation of new expanses and the bringing of order to chaos. After all, the vast, mud-covered forests and steppes that lay between Europe and Asia were in a state of disorder — there were no points of reference: no mountains, towns, fortresses; there were neither borders nor *stanitsa*s,* only snow and wild forests, and tumuli, and hordes of nomads. This expanse had neither history ("a past preserved in writing"), nor a true faith (idols proliferated among the tribes), and, up until now, nobody had *osmyslil* it, that is, become aware of it. A double task faced the monasteries: it was not just the earth that had to be cultivated, but the semantic fields as well. In a word, out of

---

*Border guard posts. *Tr.*

chaos they had to create a world with the help of language . . .

. . . which had come about through the merger of ancient Bulgarian (called ancient Slavonic) with different variants of the Russian of that time: from speeches at public meetings and banquets to legal texts and *byliny*.* The variety of dialects belonging to Slavs who made up Rus gave the Russian language a wealth of synonyms (an abundance of words meaning one and the same thing, depending on the region); style was fashioned on biblical sentences, lyricism came from women working the fields, while pointedness came from *muzhik*s in the market. But the most important element was rhythm – the measure of the prose. Rhythm added reality to order just as a warrior's steps measure out every inch of land and a pulse measures the flow of time. The rhythm of the language imparted order to the world.

3

Let us return to Father Theodosy's cell so as to look more closely at the figures seated there. There is Ilarion – "*muzh blag, i knizhen i postnik*" ("a pious, well-read man who fasted"), as the chronicler describes him, the author of the *Sermon on Law and Grace* – the first monument of Russian literature – and builder of the first cell in Rus – a grotto on the banks of the Dnieper, where he dug two toises into the depths of the earth so that he could pray in isolation there. Prince Yaroslav must have valued Ilarion because in 1051 he made him Metropolitan of Kiev (the first Russian to sit on this throne), in spite of Constantinople. Perhaps the *Sermon on Law and Grace*, written two years earlier, influenced the prince's decision.

Ilarion's treatise was the first attempt at formulating the so-called "idea of Rus" – the historiosophic concept according to which Rus

---

*Ancient Russian epics.

72

(later Russia) has a special place in world events; in other words — it has its own mission to fulfil. Ilarion referred to the biblical story of Abraham and constructed a series of oppositions: from the concubine Agar and the wife, Sarah — slave and free woman — Old and New Testament — Judaism and Christianity . . . to the law of the title, and grace. Without delving further into this monument (a task for a separate essay), let us turn our attention to the elements which guaranteed it longevity in Russian thought, making it a sort of archetype. Firstly, it set down the cornerstone of Orthodox faith in the power of God's grace, as opposed to human laws, as light is opposed to shadow, preparing the grounds for disregarding law in the name of the grace of those anointed by the Lord. Hence the later aversion to the West, the heirs of Roman laws. Secondly, it built the foundations for anti-Semitism, dividing people into the tribe of Isaac and that of Ishmael — the sons of truth and the sons of falsehood. Some justify Ilarion, saying that he did not have the Jews in mind, only the Khazars, the enemies of Rus. Thirdly, it built up the structure of Russian messianism, as if the future of Christianity belonged to the Russians, and it divided world history into a time before Russia's baptism and after. There are those who, at this point in the *Sermon*, see the announcement of the end of history and the beginning of present times. Fourthly, it linked words into new concepts: *russkaya zemlya* [Russian land], *yedinodyerzhec* [monarch] . . . which described the national identity of the peoples inhabiting these expanses and the system of power ruling over them. And, fifthly, it appropriated the throne of St Constantine to Rus, which Filofey later took up in his concept of Moscow as the "third Rome". All these elements, in one way or another, became variants of the "idea of Rus": from the above-mentioned Filofey to Dostoevsky or Solzhenitsyn. It is not by chance that now, when once again there is much talk about the "idea of Rus", Ilarion's treatise is being published in new translations. And one more thing: the artistry of the *Sermon*. Ilarion also set an example here — philosophy through art — enclosing the discussed contents in an artistic form while using simple language, because language in Russia was, after all, just in the process of being born and this excess of words, created from one root with the help of various suffixes, did not yet exist. And because of this, the world was not yet falling apart into details and nuances, into all sorts of diminutives, augmentatives, compounds . . . The world, in the *Sermon*, can be seen plainly and clearly, if not unequivocally.

After the death of Prince Yaroslav, Ilarion stepped down from the throne of the Metropolitan of Kiev (perhaps he was forced to do so) and returned to his cell, around which — in the meantime — Pecherska Monastery* had sprung up. And this is where we found the former Metropolitan writing books.

4

Next to Ilarion is the great Nikon . . . his silhouette, unclear to scholars, is barely visible in the corner of the cell, as if the small flame of the *lampada*** was picking it out of the semi-darkness and projecting it onto the pages of the chronicles. We see him here at the side of the saintly Antony in Ilarion's grotto, when the latter held the office of Metropolitan of Kiev. We see him in Tmutarakanya, where he escaped after his argument with Prince Izaslav, son of Yaroslav the Wise; then again in Pecherska Monastery . . . And always in someone else's shadow — be it Antony's, Theodosy's — just as an author can be detected behind his characters or a painter of icons in the depths of his icon's eyes. Nikon can be called the father of the Russian chronicle, although he was not the first.

In Rus, writing chronicles was the occupation of monks. The cell

---

*The monastery of the Grottos. *Tr.*
** Icon votive light. *Tr.*

enabled the monks to concentrate, allowing them to rise above the Russian landscape and see it from a bird's-eye view — in its entirely. Painters of icons call this a "raised horizon", as it is enough to raise the horizon a little higher to find yourself above a sight without actually moving from the spot. What could the chronicler see from the height of his cell? A flat plain, endless forests, extensive steppes and rivers like roads with boats on them sailing from the North towards Byzantium and carrying slaves for sale . . . A truly undefined sight — and timeless. In order to preserve it, the rivers had to be named, as well as the tribes who lived there, and their dialects, and every frame had to be dated. The model was prompted by Hamartolos's *Chronicle of the World*, from which the prologue covering the creation of the world to the birth of the Russian Land in 852 — when Rus invaded Tsar'grad — was drawn; while local events were compiled from *byliny*, hearsay and old writings — from the legendary Rurik to the subsequent scribe, because each scribe tended to end with himself. Nikon created the chronicle genre itself: a net of dates in which events could be caught. Time was the warp on to which events were strung: invasions, massacres, ravages . . . But — careful! — time in Rus was perceived differently from today: it was back to front. The writer had the past in front of his eyes, the future behind his back. Standing behind the writing desk, he saw the napes of his predecessors, who were facing — as he was — their ancestors. The scratching of pens brought to mind the rustle of sand . . . one writer picked up the thread from another, sometimes this would be broken, especially when outsiders invaded, so as to be taken up again, after some time, in another cell, on the confines of the Russian Land. That is how the collective literature of Ancient Russia came into existence, how the Russian style of "monumental historicism" — to use Likhachov's expression — which also embraced architecture, icons, music and a vision of the world, existence and political etiquette was born; a style, in which the history of Rus was shaped and often subjected to the rules of the genre. For example, under 1065, the chronicler notes the appearance of a comet: ". . . and an enormous star, burning blood-red, appeared in the sky after sunset every evening for seven days. This was a bad omen. Wars began and so did the pagan invasion of the Russian Land; that star, a bloody one, foretold the spilling of blood." In actual fact, the comet appeared a year later, in April 1066, but it was more important for the chronicler that the date of the event should coincide with the betrayal of Prince Vsyeslav, who, together with the pagans, attacked Rus . . . The chronicler did not re-create reality, he created it, deriving meaning from event. And, at times, he became fixed within it himself, like Nikon under the pen of his pupil Nestor — in Father Theodosy's cell.

5

And so to Theodosy, the master of the cell. This character can be seen most clearly — from adolescence to grave — thanks to the *Life* written by Nestor. Ever since he was a child, he was turned in on himself, often *yurodivy* — or God's fool, as we say — at odds with his mother and not understood by those around him. He finally landed up in Ilarion's grotto. There, Nikon had him anointed as a monk. In time, the pious Theodosy stood at the head of the brotherhood, organized Pechersky Monastery and introduced the study rule. Laying the foundations of monastic community in Rus, he taught: "Enclose yourself, brother, from all sides as if from brigands, with a fear of God and prayer; stand guard not to distract your thoughts when you are in town among people but, remaining centred within yourself — as if in a cell — contemplate approaching death as if you were in a desert." After death, he was canonized and revered here as the spiritual father of monastic life.

The history of the first monastic community in Rus is told in *The Kiev-Pyechera Paterikon*, which is also an example of the birth of a subsequent literary genre — the lives of saints. According to the rules of this particular genre, an individual creates his own life and then someone else writes it down, simplifying it somewhat. Unlike sermons and chronicles, the lives of saints give an insight into the private lives of people in Ancient Rus, call to mind their sins and intimate details . . . It is often impossible to know where the actual life ends and the recorded life begins and who is the author of a given episode: the saint or his scribe. For example: is it possible to live buried in the ground up to the neck as did Yoann Zatvornik? The collected lives of the saints were called *paterikon*s and one can see in them, as in a mirror, the realities of the times and an outline of the morals, the ideals of saintlihood and the whims of deviation. The significance of *The Kiev-Pyechera Paterikon* is singular. Rus, barely awakened, looks at itself in it and forms itself accordingly; from the lives of the *smerd*s [serfs] to courtly etiquette. Pyechera Monastery was, at this time, not only a school of prayer, fasting, craftsmanship and obedience, but also an important centre of the written word and political thought. Here, Orthodox liturgy and an attitude towards the Latin faith were shaped; here, the concept of the unity of the Russian Land and the image of Poles, its enemies, were born. It is not by chance that a demon appeared to brother Matvey in the shape of a . . . Pole. Finally, it is here that various superstitions grew rife (such as ritualistic murders by Jews, for example), the majority of which have survived to this day . . . (The Patriarch of Moscow and of all Russia recently asked the General Public Prosecutor whether the slaughter of the Tsar's family had the traits of such a murder). To put it briefly, Pyechera Monastery was a nursery for both the Orthodox faith in the Russian Land, and for superstitions, icons, books, and saints. And from here all this went North . . .

With the break-up of Rus, the number of monasteries grew — in Tver, Kostrom, Yaroslav, Nishny Novgorod and Moscow — because every independent prince wanted monks at his side who would pray for him and advise him and glorify him in chronicles. Later, under the Tartar yoke, Rus survived in the monasteries as did its history in manuscripts. In the 14th century, far from people, among remote forests and impenetrable marshes, a new kind of Russian monastery came into being called *pustyn'* where monks who had tired of the world's vanity lived. One of these monks was Sergey Radonezhsky, the founder of the Monastery of the Holy Trinity not far from Moscow, from where the "gathering" of the Russian Land began. First of all, the saintly Father blessed Prince Dimitry for the victorious battle with the Tartars, and then his disciples took to colonizing the northern tracts of Muscovy – from Beloozero [White Lake], through Valaam on Lake Ladoga to Solovky on the White Sea – so as to build there, over subsequent centuries, a state within a state, in which ". . . the monastic brotherhood – a sort of aristocracy in *ryasa** – ruled thousands of humble slaves . . ." – as Kluchevsky wrote, but this is another chapter of our story.

6

St Theodosy left behind him his *Message to the Prince about the Latin Faith* – a sort of spiritual testament. In it, he wrote: "I, Theodosy, wretched monk, servant of the Most Holy Trinity, the Father and the Son, and the Holy Spirit, was born of and taught by Orthodox parents to stay far from the Latin faith, not to imitate its rites, not to partake of its communion, not to listen to its teachings, and to abhor its customs: not to give my daughters in marriage to those of the Latin faith, nor to take their daughters; not to fraternize with them, greet them, or kiss them; not to eat from the same plates as they do and not to drink with them, and not to partake of their food. And when they do ask us for food, to give them to eat and drink only from

---

*A cassock – c.f. *podryasnik*. See Glossary. *Tr.*

their own vessels. And if they have no vessels of their own, to give them ours to use but to wash them out carefully and say a prayer over them. For they believe falsely and live unclean lives: they eat with dogs and cats, they drink their own urine and eat lizards and wild horses and asses and snakes and carcasses and bear meat and beavers' tails. And their monks eat pork fat and fast on Saturdays, and, having fasted, eat milk and eggs in the evening. They ask for the forgiveness of sins not from God but from priests – for money. And their priests do not take wives but beget children with servants. Their bishops sleep with concubines and go to war. They do not kiss icons or holy relics. They lay their dead with their feet turned towards the west. They baptize by immersing once, we – three times. When we baptize, we anoint with myrrh and oil, while they pour salt into the mouths of those being baptized. They say the Holy Spirit proceeds from the Father and the Son. We do not say: and from the Son. And they have many such things, illegitimate and depraved; their faith leads to ruin, their deeds are worse than those of the Jews. Therefore, beware, son, of the false believers and of all feasting with them because our land, too, is full of them. Only he who lives the Orthodox Faith will save his soul because there is no other, better faith than our pure and holy Orthodox Faith. Remaining in the Faith, you will save yourself from sins and the torments of hell and you will gain eternal life and be happy with the Saints. But those living different faiths: Catholic, Muslim or Armenian – will never see eternal life."

7

St Theodosy's *Message* is alive in the Russian Orthodox Church to this day, especially in monasteries. Its arguments have often been repeated by the holy fathers. Let us mention Amvrosy, and *starets*

Optinsky, who, in his letters to the faithful, warned against the Latin heresy, or St Yoann from Kronstadt, who fought against ecumenism, saying that it was Satan himself who was implanting thoughts of the unification of Christian faiths in the world, thus leading to indifference in respect of the one and only Orthodox faith, its rites and dogmas. On the eve of the Revolution, Archimandrite Ilarion's (Troytsky) book entitled *There is no Christianity without the Orthodox Church* appeared in Russia, and in it the eminent 20th-century Orthodox theologian writes: "The truth of the Orthodox Church became distorted in the West after the secession of Rome from the Orthodox Church, and the Kingdom of God there ressembles a kingdom of this world. Catholicism, with its mercenary attitude to God, with its reckoning of good deeds and imitation of salvation, falsified the Christian idea of the Orthodox Church in the minds of the faithful.' In 1925, Archimandrite Ilarion was sent to the Islands where he gained great authority among the *zeka*s and co-authored the famous *Messages of the Solovetsky Starets*es − a spiritual testament for the years of persecution.

8

During the first years of SLON on the Islands, St Onufry Orthodox church (the only one retained) was in use and the Orthodox faithful could pray there. In the autumn of 1925, a Uniate clergyman, Father Aleksandrov, was granted permission from Eichmans, the commander of the labour camp, to celebrate Mass there according to the Catholic rite. Unfortunately, the Mass was not celebrated because the monk Agapita, the administrator of the church, as well as the other monks . . . were in opposition. In the summer of 1993, Father Professor Cekiera, a professor from Warsaw, came to Solovky in order to celebrate Mass for Catholics who had died on the Islands during the days of SLON. But this time, too, the Solovetsky community would not agree to a Catholic Mass in their church. Father Cekiera celebrated Mass in our house, at my writing table.

VIII

"You ask me what I do here in my spare time. I read a lot, pencil in hand, noting thoughts which I intend to expand some time in the future."

Joseph de Maistre

1

Winter arrives differently each year. Suddenly, in October, when the remaining leaves are still hanging on trees, snow pelts down like pearl barley; heavy and sticky, it covers the earth and gives rise to the hope that the waterworks won't freeze. Or there are foul rains up to December, cold and dark, and mud all around. Another time, frost covers the bare ground, which hardens, glazes over, and rings out. Then again, white powder settles, decorating every branch like Vologod lace. Sometimes it hurls down tiny pieces of ice; the wind is cutting and flowers resembling Dürer's thistles are drawn on the window panes. Other times, we are suddenly buried up to our ears, then the snow melts in mid-January and drips everywhere, and there is black ice like cake icing. But most often it snows continuously and we are buried in the snowdrifts. The sea, too, freezes in different ways, depending on the wind. When there are heavy storms, *shuga*, or brash-ice in our language, gathers by the shore – an icy porridge – and it grates with every wave. When it is calm, the White Sea is

82

covered with a thin sheet and snow might fall, not allowing the ice to harden. Then you walk on skis and wet tracks follow you . . . water seeps through and you get stuck. It is best when frost holds for a long time, there is no wind and it doesn't snow. The sea then freezes to stone and can remain that way until May. A traveller from the last century, Sergey Maksimov, wrote in *A Year in the North*: "First autumn storms, then ice, cut off any access to the Islands for the whole of autumn, the whole of winter and the whole of spring, and there is no contact with the world. At this time they let the convicts out of the prison cells and some walk around outside, others visit the Orthodox church . . ."

2

For centuries, political dissidents and inconvenient people were deported to Solovetsky. Among others, the following served time here: Artemy, the former Igumen of the Monastery of the Holy Trinity, accused of rationalism, and his accuser, Archpriest Sylvester, the former supporter of Ivan the Terrible and author of *Domostroy* (The Discipline of Family Life); Avraamy Palitsyn for his traitorous sup- port of the Poles; "the tsar of all Russia", Simeon Bekbulatovich, a Tartar prince who had the misfortune to get entangled in Russian politics; Count Tolstoy, head of the penal tribunal, who deported a multitude of people to the Islands; and Count Musin-Pushkin who had deported Count Tolstoy here and later was deported himself; the self-styled Tsar Ivashka Saltykov; the despicable scribe Volk for his "thief's letter" in which he stated that the Emperor Peter was an Antichrist; the last ataman of Sich of the Zaporogs [Cossacks], Pyotr Kalnishevsky, who, having served a quarter of a century here, on his release at the age of 110, asked to be permitted to stay on the Islands; God's slave, Dmitryev, who spent fifty-eight years in its prison cells,

83

forty-eight of which were in solitary confinement, for Khlyst heresy; the Skopets* Sozonovich, who castrated a couple of dozen prisoners and several guards to boot, and founded a commune of castrates in his cell; the Pole Jeleński, to whom I will dedicate a later chapter; the Decembrist Gorozhansky; and Gannibal Pushkin, the poet's uncle, and . . . it is impossible to list them all.

The Solovetsky prison — according to Gernet, author of the basic *History of the Tsarist Prison* in five volumes — was the oldest and harshest prison in the Empire. The condemned were held in the depth of the walls and towers, in stone niches which brother Trifon, the builder of the monastic wall, designed for the storage of gunpowder and munitions in the event of a siege. These were small quarters (three arshins [71.12 cm] in length by two arshins in breadth), with a stone bench to sleep on, and a slit in the wall with three bars and two meshes in place of windows. Eternal semi-darkness, damp and cold reigned within. Imagine, reader, that you have been thrown in there, shackled, with your tongue and nostrils torn out and . . . indefinitely. Or, even better, imagine that they are holding you in *zemlyanaya tyurma* (an invention of the Solovetsky community!), that is, a cave in the ground, laid out with bricks and covered with a wooden trap-door, held down by stones and earth; bread and water are lowered down to you through a hole; you shit and pee under yourself until you realize that ". . . you are only excrement and dust". It is only at the beginning of the 19th century that a separate building was constructed for the prisoners, not to make things any easier for them, but to make it easier for them to be guarded. Maksimov wrote: "The earth prisons (which Peter the Great so greatly valued) were replaced by special cells for secret prisoners located in the cellars of the building. There, on the lowest level, in blind recesses measuring one and a half square arshins, where it was impossible to lie or sit

---

*A cult of castrates. *Tr.*

with outstretched legs, there, with a chain around their necks and iron balls at their feet, the most important offenders, condemned to eternal silence and constant solitary confinement, were kept. Most of them lost their minds. Other prisoners, not so important, were forced to do the monastery's dirty work; these included children . . . On 11 June, 1829, ten-year-old Ivanushko landed on Solovky for fifteen years of "hard labour under the strictest surveillance". After many years, some prisoners had their chains removed and were allowed to live in penance among the brothers in the cells.

Living in penance – the formula of the prison was close to that of the monastery. No wonder the prison and the monastery integrated here and the monks took on the duties of guards. They kept an eye on the purity of faith, rites, traditions, etc. Hence the particular attentiveness to silence – dissidents, above all, were held here. Looking through the list of convicts from 1786, I noticed that there was a note next to almost every name not to give him *chernilo*, paper and other writing implements. Those, on the other hand, who spoke their thoughts out loud ". . . without superfluous explanations and moral teachings, had a stick with cords – of the sort that was used on wild animals caught alive or pushed into horses' muzzles to stop them from biting – put across their mouths, and this was only removed when the convicts were given food; words spoken by them during this time were noted down and sent to a secret office."

3

Among the dissident-convicts there were disciples of various shades of the old-believers' rite as well as sectarians of all kinds: Khlysts, Skopyetses, Chelaputs, Pryiguns, Beguns, Perduns* and one has to be

---

*Whippers, castrates, triflers, jumpers, runners, farters.

very knowledgeable to come to grips with them all. Take the Perduns, for example, a sect founded by Gavrilov, a monk from Athos who preached that what we eat nourishes the devil in us and, as a form of purification, he advised ritual farting combined with prayers . . . which the contemporary French historian Ingerflom interpreted as a relic of the Perun (Thunder) cult which associate farts with thunder!

Or the Khlysts, that is ". . . the independent expression of the Russian soul", as we read in the *Orthodox Encyclopaedic Dictionary*, "influenced, on the one hand, by the pagan faith of our ancestors and, on the other, by Bogomil ideas propagated in Russia thanks to apocryphal literature". This literature, let us add, came to Rus together with Christianity (icons, books, clergy) from Okhrid, a Bulgarian patriarchate dominated, at that time, by the Manichean (Bogomil) heresy which, from there, infiltrated West in the form of the Patarins, the Cathars and the Albigensians, while in Rus it smouldered for centuries in . . . the monasteries. It took Nikon's reforms, which destroyed old books, to provoke counteraction and to lure the heresy out of monastic cells and into the world. This, not infrequently, led to the spillage of blood or to the stake. For another eight years, Solovetsky monastery, besieged by the Tsar's armies, defended the rite of the old faith . . . And then later, even after the success of the reforms, the monasteries were sometimes the hotbeds of other heresies, especially the Khlyst heresy. The reliable Kutyepov, author of *Sects of the Khlysts and Skoptsy*, counted a couple of dozen monasteries, including upteen in Moscow, contaminated by *khlystovchina* in the 18th century. The sect was started by Danilo Filippov, who, in 1631, threw books belonging to the church into the Volga and proclaimed twelve commandments. The first ran: "I am God, foretold by the prophets, descended to earth to save people's souls. You will not hold other gods before me." "God's people", as the Khlysts were called, believed that God becomes incarnate in each of us, as He once did in Jesus Christ – it is enough to *radet'* and *kruzhit'*. (This was a collective ritual of "whirling" that led to altered states of consciousness, sometimes hallucinations, epilepsy and the like.) For these devotions, often culminating in orgies, the Khlysts organized communities called "ships". Preaching that sex was a sin, they claimed that without sin there can be no penance and without penance, no salvation, and so marital intercourse, which concealed sin, was worse than the sin itself. In the Khlyst "ships", everything was communal: from bowls to women.

A contemporary philologist states that the Khlyst "ships" − where God was present at the rituals and the faithful repeated the same texts in unison, whirled in an enclosed space and experienced orgasm together − is one of the strongest metaphors of human community known in anthropology and history. The traditional Russian *obshchina*, with its communal field, rite and law, set the family and matters of sex aside − the collective did not touch them. The Khlyst ideals, on the other hand, while sealing the community, found experimenting with the family and sex attractive. To stabilize this experience, faith was necessary. True communism can be achieved only in an erotic and mystical community.

4

In 1772, in the village of Bogdanovka, a concerned policeman registered thirteen *muzhik*s ". . . without balls, the alarm was raised, the offender escaped . . ." That is how the history of one of the strangest sects in the history of the world begins, the sect of the "white doves", in which Russian radicalism found its fullest expression. Individual cases of self-castration for religious purposes, such as that of Origen, occurred earlier, and, in Rus, a couple of monk-castrates among the Pechersky community, Yefrem, later Metropolitan of Kiev, for example, or *inok* Moisey, whom a Polish woman emasculated, are described in the *Paterikon*. But it is only towards the end of the 18th century in Russia that castration took on the form of a religious sect, emerging from Khlyst "ships" as a new order. At its head stood *starets* Selivanov, God and Tsar in one person because he claimed to be the incarnation of both God and His Highness Peter III, combining mysticism with politics. Selivanov preached that the End of the World was approaching and that it was enough to castrate 144,000 brothers and sisters for the Last Judgement to take place . . . The Judgement was to take place in Moscow under the leadership of Selivanov, who, by that time, would be on the Tsar's throne. People would be punished for *lepost'*, that is, for sexual intercourse, a terrible sin which was devouring the world and turning people into beasts instead of angels. In order to become an angel, one had to atone for one's sin, that is . . . castrate oneself.

The play of words in the Russian language: *iskuplenie/oskoplenie* (redemption/castration) conveys the sense of the metaphysical meaning of the redemption of original sin by the castrates. According to their teachings, the first people were sexless, that is, they had no sexual organs. But they did have complete freedom – they were only forbidden to touch the tree of knowledge. God punished them dearly for breaking this injunction: organs appeared on the bodies of Adam and Eve which were copies of the tree of knowledge. The trunk grew as the penis, the apples as breasts. Only surgical intervention, that is, the ablation of the sinful parts, could save man from original sin. The operation was performed with a white-hot iron and was called "baptism of fire", "sitting on the white horse", or sometimes "the seal". A distinction was made between the "little seal" – the removal of testicles in men and of nipples in women – and the "Tsar's seal" – the ablation of the penis and its base, and of the breasts "down to the bone". Women also had their vulvae removed, which led to their vaginas growing together. It is difficult to tell who is a woman and who a man among the naked castrates on old police photographs (I have them in front of me!). Truly, sexless angels.

Selivanov's teachings found a following. Denouncements were not long in spreading. Here, there and everywhere, new castrations were reported. "Ships" of castrates were springing up like mushrooms after rain . . . in the provinces of Orlov, Kaluga, Kursk, Tulsk, Tambov, Moscow, St Petersburg. Peasants, soldiers, merchants, village crones and townswomen were all having themselves castrated. It soon became evident that the castrates' lifestyle, with its abstinence and vegetarianism, was conducive to making money. Wealthy "ships" bribed the police, expanded business and held influence in Court. Starets Selivanov, after a brief exile to Siberia, returned triumphantly to St Petersburg and was pampered in higher circles just as another *starets*, Rasputin, was a hundred years later. Then circumstances became less favourable and the castrates were persecuted, exiled and tortured. Selivanov was locked up in the Spaso-Yevfimievsky monastery in Suzdal where he came across . . . the "ship" of our Polish compatriot, Jeleński, about whom more in a moment. Despite repression, the sect grew and new "ships" sprung up in the most unlikely places: in the garrison of the marine infantry in Krondstadt, in the 95th Regiment on the Caucasus, in the cells of Solovky . . . Here, too, on Solovky, traces of the last castrates can be found – in the archives of SLON.

The philologist notes: "Castration binds a person to a community more strongly then any economic or ideological tie. Dependence on the community always clashes with the power of sex – love for the individual, not for the community. Castration does away with this problem. Castration closes the door to the partner and opens it to the collective body. Castration makes communism possible, even necessary."

5

We know little about the Polish castrate, Józef Jeleński, author of a theocratic-castrate utopia, imprisoned on Solovky from 1794 to 1801 – especially about the period preceding his stay there. Some say that he was the King of Poland, Stanisław August's chamberlain, some that he colluded with Kosciuśzko, others scorned him as "a homeless, Polish intellectual who tried, unsuccessfully, to make money here". In evaluating Jeleński's role, historians also differed: some declared the Pole the first Russian revolutionary and his treatise "the highest achievement of progressive 18th-century thought", others declared him a mystic and madman. Let us look at these few known facts more closely.

Józef Jeleński (1756–1813) was born to an impoverished noble family from near Minsk. After his parents' death he sold the remainder of the estate, quickly lost the money, then came to St Petersburg. What did he do there? It is difficult to say. Some sort of ventures, small business, gambling . . . Perhaps he conspired . . . There were times when he didn't eat for two days. In May of 1794, on the basis of Captain Cybulski's denunciation, Jeleński was arrested. Among the papers confiscated during the search, a proclamation about the abolition of serfdom was found, published in Cracow. The Pole converted to the Orthodox Church under the name of Alexey so as to avoid the death penalty and was then exiled to Solovky, under strict surveillance. Here (in his cell), he wrote his famous *Blagovest*, that is *Good News*, which astonished Archimandrite Yon with its tone of arrogance. For Jeleński demanded no more, no less than that the Empress Catherine abdicate from the throne, ". . . otherwise the whole of Russia will be bathed in blood". It is interesting that *Blagovyest*, which blended demands of the Polish manifestoes with Pugachov's proclamations, was written in the style of ancient Orthodox writings, with a clear note of misogyny. It was here, too, on the Islands, that Jeleński had himself castrated . . .

(Stop! Let us pause here for a moment. Different researchers have tried to interpret this act in different ways. Frumenkov, the author of *Prisoners of Solovetsky Monastery*, for example, explained Jeleński's action by saying he went insane at the news of the fall of Kościuszko's Uprising. But then, nobody today can say for certain what motivated Jeleński. Perhaps, in his way, he wanted to get out of the cell-body. Perhaps the castrates, his fellow prisoners, told him that our body is a prison and that the way out of it is "on a white horse". The Pole later wrote: ". . . and my arms grew longer, and my legs became huge, and thus the whole of me became enormous and I expanded, as if God had put heaven and earth and all creatures within me".)

After Catherine's death, Tsar Alexander took pity on Jeleński. On His Highness's orders, Jeleński was given lodgings in Alexander Nevsky monastery in St Petersburg, in the Metropolitan's quarters. My compatriot was by no means idle in the Russian capital: he grew close to the most famous mystics of the time – Alexander Labzin, creator of the Masonic lodge "The Dying Sphinx", Alexander Golitsyn, the Minister of Education, as well as the God of the castrates, Selivanov – then he, himself, seated a couple of dozen Russians "on a white horse" so as to finally become the sect's chief theoretician. Then, in 1804, he handed over to Novosiltsov, the Tsar's talebearer, his *Message* – a project for a complete reconstruction (*perestroika!*) of the Russian Empire. A truly exceptional document. Here, in a few words, is the gist of it:

Russia, declared Jeleński in the *Message*, is the nation chosen by Our Church to begin the Great Change – from here, the whole world would be transformed. The change would begin with the army and the navy: each commander of a military unit or ship would be allocated a prophet-castrate, an advocate of the Word, and a confidential monk-castrate, commentator of the Word, who was to decide about war operations, guard over military discipline, morals and . . . castrate the soldiers. Jeleński emphasized the system of control: the confidential monk would control the military commander, the prophet (obligatorily illiterate!) would control the monk, the prophet would be controlled by a senior monk, who, in turn, would be controlled by a higher prophet and so on . . . right up to the First Monk, meaning Jeleński himself, who would stand at the head of the Chiefs of Staff of the Russian army and comment on the Word of Our Lord, the Father and the Son and the Holy Spirit in the One Person of Konrad Selivanov, living in the Court of the Russian Tsar. Then this Order would be introduced into towns and villages and embrace the entire Empire. All this, so as to castrate them, castrate them, castrate them ... Humanity, according to Jeleński, would be divided into two groups: the castrates, meaning spiritual people, who would rule, and the rest, who were to work and multiply under the attentive control of the first group.

The philologist writes: "This is the most totalitarian project of all known to the history of Utopia. Jeleński, after all, not only proposed the transformation of the entire system of authority, both state and spiritual; not only did he intend to start the revolution with the army and the navy so as to later spread it to all the ministries, provinces and villages; not only did he want to build his regime using one of the strictest methods known to us — through the personal control of the spiritual shepherds organized in a hierarchical system. All this had been known previously already; there had been attempts to put much of this into force before Jeleński and after him, too. But only in his project were the politics of the body, in their most radical and irreversible variant — surgical — included with external, internal, and spiritual politics. The idea of castrating — first the commissars and then, under their control, the nation — is a Utopia which comes to the theoretical conclusion of all Utopianism. Nobody, other than the Pole Jeleński, ever unravelled the secret of Utopia so literally."

On 24 August, 1804, Jeleński was locked up in Spaso-Yevfimievsky monastery in Suzdal for "spreading the Skopets heresy". But the Pole did not stop castrating even there. Together with the monk Paysy, he organized a whole centre of castrates in the prison cells, and castrated them, castrated . . . right up to his death. A century later, another Pole tried to realize a new Utopia here. His name was Felix Dzerzhinsky.

6

I have finally discovered the source of the gossip which is persistently going around Solovky. Apparently, I have been exiled here because of . . . "Solidarity". Panteleimonovich, a former *politruk* [political instructor], known for his fabrications, has been spreading these rumours. Paltus, when he brought me the book entitled *The Collapse of "operatsia Polonya"* ("Operation Poland"), *1980–81*, which Panteleimonovich had given him to read, told me about it. There was a stamp from the military library in the book; the former political instructor must have kept it as a souvenir. Maybe he used it during his political instructions, or to help him fall asleep? There is a note about the author on the cover: Vadim Trubnikov, graduate in Philosophical Sciences and deputy editor of the foreign section of the monthly magazine *Kommunist*; in 1985, *The Collapse* was awarded the Journalists' Association of the Soviet Union's prize for best non-fiction book of the year. I flicked through it. Names which were known to me: Kuroń, Wałesa, Frasyniuk. And the old times: opposition, the Gdańsk Shipyard 1980, "Solidarity", state of war, conspira—? A part of my life, suddenly seen from the other side, through the eyes of Solovetsky seamen, yawning from boredom during political instruction with Ilya Panteleymonovich. Paltus had been one of them.

There is no way you can read it. Garbled agit-prop slang, strewn with quotations from *Trybuna Ludu* [People's Tribune] and *Żołnierz Wolności* [Soldier of Liberty], in unison with a Soviet commentary. What a mish-mash there must be left in the heads of those Solovetsky seamen. Nobody ever set things straight for them, after all! If you listen more carefully to what they say in Russia today, you can distinguish distinct drifts in the general conversation. Here, for example: Brzeziński. In *The Collapse*, he has been made to be the main director of *"operatsia Polonya"* and a schemer who, throughout his life, had been contriving to break up the Soviet Union. And ten years later, Solzhenitsyn was saying the same things on TV when talking about the break-up of Russia. It is not surprising that people like Paltus and his pals from Panteleymonovich's political instruction course don't trust the Poles. New ideas don't reach here, in the depths of Russia, and if they do, they are greatly distorted. Here, old notions abide or none at all. Looking through *The Collapse of "operatsia Polonya"*, I noticed some thick underlining in a red ballpoint pen. All concerned . . . *Kultura.*

27 October

À propos "Solidarity" . . . I am thinking about that other "S" as it was the 1980s, not as it is described today. The image of that other "S" in today's Polish papers (which I read here from time to time in not too large a dose) is becoming ever more splendid – and less real. Sometimes it is nostalgia, as in the case of Smecz ("the flutter of flags on shipyard cranes"), sometimes a journalistic ploy or forgetfulness. Often those writing or speaking about that "S" idealize the recent past so as to paint a darker present . . . For example, Herling-Grudziński: "The introduction of a State of War has terrible consequences to this day. It is a source of awful sickness in social life – a life which was united before 13 December and then, as a result of the Martial Rule, systematically spoilt, taken apart, decaying even." I took the quotation from a conversation entitled *The Plague of the State of War* ("Tygodnik Powszechny", 12/1997) in which the author of *Miracles* and *The Plague in Naples* draws reality in black and white on the margins of these two tales: up until 13 December it was the Miracle of "Solidarity", after 13 December it was the Plague, which persists to this day . . . Hmm! I know the Poland of today only from newspapers and from Polish tourists who rarely come here, so I am not going to say anything. Whereas I do remember the old days from having been there myself: in the Gdańsk Shipyard; in the MKZ [Solidarity headquarters] on Grunwaldzka Street, and in the underground.

I don't recall any miracles although there was more than enough dirt even then. Take, for example, the battle between Lech Wałesa and the "star collection", meaning Gwiazda's [Star's] sympathizers; it was ruthless on both sides. Ms Ania (Walentynowicz) would pester us in the *Solidarity* editorial office to print articles in the paper about Wałesa being a SB [Secret Service] agent. The other side, that is the Chairman of NSZZ [Niezależny Samodzielny Zwiazek Zawodowy – Independent Trade Union] was also unscrupulous. And what about the aggressive "true Poles", who demanded KOR's blood and cleansing the Union of Jews? And Father Jankowski, the spiritual papa of the Gdańsk Shipyard and "S"? I remember an episode: after publishing an article about Edward Abramowski, we had a visit from what could almost be called a storm squad. This was a delegation from the Committee for the Building of a Monument to Commemorate Dead Shipyard Workers, demanding that I report to the Shipyard and explain by what right I was propagating Judaeo-Masonic ideas in the magazine "S". That is why I cannot agree with those who would idealize those times. The Plague had already struck. Because the Plague is a sickness . . .

Phew! I promised myself I wouldn't touch on Polish subjects and there – I haven't kept my word. That book from the Solovetsky political instructor, Ilya Panteleymonovich's little library has evoked some ghosts.

IX

Being a foreigner, outside of local conflicts, I study the history of this country without passion and watch today's events from a distance . . .

Joseph de Maistre

1

Ondatra zibethica. That is, musk-rats, water rats. Brought to Solovky from Michigan in the days of the labour camp and farmed on the islands of Long Bay for their valuable fur. The *zeka*s called them "Soviet sheep" and used to steal their meat. Now the musk-rats live here in the wild. They have multiplied. Smirny told me how, in summer, ten of them climbed into his *morda* (a sort of fish net). They had lifted the net to the surface of the water and poked their snouts out, panting heavily. The *muzhik*s submerged the *morda* with poles. The water wasn't very deep here – half a metre – so they could see what had happened quite clearly, as in an aquarium. Musk-rats can stay under water without air for a fair time. So they stayed there calmly. Suddenly, after a couple of minutes, one of them threw itself at another and, in the wink of an eye, had bitten it to death. This was a signal. There was turbulence in the *morda* and blisters of blood floated to the surface of the lake. The musk-rats were fighting a vicious battle, everyone against everyone. After a while, they were all dead . . . Today, the *muzhik*s are here, like musk-rats in a *morda*, and their *nachalstvo* [authorities] suffocate them, pushing them down with rods of reforms. It only remains to watch and see when they will start to bite each other.

2

Up until the time when the monks came to the Islands, and the monastic chroniclers with them, the shores of the White Sea, from the Suma to the Vazhuga, were inhabited by Finnish tribes, called *Karelskie ludy* [Karelian People], who considered themselves the owners of these lands, and by settlers from Novgorod who gradually took the lands for themselves. Both the former and the latter held claim to Solovky but nobody had enough courage to live here for good, and only in summer, sporadically, would they fish here and kill seals. The attentive reader of *Solovetsky Paterikon* will find, in the lives of the saints, in their miracles and exquisite visions, more than one trace of conflict with the Pamorsky tribes who did not immediately want to agree to hand over the rich herring fisheries to the monks. The dispute frequently required intervention from the heavenly powers; on Sekirna Mountain, for example, angels flogged the backside of a Karelian peasant woman, in this way teaching the poor dear that the Islands belonged to the Orthodox monks. Of course, the pious monks did not stop at guarantees from supernatural power, but made sure they had the warranty of worldly authorities. As early as 1450, the first document was signed in which Great Novgorod handed over the lands, forests, lakes and deep seas of Solovky to the monks. With this – claims Kluchevsky – "began the interesting process by which the vast coastal territories of the White Sea were amassed in the hands of the Solovetsky monks, a process which, no doubt, influenced the history of this country."

The first lands to be ceded, as early as the 15th century, were the Pamorsky and Karelian shores of the White Sea and among the first gifts were the villages on the banks of the River Suma, offered to the monks by Marfa Posadnitsa; then, in the 16th century, Solovetsky monastery stretched its hand out to the far Tersky coast of the Kola Peninsula and two of its largest rivers – the Umba and the Vazhuga. The Muscovite princes, after the victory at Great Novgorod, not only supported the old endowments, but bestowed a pile of new ones, and it is worth remembering the chapter in Ivan the Terrible's document dated 1539, which gives the Igumen the right to judge peasants living on monastic land. Meanwhile, the monastery constantly demanded new lands because the community's main source of income came from the extraction of sea salt associated with the burning of coastal forests. And thus, in the middle of the 17th century, the most important Russian settlements on the estuaries of the Pamorsky rivers – the Umba, Vazhuga, Kereta, Kema, Shuya, Vig, Suma, Kolezhma, Nyukhcha, Unezhma, Lyamtsa, Purnema, Kuya and Una – were in the hands of the Solovetsky monks. It is not beside the point also to mention the rich contributions made to the community's treasury – in gold as well as in other valuables – and the exemption of the monastery from numerous taxes in return for the monks' surveillance over the confines of Rus and keeping guard over the prison.

In 1764, the Empress Catherine II secularized the Pamorsky property of the monks and turned it over to be managed by the College of Economics. In compensation, as a sweetener, she granted the community ownership of the Solovetsky Archipelago. Oppression of the peasants eased . . . somewhat – according to contemporary historians. The monastic chronicler, Melety, comments on the event: "The monastery was poorer, to be sure, and considerably so, but at the same time it gained a moral advantage for the brothers who were thus freed from conflicts associated with the administration of property and found the peace necessary to lead the pious life of a monk." Hmm, as for pious . . . that could be disputed; suffice it to read Myelety more closely or to study the monastic rule, paying especial attention to the points relating to the interdiction of keeping vodka and money in the cells. One thing is certain, the monks were faced with a few lean years . . .

3

Towards the end of the 19th century, Nemirovich-Danchenko, a well-known traveller and writer, arrived on the Islands. Solovetsky monastery stunned the newcomer with its splendour. In his book about Solovky, Vasily Ivanovich states that the extraordinary wealth of the monastery was based on the "free" (please remember!) labour of pilgrims and generous offerings. Here are some facts:

If one counts thirty kopeks per working day of each of the 400 *godoviks* – that is to say, voluntary workers – vowing to work for a year in praise of blessed Zoshima and Savvaty, usually in gratitude for salvation from a storm, sickness or demon, the monastery saved 43,800 roubles a year.

If one counts ten kopeks per working day of the 100 boys handed over in praise of blessed Zoshima and Savvaty by their parents, who could not afford the upkeep of their offspring, the monastery gained 3,650 roubles a year.

If one counts eight roubles for each of the 15,000 pilgrims who brought ten roubles each (minimum) in praise of blessed Zoshima and Savvaty while their upkeep cost the monastery two roubles, the monastery increased the sum by 120,000 roubles. If one adds 10,000 roubles for the pilgrims' accommodation in the guest house in Arkhangel and 15,000 roubles for their transport to Solovky, then the weight of the monastic purse increased to 200,000 roubles a year. Plus 25,000 roubles interest on capital.

It should be noted that apart from flour from Arkhangel and coal from England, the Solovetsky monks did not buy anything because they produced whatever was necessary on the spot and sold any surplus, from which the monastery gained another 30,000 roubles.

The value of all their property – transferable goods and real estate – should also be rounded off as being at least 10,000,000 roubles: the islands themselves, their lands, forests and deep seas, as well as churches, *skit*s, living quarters and farms, industrial equipment, ships, docks, herds of horses, herds . . . in order to comprehend the wealth of this "working commune of ascetics", as Nyemirovich-Danchenko described Solovetsky monastery at the turn of the 20th century.

4

In the 20th century, the administrative system on the Islands and the administrators themselves kept changing, like figures of coloured glass in a child's kaleidoscope, but the principle of free labour remained (basically) the same. Cunning rogues of all sorts took advantage of the short period of disorder, Revolution and Civil War, to plunder monastic riches, then, with a couple of fires, the extent of the theft was covered up and construction of a New Order was undertaken. In 1923, SLON, that is Solovetsky Lager Osobovo Naznacheniya – the first enterprise of this sort in the Soviet Union, an experimental enterprise, you might say – settled on the Islands, on the remains of the monastic property. Monks, priests and their wives, the unslaughtered remainder of the aristocracy, the bourgeoisie, kulaks and other contras, the opposition on the right and contenders to power on the left, and also harlots, decadent artists, drug addicts, parasites and hoodlums were put to work. Making use of prisoners' labour on the Islands was nothing new; suffice it to mention the priest, Simeon (Maksimov saw him in 1856), the heretic chained to the wall of the bakery who endlessly kneaded dough for the brothers' bread, or other "wretches in chains condemned to dirty monastic labour". Besides, SLON took advantage not only of the monks' experience in organization and administration, but also of the workshops, guilds, docks, warehouses and, finally, the monks themselves as overseers. Apart from traditional monastic activities — fishing, gardening, forestry — new things were also tried out; for example, the production of agar-agar, in which the philosopher Florensky specialized, the rearing of musk-rats, publishing, and scientific work. It is impossible to list all the activities of SLON, especially as people became fewer and times changed, as did demand. But the most important included: the production of lime, alabaster and bricks, the extraction of peat, the collection and processing of seaweed, the tanning of seal skins, the tailoring and shoemaking crafts, the carpenters' guild, the toymakers' guild . . . yes, yes, in SLON more than 300 *zeka*s, that is more than work all together on the Islands today, were employed in the production of rag-dolls! While the labour camp *selkhoz*, which employed over 1,500 prisoners in the rearing of horses, cattle and pigs, in dairy work and gardening, had its own club, reading room and shop. The camp hospital, which catered for 100, had five wards: a ward for internal medicine, a surgical ward, a ward for tuberculosis, a neurological ward and a maternity ward, as well as its own kitchen, storehouse and shelter for children. In the days of SLON, there was also a theatre with three stages on the Island, where five shows a week were performed, as well as a cinema, a central library with scientific collections (about 30,000 volumes), and a club with a reading room, a games and recreation room, open to the *zeka*s throughout the day until eleven o'clock at night. (In 1925 alone, there were 139 theatrical shows, 40 concerts and 37 film screenings, and numerous lectures, discussions and literary evenings.) A separate enterprise even collected useful refuse, sorted it out and sent it into Kem, whereas now, wherever you look in the *posyolok*, there is scrap metal, pieces of glass and whole blocks of reinforced concrete scattered around.

5

The publishing and scientific work undertaken in the SLON *zona*s deserves a separate chapter. The weekly paper *Novye Solovky* [New Solovky], to which one could subscribe anywhere in the whole of the Soviet Union, came out regularly here, and *Solovetskiye ostrova* [Solovetsky Islands], an illustrated monthly of 250–300 pages, enjoyed the reputation of being the most independent magazine in the USSR. Apart from prose, essays and poems, it published articles by the Solovetsky Geographical Society which brought together learned *zeka*s and *volnonayomnye* [free workers]. These works still prove useful to those researching the North, not only for the information contained in them, but also because they are an example of some serious work, since the Society's scientific output over a couple of years easily beat the Solovetsky museum's output over thirty years. The scope of the *zeka*s' scientific interests was enormous; it is enough to mention the titles of a few of their publications: *The Biology of White Sea Fish, Fishing Equipment on the White Sea, Climate of the White Sea, Birds of the White Sea, Archeology of the White Sea, Problems Concerning the Protection of Animals on the Islands of the White Sea, History of the Kem Region, Coastal (Pomory) Inhabitants – their life and activities, History of the Coastal Village/Countryside, Peat of the Solovetsky Islands, The Effects of Wind on Solovetsky Forests, Erosion of Solovetsky Soil, The Monastic Prison on Solovetsky, Bone Artefacts of the Monastery, Statistical Data of the Economy of Solovetsky*, and so on and so on . . . From 1926, "Documents of the Solovetsky Geographical Society" appeared under separate cover as a supplement to the camp monthly. All in all, twenty-three items were issued, including Vinogradov's fundamental work on Saam labyrinths and the first dictionary of *blatnaya muzyka** . . .

---

*See Glossary.

6

Towards the end of 1939, the last *zeka*s were evacuated from Solovky and the Islands were turned over to the Soviet army; nevertheless, the *zona*s remained, as did reels of barbed wire. Only the names were changed and instead of *zona osobovo naznachenia* [special purpose zone], the *zakrytaya zona* [forbidden zone] was created, and its regime remained in force to the end of 1989. Two fat letters, z.z., still figure in the passports of a good many Solovkians. And until recently, you still had to have a personal invitation in order to be issued a ticket to Solovky. The principle of free labour remained unchanged: soldiers slogged for a bowl of food, sometimes for a bottle of vodka. Slowly both old and new order were consigned to oblivion, most of the crafts, guilds and skills were neglected, while the farmed muskrats ran all over the Islands and started to live in the wild. The Solovetsky army looked after itself, especially its food – the cattle and pigs. Apart from that, military engineering was repaired as, at the same time, were the Solovetsky roads. Transport – both sea and air – communications, power engineering, the hospital and two clubs were also under army management – all within the limits of service – with no pay. At the same time, civilians were beginning to settle on Solovky; first of all alongside the army, as if to help, then on the army, like lice – according to former political instructor Panteleimonovich's words – and not only were they parasites on the soldiers' toil and of allocations from the defence budget, but they also took provisions for nothing – provisions which had rotted in storage. As time went by, more civilians arrived on Solovky. First of all, from Zhizhgin, from where, in the 1960s, the agar-agar factory was moved to the Islands together with a couple of dozen workers and their families who had been deported there. They were followed by seasonal gatherers of sea-grass, *bich*s without a posting, free as birds. Some settled here permanently. Then intellectuals poured in, failed scholars, artists without flare, historian-winos – all came to work in the museum, a snug little job. In the mid 1970s, the museum was transformed into a *zapovyednik*, or a nature reserve. But what beat everything was when, in the years of *perestroika*, the entire Archipelago was embraced by the central plan for development and urbanization in the style of Soviet gigantomania. Great budgets were allocated which, as usually happens with such plans, brought with them bands of loafers, schemers and thieves. Heavy construction equipment was transported to Solovky alongside hundreds of tons of materials and PMK (*peredvizhnaya mekhanizirovannaya kolonna*), that is, several brigades of down and out workers: condemned under article 33 (for drunkenness at work), or conscripted from the militia, like slaves. The new arrivals put together a few barracks from silicate air bricks and began the construction of a huge sewer purification plant designed for tens of thousands of inhabitants and an even larger bakery works, according to the principle: the greater the construction, the more there is to steal. Then a concrete ring road was lanced through the forest, sand pits were dug up alongside it, the sea shores were strewn over with all sorts of rubbish, and, at the same time, a few houses sprung up along Florensky Street. Good-for-nothings multiplied in front of your eyes like musk-rats. In the summer of 1989, the army left the Islands. The old order was coming to an end and rumours about reforms started to circulate. Then grants were cut and all construction work was halted, walls half built. General *prikhvatizatsiya* took place – nationalization inside out. Everything that lay around and did not belong to anybody was grabbed: concrete slates, telegraph poles, buildings, workshops and warehouses, mazut, tar paper and barbed wire. Even chairs were taken from what used to be the cinema and the screen pulled down from the wall. Finally, the PMK was completely taken apart: from bulldozers down to paper-clips. Only the people remained, unemployed . . . Today, there is no faith, or power, left on the Islands in whose name people could be made to work for free: no religion, no labour camp, no army. Now everybody here asks for *dengi* – without work. There, a *muzhik* comes along croaking for a tenner because he hasn't got enough for a bottle of vodka. "Chop some wood," I tell him, "then I'll pay you".

"It's not worth it."

7

And so, a digression. In 1811, de Maistre wrote to Count Rumyantsev: "In these times, when both anchors – religion and slavery – have simultaneously lost the power to hold your ship, storms may carry it away and wreck it. One should think hard before undertaking anything regarding the abolition of serfdom; sometimes the smallest legal concession is enough for misery to begin: first, it will be fashionable, then desirable, and, in the end, it will be madness. And, beginning with a statute, it will end in rebellion. As a consequence of such unexpected freedom, the serfs will go straight from superstition to atheism, from dumb obedience to unbridled licence. Freedom acts like a strong wine on such dispositions and quickly goes to the head of one who is unaccustomed to it."

I'll remind you that Joseph de Maistre was the King of Sardinia's ambassador at the court of Alexander I from 1802 to 1817, as well as being a thinker, writer and keen commentator on both political intrigue and Europe's theatre of war. Besides, he observed the world from a distance, like opéra bouffe, as he admitted himself on the margins of official despatches. And it is not surprising, for he saw the vagaries of fortune, which brought down dynasties, armies and cities, the baseness of heroes, the disloyalty of servants. His letters from St Petersburg not only give a picture of the times, rich in events such as Napoleon's march on Russia or Alexander I's attempt at reforms, but also give a cutting commentary to them. The words quoted above come from *Notes on Freedom*, which refers to the project of Speransky, one of the first Russian reformers, who proposed that all those subject to the Tsar should be equal in the eyes of the law and that all authorities, from rural communes upwards, should be elected . . .

X

. . . there is nothing more absorbing than to watch the Russia of today.

Joseph de Maistre

1

"Zdyes' vlast' ne sovetskaya, a solovetskaya" ("Here we do not have Soviet power, but Solovkian power"), Nogtev, the head of SLON, liked to repeat, emphasizing the singularity of the regime here. I've often heard this saying here. The post-labour-camp administrative machine of the Islands, a Party-military bastard, was created by crossing two regimes – one military, the other civilian – and was made up of two organs – the executive and the legislative. The Party recommended people, then played with them, pulling the strings. This freak with three legs (army, museum, *posyolok*) and with blurred scopes of activity, survived up to the days of *perestroika* when the functions of the presidents of both organs were merged into one: the *Glava* of Administration. This was warrant officer Nebozhcnko. In 1991, the place of the army in the Solovkian triangle of jurisdiction was taken over by the monastery, and the Islands were given the status of *osovo okhranyaemaya territoriya* (Special Nature Reserve). Then, before my eyes, the Soviet Union fell apart, the Communists scattered, the parliament in Russia was renewed twice, the war in Chechnya exploded and

subsided, a President was again elected, but Nebozhenko, to this day, runs Solovky as he always has — just as he likes.

"*Zdyes' vlast' ne moskovskaya, a svoiskaya*" ("Here, we do not have Moscow's power, but our own"), one could say, paraphrasing Nogtyev. In other words: local government made up of our own men. There are twenty-five *chinovnik*s [state officials] on Solovky — wives of former officers and Nebozhenko's buddies. Once three were enough! While the situation was being clarified in Moscow, here they were finishing off what was left of the state cake: shady credits and tax deductions for their own people, usurious turnover of monies which had been intended for wages and pensions . . . (Traders in vodka, for example, pay only twenty per cent tax compared to those selling other provisions with the result that a bottle of "Russian" costs as much as three loaves of bread and the profit, bypassing the cash register, goes straight into the pocket . . .) Instead of subsidizing the school, the *chinovnik*s themselves study law and administration by correspondence and, using funds destined for veterans, buy themselves apartments on the side . . . Consequently, there is general bankruptcy on the Islands, businesses have gone bankrupt, *muzhik*s die like flies, from booze or undernourishment, children rummage in dustbins or steal, and only Nebozhenko and his clique of talebearers live by the trough, and grow fat.

2

5 November
"*Doloy Nebozhenko!*" ("Down with Nebozhenko!") — such was the rallying cry of the protesters at the door of the Island's Administration. I should point out that the rally was held as part of a protest throughout Russia against the withholding of salaries, retirement and old age pensions. The state's failure to pay out had taxed the limits

of human patience: employees of communal services have not been paid since the winter before last, doctors and teachers since May, and retirement and old age pensions had last been distributed in summer. Rumours are going around the Islands that the *Glava* of Administration is depositing sums allocated for these payments, in order to gain interest. The sea is freezing over, the season for navigation is drawing to an end, and the inhabitants of Solovky cannot buy goods for the winter. They can't even get bread on credit in the shops any more. And how are they to get firewood for heating? I'll just add that there weren't any mushrooms or herrings this year, the potatoes were blighted, as was meat, and the reader can imagine the Solovkians' despair.

Today, since morning, a damp snow has been falling in huge flakes. And melting straight away. The White Sea has been stormy for a week now. A gusty, icy wind almost knocked me off my feet when I emerged from behind the monastic wall on to the open expanse of Holy Lake. In front of the Administration building, there is a sticky, glutinous slush. They started to dig a ditch here in the summer and stopped work halfway through. A lot of people have gathered in front of the *Glava*'s door; about a hundred people are churning the mud. Old men of Solovky, gnarled, bent over, wrapped up like rag-dolls. I notice people I know. The hospital staff is complete, that is, the hospital head, two nurses and the *banya* cleaner. Next to them is a small group of teachers, the veterans' committee standing in a row, several employees from the power station, Nadezhda Kirillovna from the library, the woman from the *banya*, a radio reporter, a forest warden, Foka, and "shit sauce", as the owner of the rubbish removal truck is called. Somewhat further along, under the green platform of rotting boards – a relic of Brezhnev's "period of stagnation" – *muzhik*s in quilted working tops, felt boots and *ushanka*s,* suffer dismal hangovers, the unemployed of Solovky. The people are seething, drowning

---

*Hats with flaps over the ears.

everything in *mat*. Nobody knows what will happen next. They are waiting for Nebozhenko; he promised to come out. Apparently, he is phoning Arkhangel to find out when they are going to send the money. As if he couldn't have done so earlier.

"Down with Nebozhenko!" a growl came from beneath the platform.

Valentin Viktorovich appeared in the door of the Administration. Thick set, leather jacket, puffy face, protruding eyes half-hidden under the peak of his chequered flat cap. The small crowd grew silent, drew closer, fuming, pressed forward. Nebozhenko backed away and tensed.

"Well, what do you want?"

Cries broke out. Women shouted over each other, shrilly: that this was it, they couldn't go on like this, that they'd been driven to the limit, that even during the war things had been better because at least bread rations had been distributed, but now they'd have to eat dogs and cats, and there weren't even enough boards with which to make coffins while they, in Administration, were stuffing their faces . . .

"Ah, so that's it," roared Nebozhenko, turning red. The women turned silent, the snow was falling, and Nebozhenko was thundering that he could make mincemeat of them in court for insulting an official on duty, and that there was law and order in Russia now and they were to keep their hands off state authorities, that these were plots before elections, that they were looking for a scapegoat but he, Nebozhenko was not going to be a goat. That's why, calmer now, he was asking for questions and would answer them all, one by one. Without insults, shouting or demagogy.

The head of the hospital, Lina Ts., spoke out saying that there were twenty-six beds in the hospital but food only for four, that there was a shortage of medicine, the needles had disappeared and all 90% proof alcohol had been stolen. There was barely enough coal, too, to last a week so they were heating just enough to prevent the drips from freezing up. Yesterday, one of the nurses fainted from malnutrition. And not everybody can afford an aeroplane fare these days so, if the hospital on Solovky were to close, it would be like pronouncing a death sentence on the old folk. They'd phoned from Arkhangel that they had sent the money, but the hospital hadn't received a rouble. So where had it got to?

The *Glava* sent for some papers to give them proof in black and white, and, in the meantime, employees from the powerhouse spoke out saying that the engines were on their last legs, that the smallest breakdown would knock them out for good. And without power, water would freeze up in the pipes and the whole waterworks would fall apart in an instant. People were seething with anger and ready to stop working, and don't let anybody talk about the illegality of power plant strikes, because they won't call this a strike — they simply won't show up at work because of hunger.

They brought out the paperwork. The *Glava*'s hands were shaking, the pages rustled. He searched, read, quoted some figures . . .

"Hang you, you bitches," a drunken *bomzh* suddenly howled, leaning out from behind the platform and, staggering, made for Nebozhenko. Luckily for him, his comrades held him back by the tail of his coat, pulled him about a bit, punched him in the face and made his nose bleed, until he calmed down. He carried on muttering, half sobbing, that they should all be got rid of, the cunts, from top to bottom, from Moscow to Solovky. Nebozhenko pretended not to see anything and carried on reading.

People started getting bored. Who's interested in figures on paper? They started to trickle away. The wind gusted more strongly, the snow stuck more thickly. A handful of people remained on the small square in front of Administration; beneath the platform, it was empty. The *Glava* finally finished but came to no conclusion, and summed up:

"There's no money!"

Someone dealt a swinging kick at a dog running past. The dog gave a short yelp, pulled its tail between its legs and crawled beneath the platform. The crowd melted away like snow, the people were washed away by the darkness. I remembered the anger of the late Lokh Rudy, who often repeated that things would finally have to be put in order and all the s.o.bs hung: monks, head-*chinovnik*s, and parasite museum employees. The Russian *muzhik* is patient, but when he loses his temper, he'll raise hell, fume like foul smoke and eat your eyes out . . .

3

Elections are being held all over Russia at present, Russian-style: fanatically. There are elections on TV, elections in the papers, elections in the *posyolok*; wherever you go, a kitchen or *banya*, everywhere people are talking about the elections. The battle for the Duma had barely finished when a fight for the President's chair broke out. The President hadn't even recovered his bearings after the campaign, when bets were being made for the Russian provinces. The papers, radio and television are all blowing the same trumpet; finally, for the first time in history − what an event! People are racing to the vote, every village wanting its own duma. From Chukotky to Klin, from Magadan to Solovky, they are electing presidents, governors, mayors and all sorts of heads. It is worth taking a good look at the elections on Solovky for two reasons: firstly − it is an historic occasion on the Islands without precedent in their history; secondly − the Islands encapsulate a whole set of events and problems particular to the Russian province.

4

Elections on Solovky. The day before yesterday, I accredited myself
– officially, it goes without saying – as an international observer from
the monthly periodical *Kultura*. Ludmila Mikhailovna from the electoral commission, fat and respectable, clapped in astonishment and
shouted: "Well, *blin!*"

On the Islands, you can see everyone clearly as through a magni-
fying glass. So the insight into the infancy of democracy in the depths
of Russia is extraordinary, almost like in a laboratory. Being an impar-
tial foreigner without the right to vote and, at the same time, familiar
with all the local affairs and gossip, I am in a singular position
because, without siding with anyone, I know everyone. The Solovkians,
on the other hand, like islanders on the whole, are hardened in their
resentment against each other, effusive with strangers, prone to
gossip, and to share secrets. Maksimov even mentions the unusual
disease, *govorukha*, which affects people in the North: taciturn
because of lack of opportunity to talk, when they do start talking,
there's no end . . .

And so, making the most of this coincidence, I watched the electoral battle on Solovky from the kitchen, where, drinking tea, sometimes *shilo*, I listened to the contenders for power, their programmes,
grievances, biographies. I visited them all, one by one, in their homes
in order to see how they lived, what they had and what they still
needed. I was present at meetings and various sessions; I went to meet
the candidates for mayor of Solovky in their places of work (the
museum, the office of public services, the agar-agar factory, and also
the hospital, Leskhoz, the militia, the airport); I took part in a couple
of rallies in the *banya* and the "round table" discussion at the *posyolok*'s cultural club. And finally, every day in the evenings after supper,
I would pop in to see Vasyalich, the former Solovetsky party secre-

tary who knows everybody here: through inside information and denouncements. Vasyalich has been living on the Islands for years; he has seen and heard a great deal and can recall what people – who now say something completely different – used to do in the past.

So that is how I saw the first splutterings of democracy on Solovky. And I won't pretend that it wasn't all rather messy, and that it smelt bad. The closer it got to elections, the more dirt was pulled out into the open. The people were fermenting like *braga* [home-brewed beer]. *Muzhik*s in the *banya* conspired on Saturdays, the women rallied in shops while waiting for bread, *chinovnik*s stuck together and took a stand, the "new Russians" of Solovky bought votes for a bottle of vodka, veterans clamoured, everyone schemed in his own way, and even old folk, one foot in the grave, were suddenly possessed by the demon of politics. Only the *bomzh*s and *bich*s didn't care two hoots, the same as before. And the young people couldn't care less, as usual.

Six candidates put up a fight: Valenty N., already hardened in battle (when I asked with what party he sympathized, he replied none because he is now a *khozyaistvennik*, economic manager) and Sasha B., the head of the power station, the only contender without a higher education, a cross between Lebed and Zhyuganov, and who local *muzhik*s consider as one of their own (the central point of his programme is the demand that Yeltsin be put on trial). Further in the betting were Luba G. and Lev R., sharks of the tourist sector – she is the owner of the hotel (privatized *po blatu*), he, the head of the department of social aid on Solovky and director of an excursion company (also *po blatu*) – they hate each other and fight ruthlessly because each of them needs a *krysha* [a cover] with which to mask their business and strangle the opponent. Finally, there were Lina Ts., the head of the hospital on Solovky, and Sveta S., an unemployed lawyer (the former likes the Communists, the latter the Democrats), both abandoned by their husbands, ugly and wanting power so as to drown their loneliness and take their revenge.

Their electoral programmes? A farce. Each copied the other; they all wrote the same things, making the same mistakes, using clichéd phrases. About economic development and social care, about the protection of ecology and financial obstructions, about foreign tourism and divine providence, about subsidies, taxation and responsibility. In other words, as children say: promises, promises. Among more concrete facts, I recall the different approach of the two main contenders, N. and B., to the subject of energy resources. The Solovetsky power station is on its last legs and threatens to break down at any moment, to say nothing of the tons of mazut which leak from the pipes, destroying the extraordinary natural landscape of Solovky. Enormous sums, totally unobtainable today, are necessary to repair the power station. There are no stoves in many of the houses, including the hospital. They are heated in winter by a central system whereby hot water circulates thanks to electric pumps, and it is enough for the power to be turned off for a few days for the pipes to burst, the water to flood the houses, then freeze over . . . Power shortage in the North means death. N. proposes building windmills. Because they are ecologically clean, of the future and, who knows, maybe they would give them some dollars towards the cost. Who? I don't know, the Norwegians, Solzhenitsyn, the Orthodox Church? (Incidentally, N. is tempting the monks with tax concessions and free land as long as they vote for him; he has even started going to church and bangs his forehead against the icons and shouts about penance at meetings!) While B. promises us *malysh* [a nipper], that is . . . a small nuclear reactor (. . . and no concessions for "the blacks"). Lenin had already once said that Communism equals power of the Soviets plus electrification. Today, they have started building capitalism by the same formula.

The Solovkians don't want anything to do with capitalism, they really don't. They want to eat better, buy firewood. They miss the times when wages were paid without delay, pensions came at an appointed time, and savings guaranteed a peaceful old age. And now? Today, there are no wages, no retirement or old age pensions, and the devil already took any savings (often a whole life's savings!) during Gaidar's day. Today, there is a shortage of roubles! This is what hurts the Solovkians. Without roubles, man loses his dignity. When, during one of the pre-electoral meetings, N. promised old age pensioners a one-off credit in the shop (of 100,000 roubles, that is about twenty dollars) on all provisions apart from alcohol, the old people kicked up a row, and the old woman Vala screamed that this degraded her, even though she doesn't drink. It was cold in the hall, clouds of vapour wafted from people's mouths, the people sat in felt boots and stamped their feet. I looked around. Around me were old, worn people. Defenceless, powerless. All their lives they had been dependent on the authorities which thought for them, gave them work and food. And now? They only wished to survive until death. N. is dreaming of windmills, and the people dream of a fence around the cemetery because cows pasture on the tombs. He is making plans for a new hospital, and they weep because there is a shortage of medicine. He is talking about enlarging the airport, and the old women are asking that the *polaskalka* (the wooden hut on Holy Lake where the local women rinse their laundry in winter) be repaired, because the boards have rotted in the old one and draughts . . .

Other meetings were similar.

In the club, on the other hand, where the "round table" for all the candidates together had been set up, people didn't stand on ceremony. Everything that had, up until now, been whispered in corners, was now thrown out like dishwater from a window. What right has Lev R. to mix work in administration with private business? Who allowed Luba G. to privatize the municipal hotel and gave her the slabs of reinforced concrete from the unfinished sewer purification plant? Why did N. buy himself a house in Orel using funds which had been intended for veterans, when he already has an apartment and a house in his father-in-law's name on Solovky? Where have the milliards of subsidies gone? And so on, and so on . . . The contenders bit back. B. turned out best because he said the least. He also won the elections.

The elections ran their course without any major incident. Eighty per cent voted. For the first time, there was neither buffet nor music in the election hall. The results were announced the following day. And so, we have got a new *Glava*, and a new Duma. The councillors, hmmmm . . . there is a woman who trades in vodka at night, an *alkash* "on the wagon", a *muzhik*, who doesn't know what a constitution is . . . But they're all our own kind, people from Solovky. What now?

"Wait and see . . ." as the Russians say.

5

Christmas Eve

Outside the window, stars crackle; inside, the house smells of spruce, poppy seeds and honey. On the table, there is some "opłatek"* from Poland, borsch with "uszka",** "kutya"*** and, instead of carp made in the Jewish way, there is *ukha* made from *nalim* [monkfish]. A thick, fragrant bouillon of green burbot, pulled out yesterday from beneath the ice on Thundering Lake.

We left at dark-grey dawn, on a sleigh drawn by a tractor. Smirny, Maksy and I. Above the Island hung a duvet of cloud as if soiled by the sweat of thick sleep. Fine snow was falling, noiselessly. The lakes were asleep in the peaceful landscape. At the sixth verst, we picked up some *muzhik*s who had set off fishing for monkfish but had had a drink on the way and when, in Isakovo, they had fallen out of their sleigh, they had immediately fallen asleep in the snow . . . It is impossible to drive up to Thundering Lake so we covered the last verst

---

* A wafer which is broken and shared on Christmas Eve while those who partake of it wish each other well. *Tr.*

** A sort of Polish tortelloni. *Tr.*

*** A dessert made from the milk of poppy seeds. *Tr.*

through the forest on wide, hunter's skis; sweating profusely, we ploughed through obstructive, powdery snow which looked as if it had been piled up uninhibitedly by some heavenly shovel, while white clusters fell from the spruce trees straight down our necks and ran down our bodies in cool streams, zigzagging in trickles. Maksimka immediately disappeared up front; Smirny remained in the back, so I plodded in the muteness of the forest and white dampness. It was hard work, just as it sometimes is when one is bent over a blank sheet of paper: the same whiteness, muteness and the same sense of being buried. Suddenly, the forest opened out wide on to the lake where islands slept like flowerbeds in a winter park; down below was Maksimka's small silhouette, and deep tracks with dark stains in places where water had seeped up through the ice. Smirny, panting, arrived after a while and we started fishing. First of all, we hacked out a *yordan*, that is, a large air-hole in the ice, so that we could pull the nets out through it. Smirny drilled holes in the ice, I joined them up using a crowbar and Maksy tied the strings. We pushed the ice-floes with a spade and crowbar until they slipped under the ice and hid themselves. Then we cleared the *yordan* of any remaining brash-ice and set about dragging in the nets, which had been left here three days earlier. The nets floated out from the dark abyss of the air-hole, like hair, with silvery hairgrips of whitefish. We removed the fish delicately so as not to tear the bodies in the mesh; they trembled on the ice for a while, until the icy air sent them to sleep for ever. Sometimes we would find a burbot, dark green, slippery and fat. In this way, we went through two dozen nets from five *yordan*s, and set down ten new ones. Setting nets down under ice requires no mean experience and is somewhat like crocheting. First, you drill a *lunka* [opening in the ice], then another, a metre away. You put some string with a weight down the first one, and in the other, a long, oddly bent rod, and you twist and turn the rod in the hole until it catches the string from the first *lunka*. Then you pull the string under the ice, make another *lunka* and repeat the procedure. You need to drill about thirty *lunka*s in ice as hard as diamonds for one net. And God forbid if you come across a root because then you have to drill to the side, pull the nets through and . . . begin anew. We returned at dusk, drenched in sweat, as if from a steam bath. And the snow kept falling. The forest was falling asleep. On the way, we picked up fishermen who were emerging from the dark like the ghosts of monks or *zeka*s. We brought a sleigh full of *muzhik*s to the *posyolok*. Each was carrying a *maydan*,[*] a drill for the ice, and forest skis. They dispersed near the kremlin, in silence. People are now saving themselves — from hunger — with fish.

6

Old Vasyalich brought a newspaper in which a clairvoyant, an old woman from near Arkhangel called Vera Zashukhina, famous throughout the whole of the North for her divinations and miraculous cures, forecasts the annihilation of the Solovetsky Islands: "I saw an explosion on Solovky, like a terrible earthquake, and the bottom of the sea fell in, and the sea drowned the Islands, and an enormous wave surged towards Arkhangel and broke over the town, and there were countless victims and no end of tears." To a journalist's question as to whether the catastrophe could be avoided, Zashukhina answered as follows: "Lawlessness and baseness reign today because people have forgotten about God. And he who still remembers, does so for show because that is the fashion now. We should measure our faith in the Saviour by good deeds so that Our Lord may live not only in church but in everybody's heart. Do not forget about the Lord because everything is in His power." The newspaper with the divination found

---

[*]A large tin box with leather straps attached to it so that it can be carried on the back. *Tr.*

its way to the Islands and caused a great deal of consternation. The women aren't talking about anything else; somebody has already whispered the date of the cataclysm and they say that in 1999 the sea will engulf us . . .

XI

First of all, I love the heather,
And the sea to the horizon — far away.
And I also like to believe
The one who'll die — perhaps today.
Antonina Mielnik

1

Life is coming to an end, as in Yulka's beautiful poem, where leaves go mad in old age because winter is approaching and with it, the first Ball — the Ball of last hopes — and that is why they are in a hurry, breaking away and whirling about, not knowing that their colourful clothes are . . . death's shroud.

2

19 January

Melnitsa jumped out of a fifth-floor window in Arkhangel. Her head split open with the fall. Later on, Dubrava told how she had grown sad towards the end, had often spoken about the Islands and had vacuous, absent eyes. On that hapless day, as was usual after supper, he had gone up to his room to work a little more and she had remained in the kitchen to do the washing-up. Suddenly, a smell of fresh air filled the apartment. He had a premonition and ran out of his study. The kitchen window was wide open, the wind was tousling the curtain, and below, beneath the house, on the white snow, lay a blackish, irregular shape . . . like a rag-doll. On the table, she had left a letter in the form of a lullaby about how she would fly over the Islands, her one and only country, which she would no longer have time to touch with her hands because the wind from the North would catch and sweep her up: it would sow her on the seashore, forget her on the dunes, scatter her in the forest, lose her on the way and give away the rest to the *bich*s in the *posyolok*, as prayers for the dead. And forty days would not pass before the sky, which has set in her eyes, would again be pure . . .

3

Four days later, Melnitsa's body was flown to Solovetsky by aeroplane. At first, they had wanted to take her to the mortuary but then it was decided that her body should be laid out in Petersbursky Hotel, at the museum. The museum collective took the funeral into its hands; after all, she used to work there. Functions were allocated: who was to prepare the dishes for the wake, who was to take turns watching over the body, who was to dig the grave. They placed the coffin in the smoking room, where they go for a cigarette – with the smell of old, cheap tobacco – on two long tables borrowed from the office. Folding chairs were arranged at the sides, four to a row, just like in a cinema. Whispers in the semi-darkness, rustling and sobbing. The coffin was open: the head bandaged, the forehead indented, the face bloated, a stranger's face. I sat down among women clad in black. The whispers grew silent. Candles flickered, a film was being shown behind my half-closed eyelids. My first day on Solovky. The beginning of October. I arrived straight from Abkhazia, from the war. The mud glowed yellow, the aspen were already turning red, and the sea was greenish, like bottle glass. The air smelt of freshly salted herrings and rotten sea-grass. The *posyolok* was as if deserted; only dogs wandered around, and goats. The hotel was empty. The girl at reception was astounded that a correspondent had arrived and a foreign one at that.

"What have you come for?" she asked. "Oh, to see the sights? You should pop into the editorial office of *Solovetsky Vestnik*. You'll find the editor-in-chief there, a respectable woman. She'll show and tell you everything."

And indeed. It was Tonya . . .

The stairs in the corridor creak, new women have arrived, drunkards. They stare greedily, take a long time making themselves comfortable, cursing the cold. (Heating in the museum has been turned off because of debts.) We sit muffled up, in pelisses and felt boots. The old women slowly fall silent, sink into themselves, from time to time, one will whimper, as if in sleep . . .

. . . she gradually emerges from the small editorial office: first of all, the huge — like a mill (hence *Melnitsa*, the Mill) — solid body and face of the astonished girl, then her benevolent eyes behind thick glasses and the faint smell of alcohol, and, finally, her warm hands and timid smile. She had just put an issue to bed and was on her way to the forest so, if I wanted to, we could go together — talk on the way. We leave the *posyolok*. It is afternoon: gossamer, heather the shade of rust. Warm sand, warm moss. We talk lazily, about this and that. About everything and nothing. And that's how we talk all the way to the cemetery. There, beyond the gate, at the very edge, lies Yulka, a poet and Tonya's friend. She had hanged herself in the forest, leaving behind a small volume of poems, four children and a husband, also a poet. She was twenty-five. A large photograph on an iron cross and, on the photograph, large, black eyes.

"Have you ever wondered where you'll be buried?"

A little further along — brushwood and the grave of an unknown *zeka*. It was Tonya's idea; a mound of stone, raised by the hands of the children and grandchildren of SLON victims. Our ancestors, their spirits, live on in stones the same as they do in words. The Saams knew this . . . We weave our way among the graves; leaves rustle, the sun seeps through, there is an Orthodox cross here, a red star there, and on every tombstone a *stakanchik* [c.f. *stakan* in glossary], a small glass. You can come, sit, have a drink . . .

There was another stir in the corridor. The grannies left in a swarm. They had frozen. One of them strongly cursed the management and the entire world. The rest coughed in accompaniment. Petya-*poslushnik* arrived, slightly intoxicated. He was going to read the psalms. (The monks had refused because she had committed suicide.) He began quietly, *mormorando*, deep within, then louder, monotonously, swaying to the beat. I sank into my sheepskin. The candles trembled. The psalm ran, like a road, along the seashore: "*chelovek, yako trava dne yevo, yako tsvet sel'ny, tako otsvetyot . . .*"*

. . . we've arrived at the Point of Labyrinths. We sit on the stone and smoke.

"If you want to leave here, don't visit the Saams' labyrinths, because you'll be done for. Like me . . ."

The sea is lapping the shore, seagulls screech. We walk on. Along hardened sand, sinking in heaps of algae. *Floridaea, fucus, laminaria*. She had started talking about herself, out of the blue, chaotically. Her great grandfather had been a Pole (Przegodzki, I believe), who had been exiled to the Urals, her father an *alkash* and bard. She had adored him. Her mother, she had hated — ever since she was a child — and used to dream of cutting out her *pichka* [fanny] with scissors. Her dad would rarely come home and when he did, he was usually drunk. She would take off his shoes, help him undress, listen to his

---

* "Man, his days are like grass, and like a wild flower, he will fade . . .". *Tr.*

124

garbled poems, stories as convoluted as life, unearthly tales. Then her mother took her own life and dad disappeared. Then there were aunts, boarding school, school, boyfriend. Her first vodka, her first poems. She had found her father, who was dying in R. He died, an alcoholic, in despair . . . she grew silent. The shore meandered, lost its way in the bays, like her story. All of a sudden, Hare Islands emerged from a mirage. The sun refracted the light, hurting the eyes. After a while, she took up her story again, jumping from subject to subject. She had come to Solovky twenty years ago. With her husband and Aloshka. Sasha, her younger one, was born here. Right away, as soon as she saw it, she felt that this was the land for her. That she would stay here. Her husband couldn't take it; he took the older boy and left. Later, he returned a couple of times; finally, there was a divorce and he stopped writing. At first, it was difficult for her, alone, especially in winter: the constant dark, the constant nostalgia. The low skies oppressed, the winds blew the soul away. In the end, she grew used to it, started to drink. She worked in the museum, kept herself busy with SLON. This was frowned upon at the time; the fashion for labour camps hadn't started yet. But they set up an exhibition, the first in the Soviet Union, drew a map of the *zona*s for "Memorial" and made a film with Goldovska, called *Vlast' solovetskaya − Solovetsky power* − (in the film, off-screen, she read letters, written by *zeka*s, which she had found among some bricks on Sekirna Mountain). In summer, she would show tourists around; in winter, write poems. And Sashka grew. Year by year went by, like the men in her bed: sometimes clearly outlined, sometimes vague. Finally, she realized that the museum was not for her; they embalm memory there and want to live off tourists. She started working on *Solovetsky Vestnik*; the time was right. Nebozhenko gave her some money, somebody *po blatu* found a printing press and so it began. Solovky had its own newspaper, just as in the days of SLON. A newspaper thanks to which yesterday's SLON revived and exists today: poems by *zeka*s and by Yulka appeared on one spread, reports from SLON and pieces from the *posyolok*, profiles of the dead next to those of the living. She worked as if in a trance. And she drank more and more because you won't last long without vodka here – the nightmares will choke you. Here, the walls weep, fungi grow on corpses, and the landscape is not conducive to life – it is like a stage set from a different play. It is not so bad in the summer because there are tourists, guests, talk. But in the winter, when the people of Solovky are left alone with all this, in winter you can go mad. But, at the same time, for the elect, winter on Solovky is a special time: in winter, you can meet yourself in the snow-covered wilderness.

"Come to the Islands in winter, Mar . . ."

Petya broke off in the middle of a psalm; he had fallen asleep . . . It suddenly became so silent that you could hear the ice crack on the sea, the ice floes creak. It was already half past one. Outside, the moon was full; the world, as if covered in icing, now glistened, now lengthened shadows. I read somewhere that the Samoyeds called January nights "white" nights because the moon hangs so low then, like a lantern, and the snow and ice scatter the silver glow . . .

". . . in the winter, you can see the lining of the world here. Pavel Florensky wrote that reality in the North is thinner than anywhere else, like a jumper worn out at the elbows, and the other world shines through it. You only need to see the Northern lights to feel the cosmos on your shoulders, and the silence of a 'white' night to hear . . ." She didn't finish, as if she were afraid of saying too much.

We were returning to the *posyolok* by way of a narrow sandbar which separates Sour Bay from the sea. The sun was setting behind Dog's Bar, pouring crimson light over the shores. The moss on the dunes looked like deep-red plush. The sand crunched beneath our feet. Tonya continued talking. She had tried to run away from here a couple of times; she was even carried as far as Kolyma once. But she had returned, no longer able to live without Solovky. She didn't even know herself when she had begun to feel that the Islands and she were one, that their earth was her skin (beneath which corpses had been buried), and their history had become her life. She had walked along every path here with a poem, and the stones were her friends. Here, take this one . . . She took a few steps and, from a small cracked niche under the water, gropingly, she pulled out a stone with garnets: a large aureola of granite, as if incrusted with drops of blood. She had hidden it there herself. It really was beautiful. And mysterious, as if a half-obliterated text . . .

I was awoken by the smell of *pelmeny* with cabbage, and the sound of somebody's voice. At first, I didn't know where I was. Where were these voices coming from? Where the *pelmeny*? Where had the stone gone, where was Tonya? Was there somebody snoring next to me? It was Petya. And Tonya . . . was dead! They were laying the tables for the wake in the museum office. Women were bringing in the food. It was seven o'clock, time to dig the grave.

4

Day was barely breaking when we managed to get there, up to the waist in bluish snow. The sky was paling in the east, fluffy clouds were creeping out from behind the forest, lit pink from below. It was still dark in the cemetery and only in places, in the upper branches, hoar frost glistened. A heavy frost held fast. We lit a fire near the gate. A few dry logs, a little petrol and sparks began to fly. Then *shilo*, a *stakan*, some pork fat, to help with the work. The icy liquid, thick as oil, ran down as white light, glowed inside, sharpened our eyes. The fat was hard and salty. The world became clearer, people – closer. Misha, Zhenya, Morozov, Motyl [Butterfly] . . .

I got to know them all thanks to Melnitsa. That day, in the evening after returning from our walk by the seashore, she had invited us home for her birthday. She was forty-five. Her two rooms and kitchen, on Zaozernaya Street, were dirty and untidy. I saw her friends at the table: the wood engraver Galinsky, a Buddhist whom she was sleeping with at the time; Vasya, Yulka's husband, a poet and bard; the photographer Misha Vervald, an Estonian from the Sayan Mountains; the journalist Deisan, a would-be monk; schizophrenic Nina, the poetess; the philosopher with delirium tremens, Sergey Morozov; the deaf Kritsky, a historian and communist; her neighbour Yura, a fisherman; Dichkov, the gay accountant; Zhenka, the blacksmith with a wolf-like face; the small-time crook, Sasha; Lokha, who worked with seaweed; *bomzh* Motyl and the *bich* Rudy; Inka, the syphilitic whore; lame Katya, and a few other unforgettable faces like . . . Then, after a few overflowing glasses, I thought . . . it's something out of Bosch or Memling. Like some sort of Judgement, maybe the Last, or somebody's Hell. Towards morning, when dawn seeped into the kitchen and, from the darkness, drew out the dirt and neglect — fish heads, fag-ends in the pastry, the remainder of the guests — I could no longer understand what it was all about. What were they talking about? I'd catch individual words from the garble and the whimpering — something about apples, that they grow there, in orchards. Could it be nostalgia? But yes, they were missing the temperate zone, its climate . . . Later on, thanks to Tonya, I got to know their stories, their tangled destinies — different threads of one and the same tale; the rest — their features, details of their lives — I could add myself by living among them. Today, not many of the guests of that evening remain; somebody died by their own hand, somebody else was helped by unclean *shilo* or by his neighbours. Yura was pushed out of a boat during a drinking bout, Rudy's heart refused to work, Sashka hanged himself, Katya was butchered, and they finished Lokha off in the *zona*, the bitches. And here, finally, Tonya herself fell out of the Solovetsky tale, as from the window . . .

Misha wanted to dig in the new cemetery, where there is a lot of space and the path has been trodden down. Motyl was obstinate; he wanted to dig near the fence because we were burying a suicide victim. I mumbled something about there being a gap next to Yulka, just enough space for one body, and that the fence was close by and the sea, too. My idea was taken up. We cleared the snow and threw smouldering firebrands on the frozen earth, kidding ourselves that the earth would thaw out on its own. No go . . . We had to break it up with crowbars. Half a metre of frozen crust, like reinforced concrete. We hammered in turns until there were black sparks in front of our eyes and our hands were numb. Yulka watched derisively from the photograph on the cross. In the meantime, the sun had risen, a golden shaft in a milky mist, like an anti-aircraft beam: a vertical column of light. You can only see this in winter. The crowbars ring out, bounce off the frozen earth; steam billows from the men. Sand, at last. Now, it should be easier. Time for a roll-up. More *shilo*, more pork fat from the Sayan Mountains (Misha's mother had sent it). The fire crackled, Zhenka added wood. Zhenya, Misha, Motyl, Morozov . . .

. . . Melnitsa used to say that Solovky is *svalka ludey* − a human rubbish dump. As once a glacier had carried stones down here, so today life has deposited all sorts of human refuse: dreamers and idiots, poets, outsiders and failures, delinquents, mystics, parasites and fugitives. Life tossed them about, mistreated them and carried them further and further away from the main current which the rest of the people navigated, until they came to their senses . . . here, on these stones, sticking out of the White Sea. And they realized, with astonishment, that there was no further they could go, that they had found themselves on the edge. Some grew frightened, others started to drink heavily, yet others quietly lost their minds. Melnitsa sympathized with them all (maybe it would be more accurate to say: empathized with each one?) so deeply that the boundary between someone else's pain and her own disappeared. She identified with the characters of her tales. Yes, yes, tales, for Tonya spoke about the people of Solovky both in prose and in verse. And she did not notice that she had transformed her own life into a novel, a novel whose narrative escaped her pen. Once I began to live on the Islands, I could watch the continuation of Tonya's story which she had begun then, that first day, at the seashore. She would often visit us, sensing a soulmate, as she herself used to say — bringing a bottle, or already tipsy, and she would cry, tell stories or, sometimes, even wail. Either about a new *muzhik* and the ups and downs of her love life, rows and black eyes, or a bad conscience for having lost her sons, because Losha had long since disappeared with no news and the underworld looking for him, and the younger one, Sasha, had been put into the *zona* for the under-aged, like a thief. There were problems with the newspaper, too; they weren't giving her any dough, the swine. She was becoming more bloated, neglected, vulgar. Apparently, she had started to avoid people, especially the decent ones, perhaps from shame, perhaps from pure paranoia. She preferred the *bomzh*s, the degenerates, the *alkash*s. In summer, she would run down to the deep sea fishing boats so as to give herself to the *bich*s and knock back *shilo*; in winter, she lived where she could, at Inka's, at Katya's in the "Shanghai", and she would croak out poems, like bile . . .

It's my turn. The bed is getting deeper still; work has gone quicker in the sand. We dig singly, taking turns so as not to hit each other's spades. It is cramped in the grave, icy. The sand emanates cold. The deeper I go, the more isolated I become. The voices from above, muffled, barely reach me. And here, there is silence; only the sand crunches and sometimes the spade will grind against a stone. Sand . . . has no smell. (Where do these thoughts come from?) A dirty yellow colour, frozen, it falls off the sides of the grave in slabs as we try to even them out. I wonder whether any heat will reach down here in the summer and decompose Tonya's corpse, or whether she will lie here, in the frozen snow, as in an ice-room, until the end of the world. I don't feel comfortable here. Despite myself, I am thinking about me, my own body. I've taken part in many funerals but I've always stood there, over the grave, among the living. From below, things look different: a fragment of sky in the crowns of trees, hoar frost on the branches and, from time to time, a face leans over — Motyl's, Misha's, Morozov's, Zhenya's . . .

. . . characters from Melnitsa's poems and parts of her life. Because

Tonyukha, a truly Russian woman, was generous. She dispersed their pain within her own body, measured their anxieties with her own fear, drank with them, slept with them and only when writing about them did she sometimes separate herself from them, for a while. It got to the point that she washed corpses so as to look into somebody else's death. I remember the last time — they were washing granny Gala, I believe: she came in the morning, already tipsy, carrying a bottle. She was moved, swallowing her words, muttering something about *gutta-percha* and pouring vodka. Then, howling, she sang about the "black raven". Until snot and tears ran down her face. And when she was at the door, as if coming to her senses a little, she said that everybody should wash at least one corpse in order to feel life, to the end . . . I never saw her among the living again because she ran away from Solovky soon afterwards to return here, as it turned out, in a coffin.

The work is finished. It only remains to put some fir branches on the bed and two boards across — it's easier to pull the ropes out from under the coffin in this way. And one more *stakan*, for the road. We gather our crowbars, spades. We bank up the fire. Crows gather on the surrounding trees. The funeral procession is working its way through the snow — a swarm of people. They liked Tonyukha. Now there will be a lot of speeches, a lot of tears and a queue to the grave because everybody would like to throw in a handful of sand. Later, they will fill it in, even it out, and lay out the wreaths. The women will scatter breadcrumbs. They'll disperse.

Emptiness. Only the crows peck at the breadcrumbs.

5

The wake in the museum. The tables are laid for a hundred people but more have come . . . They are looking for chairs; there is confusion, a squeeze. The mourners are crowded; there is no elbow room. In front of each of them lies a plate of *kutya* made with rice and raisins, a *blin*. That's the custom. Then there will be dishes of steaming *kartoshka*, salted herring, mounds of *vinegret* [Russian salad], stuffed cod, fried perch, monkfish *ukha*, fish cutlets, *pelmeny* with soft cheese, *pelmeny* with cabbage, pickled cabbage, and pâtés. And vodka, of course, white vodka. And a purr of contentment among the *alkash*s: the chance of a free drink. I look around. The museum employees sit together; closer to the managing director, in the middle, is Dubrava, Melnitsa's last husband; at the sides are her former lovers and acquaintances, the bohemia of Solovky; further along are the women, the neighbours and *muzhik*s from the deep seas, fishermen, sea grass gatherers, and the local rabble, meaning *bich*s, *bomzh*s and all sorts of *blyad'*.

Vodka is poured and a din prevails. Everybody rises to their feet. Managing director Martynov waits for a moment until the noise dies down, and speaks. He speaks for a long time, bombastically, as if he were savouring his words: he speaks of the merits of the deceased, of the SLON exhibition, of clearing up the white stains of history, of the repaid debt, of our gratitude . . .

. . . of our gratitude; but, of course, after all it is thanks to Melnitsa that I am here. Then, on that first walk, a thought had come to my mind, out of the blue: and why shouldn't I come to live here? At least for a couple of years to see winter in the North, the Northern lights, and to meet myself here. Where haven't I lived? In Central Europe, in North America, in the Golden Mountains near Kłodzko, and on Fifth Avenue in New York, in the Gdańsk Shipyard during the August Strike, and under the Berlin Wall while it was being dismantled, in Moscow's White House during the coup d'état, and on an empty beach in Sukhumy during the war between the Abkhazians and the Georgians. In this turmoil of events, constantly among people, it was difficult to concentrate (to get one's bearing), but here, even nature, thanks to the asceticism of shapes and colours, is conducive to isolation and concentration. There, the hum of mass media, the din, the tinkle of glasses and chit-chat; here, the forest, the silence of stones and the empty horizon. To stop, at least for a moment – why not? And Tonya helped us. She found accommodation in the biology station, telephoned Moscow, met us at the airport when we returned to Solovky in December, found us firewood for heating . . . at last Martynov has finished. They have drunk. They have sat down. They follow up with a bite.

It has become noisy, the alcohol has done its work. Eyes have grown moist, faces have thawed out, come to life. Everybody, without exception, is busy eating. Hands reach out, jaws are at work, dishes circulating. And it's not surprising; after all, the majority of Solovkians don't have enough to eat on a daily basis. Especially the *bomzh*s. Another round. Svyeta and Luba have poured vodka into the *stopka*s. Vervald tinkles with a fork and a hundred *stopka*s are raised for Tonya. Misha is a talkative man; the *stopka*s freeze in the air. He describes the deceased's merits at the local newspaper, saying that she was a journalist of high class and that she had worked the whole paper by herself, from editorials down to the printing press, and that her *Vestnik* was read everywhere as Russia is long and wide, from Chukotka to Kurskaya Kosa, and abroad, too, in Europe, the United States, even in Australia, and that she was also a poet, and no mean one at that, and that she wrote her life in verse, and verse – with her life . . .

. . . yes, yes, I remember our endless disputes about writing and life, and how one relates to the other. About what can and what should not be said about the people about whom one is writing. About the right to reinvent reality and about the grievances of the heroes of documentary prose, and about Shalanov's prose, which was like a document, and about the poetry of Rubtsov, who was killed in the night of *Kreshchenie* [the Epiphany] (19th January) by the heroine of his poems, the woman who had become his wife. During one of these conversations, one of our last, Tonya gave me her favourite book, *Diary of the North*, by Kazakov, with her own epitaph scrawled on the cover, like a motto . . . and Vervald finishes with the wish that the earth should be as light to Tonya as a feather. The *stopka*s are tossed down.

And so on. Rounds of *stopka*s, successive speeches, ever more garbled. About Tonya's goodness, about how she would always help out with a rouble, that she took people in, cried with them, cuddled them. Natasha's mascara has run down her face. Dubrava and Deysan are in each other's arms. Motyl is touching Inka up. Suddenly, Zhenya starts to shout that someone has stolen the knives. Burtseva swears that she hasn't taken them. The *bich*s, taking advantage of the commotion, polish off other people's vodka. Someone throws up in the toilet, someone falls asleep in the snowdrift at the door and . . . perhaps Melnitsa was right – I am *otreshonny* (absent, removed) from them.

"You look at us as if we were guinea pigs," she would sometimes say when she had had a drink.

XII

I finish, Your Highness, where I started: Russia is a great spectacle, which I shall always watch with equal admiration and terror.

Joseph de Maistre

1

There used to be the monastery cemetery and a church on the hill on Zaozernaya Street. Later, in the days of SLON, *zeka*s were executed there *en masse* and buried in collective graves, new corpses thrown on to old ones. In the 1930s, the church was demolished and they began building a camp hospital. The foundations stood on bones. Nearby, they continued shooting and burying prisoners. They finished building the hospital in 1939 – a stone edifice with arcades and columns, neither manor nor office. Then the *zeka*s were deported from the Island and the hospital was taken over by the army. The oldest Solovkians remember the army personnel with nostalgia: excellent doctors, professional service, free medication. In 1953, after Stalin's death, the hospital was modernized and piles of human bones were dug out. Later on, whenever there was any sort of excavation, human scraps would frequently surface. Towards the end of the 1980s, within the framework of *perestroika*, the army left the Islands. Civilian administration took over the hospital. There was a shortage

135

of doctors, the building needed repair, there was no money, the X-ray broke down, the laboratory technician was dismissed . . . Today, there is no dentist, or surgeon, or midwife, you won't even come across a proper nurse. The only person remaining is the head of the hospital, Lina Ts. The only thing she can do is to pull a *muzhik* out of his *zapoy* [alcoholic fit] and attach him to a drip. The building is falling apart, the walls are rotting, the pipes are leaking and old Solovkians, who haven't got anybody to look after them at home, are breathing their last on board beds. But at least there is light, and warmth. Although the hospital is drowning in debt, they can't cut the power off because, after all, the old people would freeze. (Other debtors have been cut off long ago – the Museum, the House of Culture, the Fire Station and even Administration.) In these circumstances, *Glava* decreed that Administration be transferred to the hospital. The *chinovnik*s have taken over the whole of the ground floor: the social department works in the dental surgery, accounts in admissions, the secretary's office is in the maternity ward, and *Glava*, himself, has taken over the X-ray department. The local old people, as before, are dying on the first floor, and the *chinovnik*s keep themselves warm at their side . . .

2

21 March

"Dobro pozhalovat' v Solovetsky lager golodnovo rezhima!" ("Welcome to Solovky's hunger regime camp!") was crookedly written on a piece of plywood with which the inhabitants of Solovky were greeting the Vice-governor and his retinue. From the early hours of the morning, in sopping snow up to the knees, workers from the public service firm were waiting at the gate to the airport for delegates from Arkhangel. They were waiting for money, which they hadn't seen since the winter

before last. Frozen to the bone, because "even blood had stopped warming them up", and ready to lie down on the runway to prevent the delegates from leaving Solovky if it turned out that they had come without the money.

"They ought to stay here with us," Pinagorsky incited and egged the *muzhik*s on, "at least a month, without any bread . . ."

The aeroplane had barely touched down when they ran out on to the runway, not paying any attention to the director of the airport who was shouting that this was forbidden. But then their courage failed them! They stopped short, rooted to the ground, overawed at the sight of the *Chinovnik*s. Some even removed their hats. The delegates walked past at a brisk pace, to the bus.

"And our money?" ranted Kola Arkatian, a Solovetsky Armenian, a huge fellow with bloodshot eyes.

"Above all, no ranting," the MVD* colonel who was escorting the delegation, snarled back. "And who are you?"

Kola immediately softened and started to stammer that he's got three hungry children, a wife who's expecting, that they're living in a camp barrack with a rotted roof and snow is falling into empty pots . . .

"We'll explain later," the colonel interrupted him, seeing that the guests had already got into the bus. Mud splattered up from under the wheels, the smell of petrol fumes filled the air and they left for Administration (that is, the hospital). And the crowd followed, on foot.

Outside the Administration (hospital) building, there was turmoil, *mat* and mud. The smoke of "Byelomar" ["White Sea canal" cigarettes] stung the eyes. Sasha Pinagorsky was fraying people's nerves again, saying that there wouldn't be any money, that the guests would stuff their guts at Ananchenko's (a former KGB official and owner of the hotel in the old SLON prison) and would leave without a word, and we'd stay in sh— up to our ears.

_____
* Ministry of Internal Affairs.

"Eh, if they'd only give us a little," Motyl started dreaming, "we could buy a piece of pork fat, a bottle, and nip out fishing."

"You'll sooner see your own ears than your money," Pinagorsky took the wind out of his sails.

"The bitches, *blya* . . ." someone swore and stopped short because a messenger had come out and invited them inside. The people crashed into the Administration boardroom (that is, the operating theatre), sat down and froze in anticipation. The air grew thick. The Vice-governor started drily, as if he were shelling peas. He said that there wasn't and there wouldn't be any money until we earned it ourselves; that there were reforms now, a free-market and that they weren't going to nurse anybody. Now, in the power station, for example, there were thirty-two workers when four would be enough. The maintenance of one bed in our hospital was costing 120,000,000 a year while in Mezen it cost barely thirty. Over eighty per cent of the people on Solovky were taking advantage of reductions in various payments for public services so it wasn't surprising that we were going hungry. Then he spoke of the municipal reforms which were being so widely talked about all over Russia. Everyone ought to pay for their own accommodation in full, and not just twenty-five per cent as they were doing now. There had to be competition in the services to prevent any old plumber from ripping people off for a piece of piping . . . At this point, Galavanikha, the new head of public services, couldn't restrain herself and said that this was rubbish because people weren't paying rates any more – how could they if they weren't getting any wages? As for competition, well, ha, ha, ha . . . there weren't enough materials on Solovky even for one company, and there was nothing to buy the materials with because people weren't paying up, because they weren't being paid, and so on, and so on . . . Suddenly, a piece of plaster fell from the ceiling right on to the chairman's table. There was laughter. At this point, the meeting broke up so that the guests could see for themselves how people were living on Solovky. Public services declared a water strike, that is, they said that they would cut water off in the *posyolok* until they received their wages. And, indeed, first the taps hummed and a red liquid, the colour of dirty blood, flowed out, then there was a rattling, a few drops of rust and . . . that was it.

The delegates began their tour with the power station, which was breathing its last and in need of two milliards for repairs. There were empty barrels everywhere, ponds of mazut. The guests got their shoes dirty. They also wanted to see the sewer purification plant but snow blocked the way and there was nothing to see – the purification plant had been abandoned in mid-construction and everything had been stolen. But they were shown the waterworks – from a distance. They didn't notice the missing filters. Whereas the leaking hydrants made them very angry.

"This is an unforgivable waste," the Vice-governor threw in, "pouring so much water into the sea."

But the Delegation didn't know that if we were to turn the taps off the water would freeze in winter and burst the pipes, and in summer would run with rust. Before lunch, they also managed to take a look at the school and the school canteen, where the kids are fed once a day, this frequently being the only meal Solovetsky children get. At the mention of food, the guests began to feel hungry. So they were taken to Ananchenko's for lunch: there, they were given black caviar, and salmon *ukha*, and roast hazel-grouse with cucumber and sour cream salad, and fresh pears, and grapes, and wine, and nut cake to go with the coffee and Amaretto liqueur.

After lunch, there was a meeting with the Solovetsky councillors. They spoke about territorial autonomy. The Islands used to be administered by a *selsovet* and three people used to be enough; today, two dozen *chinovnik*s sit in Administration and new ones are continuously being added. There is no tribunal, notary or tax office on the Islands. And, what is most important, they do not have their own budget. And if you don't have your own money, there is no point in autonomy! Autonomy only has the right to exist if it can feed the *chinovnik*s, otherwise it becomes a sham, burdening the federal budget. Today, we can say that the experiment with autonomy in Russia was premature. So long as people have not learnt how to earn money independently without expecting *poluchka* (from the verb *poluchat'*, to receive), they cannot govern themselves (which, at present, means *sharing* the monies sent by the state). The meeting with the councillors ran surprisingly peacefully; perhaps the prospect of the imminent abolition of autonomy on Solovetsky had a calming effect on our councillors. Pinagorsky, on the other hand, whispered under his breath that at last he was going to have some peace because the Duma was making his blood boil. Suddenly, somebody mentioned that people had gathered in the club and had been waiting for the guests for over an hour now. Unfortunately, the bus had broken down and we had to go on foot, through snow and mud.

The club was crowded, despite the cold. Some people had come out of curiosity, others out of boredom; women, to pour out their grievances in front of the authorities; veterans, to show off their medals; intellectuals, to shine in public; the rest, to watch, as in a cinema. The hall was decorated in 1960s style: curtain, crimson drapes, dust . . . At the table, on the platform, sat the Delegation in its entirety. The Vice-governor began without ceremony since it was high time to ask: what is Solovky? Some people argue that the Islands should be given back to the monks; others say a national park should be created here; others still that the tourist industry would solve all the problems. At the same time, nobody was working and everyone was waiting to be paid. The roads were covered in snow, there was mud and dirt all around, heat from the leaking pipes was escaping into the open air instead of heating the houses, tons of water were flowing into the sea, the sewers were leaking, the rubbish bins — overflowing — stank, while there were . . . seventy-three workers in the public services on Solovky! And they were all complaining that they weren't getting paid. But what were they supposed to be paid for, if they weren't doing anything? This couldn't go on. The vicious circle had to be broken! And so, he, the Vice-governor, believed — to sum up his short visit on the Islands — that: firstly, territorial autonomy should be abolished; secondly, people should be taken away, especially those who weren't needed, because their upkeep on Solovky was costing three times as much as on the mainland; and, thirdly, the remaining inhabitants should be permitted to shoot at migrating birds, at reindeer on Anzer, and to cut down trees in the forests for heating purposes, since the protection of the environment was senseless when people were dying of hunger. At this point, the Vice-governor fell silent so as to give what he had said time to sink in. Oh, the people became agitated . . . Granny Zina started shouting that she had lived here since 1939, had buried her husband here and wanted to be buried here herself, and that nobody was going to take her away from the Islands alive! Kozhevin declared that only those who would also manage to get along on the mainland would leave, while *bomzh*s and drunks would stay behind because who needed them there? Nadya Ch., the local ecologist, practically began crying: how could the shooting of reindeer or the cutting down of forests be allowed? This extraordinary natural landscape, which was created over centuries, would disappear in a year. Zoya B. asked whether the honorable guests had visited our shops. They hadn't, as it turned out.

"There," she roared. "They've been everywhere but haven't seen what's most important. Things cost three times more than they do anywhere else and they're past their 'sell by' date . . ."

"It would be better to go back to the labour camp," Rikusov hissed from the back. "At least they gave you *balanda* there . . ."

The only thing they didn't regret was autonomy. On the contrary, everybody complained about the councillors although they had only just elected them themselves. To wind up, the Vice-governor promised to do what he could.

The guests left towards evening. By the airport fence, cracked by the wind, the board with which they had greeted the Vice-governor this morning — "*Dobro pozhalovat' v Solovetsky lager golodnovo rezhima!*" — lay discarded.

3

Giedroyc, the editor-in-chief of *Kultura*, sent me a copy of *Russkaya mysl* ("Russian thought") with Solzhenitsyn's interview in it. The editor wrote that what Alexander Isayevich said frightened him. This intrigued me. I read the interview once, twice. Nothing. I had obviously grown accustomed to the local horrors.

Solzhenitsyn speaks of the great divide in Russian society between the impoverished people and a small group of pillagers, in which he includes both the authorities and the newly rich, not sparing any abuse: plunderers, "dirty hands". According to Alexander Isayevich, the split today is deeper than it had been before the February Revolution and all the "pacts of reconciliation and agreement" between the authorities and the opposition are not going to be of much use when faced with the anger of the masses of paupers. Those who believe that reconciliation between the ruling party and the opposition parties is enough to put an end to the conflict do not understand the danger of the situation. The crisis can be prevented by an agreement between those who have been looted and the looters, and this agreement will only come about when the looters return their loot. Return it? Hardly . . .

Furthermore, Solzhenitsyn speaks of "preserving the people" – the only national concept for the next twenty to thirty years which could unite all the nations of Russia and all social spheres, apart from, of course, the plunderers and the "dirty hands". The principle of "preserving the people" – its health, education, culture and tradition – should be the main criterion when any official decisions are made, and should be a law that takes precedence over the constitution. The idea is not new – 250 years ago Pyotr Ivanovich Shuvalov formulated it, but neither the successive tsars nor later the Bolsheviks put it into force. Alexander Isayevich, himself, recalled it in his pamphlet *How to Organize Russia?*, of which 27,000,000 copies were published seven years ago. Unfortunately, silence ensued . . .

Then Solzhenitsyn speaks of "regions", which is what they call the Russian provinces today. Their main problem is lack of autonomy. As long as the regions do not have their own finances, autonomy will be an illusion. The dependence on *dengi* distributed from above, negates the independence of any initiative coming from below. The Duma publishes successive decrees about territorial independence, but these are of little value. Alexander Isayevich visited twenty-six *gubernya*s [provinces] and he came across people with initiative everywhere but, unfortunately, their energy was spent in the battle against the wall of administration . . .

And, finally, Solzhenitsyn complains about Russian TV, that he is denied airtime . . .

Now, in summarizing, I have understood why I'm not moved by all this. I know the things of which Solzhenitsyn speaks from the inside, on a daily basis. For every generalization that the great author makes, I perceive a concrete equivalent outside my window. And, believe me, the world outside is not only more moving than the writer's ponderings but it is also more complicated. Solzhenitsyn's picture, as that of every prophet, is, at times, biased and impassioned, and sometimes tailored to fit the thesis. Let us take the division into looted people and the small group of plunderers. Why "small"? After all, it's plain to see that this is not a "small" group but a horde of swindlers, schemers, people who take bribes and ordinary thieves, who reign everywhere, from the capital down to the smallest village the length and breadth of Russia. The line dividing the poor from the newly rich has split the whole country; every Kem has its own mafia. The process of *prikhvatizatsya* has embraced the *posyolok*s, kolkhozs and deep seas; everything is being taken apart: from bricks, pipes and boards, to wood from the forest. Tons of fish are being hauled in from the sea illegally, reindeer are being slaughtered, grasses torn from the seabed. Then, some people drink away all they earn, while others invest in businesses, that is, in so-called *kommertsiya* [commerce]. Alexander

Isayevich speaks of giving back, but he doesn't add how . . . Or the idea of "preserving the people". Correct, no doubt, except, hmmm . . . what thoughts can one have about preserving a people when there is nowhere to bury it? Old Nil was kept in the mortuary for a week because there weren't any planks with which to build a coffin. More people die here than are born. Because to survive, you have to eat, not drink. Six years ago, when I arrived here, vodka cost thirteen roubles and a loaf of bread cost twenty kopeks, so that you could buy sixty loaves of bread for a bottle of vodka, and today you pay the same for one bottle as you would for three loaves of bread. It's best not even to mention schools, the health service or culture . . . Or, the provinces. Is the question of autonomy really the most important problem here? I doubt it. It's true, I haven't visited as many as twenty-six *gubernya*s, but it's enough for me to have seen the couple of dozen coastal villages which Vasya and I visit every year as we sail along the White Sea coast. There, there are no railways or roads, no airport, and no writer ever visits. And the people there do not think about autonomy; they only want to escape from there – as far away as possible. I also have the opportunity of observing territorial autonomy; a new Duma has just been elected on the Islands, and I'm often present at its sittings. At the first sitting, a new post for a Duma secretary was confirmed and two other posts for Administration . . . And, finally, TV. Solzhenitsyn complains of being denied airtime. In 1995, for fifteen minutes every fortnight, Alexander Isayevich appeared on ORT, the main channel on Russian television. The programme was scrapped; it's hard to know whether this was because it was too boring, as many thought, or because it was too biting, as the author himself claims. I have his book, *A Minute a Day* – a record of these programmes – and I see that Solzhenitsyn didn't say anything new in the *Russkaya mysl* interview. There's no doubt that the issues he addresses are important, even fundamental, and they need to be repeated again and again, but the public prefer Alla Pugacheva's birthday or the TV quiz "Field of miracles". Nobody likes Cassandras on television . . .

4

Appendix. The motifs of the mirror and of the labyrinth exist in the core of Solovetskian narrative since the beginning of the Islands' history and are indissolubly tied up with the subject of death. Because the oldest traces of man on Solovky, the stone labyrinths of the Saams (2000–1000 BC) are nothing other than the remains of a *tropa*, a path to the other world, which — according to Saam beliefs — is a mirror reflection of this world, like a reverse image in a mirror, where right becomes left. While the Islands, lying west of the mainland, were — in the mythology of the Saams — a midway point to the next world, a halfway stop beyond the grave. That is why they buried their dead here, especially shamans and chiefs, and built labyrinths of stone so that the souls of the dead could not return to the world of the living . . . The Orthodox monks called the Saam constructions "babylons", seeing in them a symbol of man's wanderings in the innermost recesses of sin, and so they raised huge walls of stone in order to reflect upon their own sins. The world which they renounced — so they believed — was the source of man's spiritual death, whereas the death of the body, which, according to them, one should never forget was the beginning of eternal life. In other words, they died in this life so as to come to life after death . . . Then there was SLON — a labyrinth of barbed wire. Soviet reality grimaced in the Solovetsky mirror, and the boundary between this world and the one beyond dissolved . . . Today, at the end of the second millennium of our era, the Islanders are gathering fragments of these mirrors and searching for a way out.

XIII

Living in this enormous country, I feel that I, myself, am, in a sense . . . becoming enormous.

Joseph de Maistre

1

Spring, here, slashes the eyes with its light – like a whip . . . I squint, like a wolf, after the darkness of my lair – after the dark and severe winter. Radiance strikes from all sides: sparks of snowy powder dance in the air, névé glistens on the stiff grass, drops of fire hang from icicles, and, all around, the whole world sparkles as if somebody were scattering diamonds by the handful. But on the other hand: bluish shadows cut a negative of the world in the snow, ice shimmers in the semi-darkness, steam billows from lips, and there is a chill in the shade. The sea is still asleep under a thick lid of ice in which seals have puffed out holes here and there so as to bask in the sun. You have to be careful not to fall into one of these holes that are covered in snow, when you wind your way on skis among the ice hummocks. Further, in the distance, on the brink of the icy lid and open water, the horizon quivers like spilt mercury. There, storms pile the ice floes one on top of the other, creating dreamlike constructions from blocks of ice and light: roofless mansions, walls leading nowhere, pointless towers and wide open gates, dead-end streets, blind alleyways . . . à la Piranesi. In these ice floes, like in lumps of crystal, rays of sun break up into turquoise, blue and pink — if you look with the light. But if you look against the light, tears, wherein sparklers play, run down your cheeks. After many hours of wandering on the sea, I return home as if from "another" world.

2

It is *Maslenitsa,*[*] or carnival, as we call it. This is the last week before the beginning of Lent; you must not eat meat, but you can eat as much butter, cheese and fish as you like. It is one of the oldest feasts in Russia and dates back to the pagans when it was associated with the cult of the Sun and the end of winter-Marzhana.[**] Later on, it was included in its calender by the Orthodox Church. It usually falls in March, when the snow *maslitsya* (becomes butter/shines) in the sun and the forest roads *zamaslilis'* (become greasy/glisten) — as Ivan Shmyelov wrote, using words to associate the carnival with the thaw. In the past, they used to *gulyat'* the entire week: on horses, sledges, or backsides, down any old hill, at table, under the table, until they couldn't take any more. And today, too, they eagerly celebrate the carnival, as long as there is something to drink.

Maslenitsa, above all, means *bliny*. These are like pancakes, yet they are something more because you can "wrap yourself up in a *blin*" and swear *blin* at someone; and wakes begin with *bliny*, and weddings finish with *bliny*. Sometimes *bliny* are made using wheat, sometimes using buckwheat; they're usually made with yeast, but I've also eaten unleavened ones. I'm giving the recipe in case some reader

---

[*] Feast of Butter. *Tr.*
[**] Marzhana — a straw doll, the symbol of winter, carried through the villages during spring celebrations. *Tr.*

finds it useful. Here it is: sift the flour into an earthen pot containing the yeast, milk and egg, add some salt, pepper and a pinch of sugar to taste, mix to the consistency of thick *smetana* [soured cream], and stand in a warm place to allow the dough to rise. Push the dough down twice when it overflows from the pot. After three to four hours, heat some fat in a frying pan, thin the dough with some hot milk, and pour into the frying pan – making it very thin, as thin as possible. *Bliny* should be transparent! Translucent! Place one on top of another, spreading with butter so that they don't stick. Serve with whatever takes your fancy. We eat them savoury: with black and red caviar, with *smetana*, and soft goats' cheese with garlic, with monkfish livers, with cuts of herring, with minced perch and salted *khrushche* [boletus]; but we also eat them sweet: with condensed milk, bilberries in syrup, cranberry jelly, preserves . . . Take a *blin*, wrap a cut of herring therein or spread with caviar and, dipping in *smetana* (or melted butter), place in your mouth. You can wrap two at once, or even better, three, like Chichikov does in Gogol's *Dead Souls*.

Maslenitsa ends on Repentance Sunday. The Orthodox ask forgiveness of each other, fall at each other's feet, bow low. The rest watch them, hesitantly, shiftily, because they don't know what all this means . . . to ask forgiveness of strangers? But others carry on having a great time, forgetting about this God-given world– or is it perhaps the God-given world that has already forgotten about them? In Russia it used to be said that people like that are celebrating "German *maslenitsa*", which means: they're drinking during Lent.

3

"I'm awakened by a sharp light in the room: somewhat unfamiliar, cold and depressing. Oh, of course, today is Lent. The red curtains with hunters and ducks on them have been taken down while I was asleep; that's where the strangeness and depression in the room come from. Today is Pure Monday, and everything in the house is being cleaned . . ." That's how Shmelov's *The Lord's Year*, one of the most wonderful books of the Russian emigration, begins. Father Yosif gave it to me a few years ago – it must have been before my first Lent on Solovky – so that I'd know how they used to fast in Russia. He learnt from it himself and now reads it in his cell during Lent. For Ivan Sergeyevich knew how to capture ancient Russia better than anyone. The philosopher Ilyin was right when he wrote *à propos* Shmelov that it is only possible to be so creative in a cell (*kelya*), in silence and in a mystical state, because only a man alone in his cell sees everything – both far and deep . . .

". . . in the vestibule are bowls with yellow salted cucumbers which have parasols of dill stuck into them, and bowls with pickled cabbage sprinkled thickly with aniseed – delicious. I take a morsel to my mouth – how crunchy! And why break the fast – I wonder – and lose your soul, when you can fast so deliciously. Why, there will be fruit compotes, and potato croquettes with prunes and dried apricots, and poppyseed bread, and pink cracknels, and 'crosses' for *Krestopoklonnaya*[*] [Adoration of the Cross], frozen cranberries, and nuts in honey, and sugared almonds, peas in syrup, and pretzels, rolls with raisins and rowanberry *pasyla* [a kind of sweet pastry], candied fruit peel, and halva. And what about buckwheat *kasha*, fried with onions and washed down with *kvas*! And Lenten *pelmeny* with *khrushche*, and buckwheat *bliny* with garlic on Saturdays, and *kutya* with nuts and raisins! And what about almond milk with white jelly or cranberry jelly with vanilla, or . . . huge pies on *Blagoveshcheniye*[**] [the Annunciation], stuffed with sturgeon! and *kulya*, a superb soup, with blue caviar and pickled cucumbers, and apples in syrup every

---

[*] The third Sunday in Lent. *Tr.*
[**] Lady Day or Annunciation: Being on April 7, this is often, though not always, during Lent. *Tr.*

Sunday, and biscuits fried with hempseed oil, with a crunchy crust and a warm, hollow inside! Will they be there, where we're going after death, such fasts?"

The philosopher Ilyin called Shmelov's work the "cell" in which the writer used to lock himself away in Paris so as to chisel that other Russia into sentences. Half a century later, a monk on Solovky is reading Shmelov in his cell so as to see that other Russia.

4

Foreign travellers were amazed by the rigour of Russian fasts. The Dominican Ioannes Fabri once wrote: "We were shaken by what we heard about their fasts because, comparing our traditions with theirs in matters of Christian religion, ours came out most unfavourably." Paul of Aleppo, the son of the Patriarch of Antioch, who came to Moscow with his father in 1656 in connection with reforms in the rites of the Orthodox Church, complained: "It is unfortunate that we arrived here during a period of fasting because, not wanting to be different from them, we ate a hideous paste of overcooked broad beans with no oil and suffered terrible tortures every day." And Neuville, a Jesuit, noted with a touch of malice that Russians would like to enter paradise starving themselves. From foreigners' accounts, it appears that none of them tried to understand the meaning of the fasts here, or their principles. Let us take Masson, who, having spent eight years of his life among Russians, wrote utter nonsense; as if their Lenten menu would allow . . . fish. We don't know much about the Orthodox fast today either. Even Russians themselves argue over the details of the rules, they haven't fasted for so many years. So maybe it is worth saying a few words on the subject.

In the past, in Rus, people fasted strictly and fervently. Apart from Lent, there were three fasts of many days: *Petrov* on the feast of Sts

Peter and Paul, *Uspensky* on the Dormition of the Virgin Mary and *Filipov* before Christmas; as well as several one-day fasts and Wednesdays and Fridays. Archimandrite Yoann, author of the dissertation *The Discipline of Penance in Ancient Rus*, writes how the fasts gradually grew stricter until ". . . they entered the Russian mentality so deeply that they became the basis of the nation's religious life". The rules of Lent were defined in St Savva's *ustav yerusalimsky*, where he allowed people to eat once a day, in the afternoon, and twice on Saturdays and Sundays. In the first and third weeks of Lent *sukhoy-adeniye* obliged one to eat raw food with no oil – bread, dried fruit, raw vegetables and, instead of wine, a mixture of pepper, cumin and anise or *kvas*. The remaining weeks (apart from Wednesdays and Fridays) the food was cooked; with oil on Saturdays and Sundays. Dairy products were excluded. Fish was allowed only on *Blagoveshcheniye*, if that feast did not fall during Holy Week, when dry food was obligatory; nothing at all was eaten on Good Friday. The rules of Lent also forbade alcohol, smoking tobacco and sexual intercourse. The hardest aspect for the Russians, according to sources, was to manage without vodka. Prince Vladimir used to say: "*Rusy veselye pitye, nye mozhem bez tovo bity.*" ("Russians have joyful drink, we can't live without it.") Apart from temperance in eating, drinking and sex, it was proper to bow. Two hundred and forty times a day, according to the rules: in the morning – sixty times, in the afternoon – a hundred times, and in the evening – eighty times. There were those who bowed even more frequently, three hundred, four hundred times. Paul from Aleppo counted that the faithful in one of Moscow's temples bowed one thousand times during the reading of St Andrey Kritsky's *Canon* on the Wednesday of the fifth week of Lent, and he emphasized that he wasn't counting the bows before or after the *Canon*. Moscow, during this time, was as if dead: *kabak*s were closed and sealed on the Tsar's orders, people rarely left their houses, grand outfits and carriages disappeared from the streets. Tsar Alexey Mikhailovich himself kept a strict fast: he didn't receive anyone or go out anywhere; for the first three days he ate nothing and spent most of his time in the temple: on Wednesday, in the evening, he ate a sweet compote and had some sent to the boyars; on Thursday and Friday he didn't eat anything again; on Saturday he partook of Holy Communion, and, during the remaining weeks of Lent, he ate cabbage, mushrooms and berries, with no oil, and drank only *kvas*; on Mondays, Wednesdays and Fridays, he didn't eat at all . . . The people took the Tsar's example, from magnates down to *smerds* [serfs] and even little children fasted, ". . . because the Orthodox people", Archimandrite Yoann writes, "offer themselves to fasting with fervour".

Of course, it is easier to see that which is on the outside: the measure, observance, frequency . . . That which is intangible is born within – in isolation. In the past, in Egyptian and Syrian monasteries, the monks would go into the desert during Lent, each one separately. St Theodosy, the father of all monks in Rus, took up this habit and would shut himself away in a cave in the rocks for the duration of Lent, only returning to the brothers ". . . on the eve of Lazarus, for it is then – [the chronicler explains] – that the forty-day fast comes to an end". Icons show the Pechersky *starets* holding a scroll with the inscription: "*Postom i molitvoyu popechemsya o spasyenii dush*" ("By fasting and prayer we take care of our soul's salvation"), in remembrance of the fact that Our Lord also overcame Satan in the desert by fasting and praying, setting an example as to how we should chase our own demons away . . . Later, over a period of centuries, a complex ritual of Lenten penance was worked out in Russian monasteries where, alongside temperance and mortification of the flesh, spiritual exercises, silence and meditation played an important role. Paysy Velichkovsky, Theofan Zatvornik, Ignaty Bryanchaninov and other Orthodox *staretses* wrote entire guidebooks to spiritual teachings, showing an extraordinary knowledge of human psychology. Lay people – rulers and merchants, and poets – were also drawn to monasteries during Lent so that, in the silence of the cell and far from daily matters, they could find within themselves "the inner man" as Father German says.

And, finally: fasting in art. No writer of the lives of saints and no painter of holy icons in Rus would begin work without fasting. And Alexander Sergeyevich Pushkin wove into one of his last poems, St Efrem Sirin's prayer, which, during Lent, the Solovetsky monks, bowing low, read in the temple everyday at dawn in semi-darkness:

> *Vladiko dnei moykh! Dukh prazdnosti uniloi,*
> *Lubonachaliya, zmei sokritoi sei,*
> *I prazdnoslovia ne dai dushe moey.*
> *No dai mne zryet' moi, o bozhe, pregreshenia,*
> *Da brat moi ot menya ne primet osuzhdenia,*
> *I dukh smirenia, terpyenia, lubvi*
> *I tselomudriya mne v serdtse ozhivy.*[*]

5

It happened during Lent, a couple of years ago . . . After many days of fasting, in its strictest, monastic form, I noticed tension among the faithful — the *poslushniks*, pilgrims and church women — growing day by day, no doubt induced by hunger and rituals, which lasted many hours in clouds of *ladan*, collective ecstasy and half-mystical hallucinations. Rozanov wrote about this, proving that a few weeks of monastic regime were enough to turn a beefy athlete into a neurasthenic. Towards the end of Lent, they were all on the verge of that "thin sleep" in

---

* "O Master of my days! allow not the spirit / of dreary lassitude to enter my soul, / The stirrings of lust, that secret serpent, and wasted words. / But allow me to witness, O God, my transgressions, / Help me not to judge my brother unwisely, / And in my heart revive the spirit of humility, patience, / Love and the spirit of chastity. (translated by Irina Brown.)

which monks have visions of saints, Our Lady or the devil. In this way, Good Friday arrived . . . Morning Mass. Ecstasy reached its peak, to the point of hysteria! And suddenly hatred erupted . . . fanatical, ominous. Hatred of the Jews who crucified Him. Rage, cries, sobs.

"*Yudeye, bogoubyic sobor, Yudeye, bogoubyic sonmishche,*" they shouted endlessly. "*Dazhd'im, Gospody, po delom ikh, yako ne razumyesha Tvoyevo sniskhozhdyenya . . .*" ("Jews, assembly of deicides, Jews, bunch of deicides! Render to them, Lord, according to their acts, for they do not understand your misericord . . .")

. . . I couldn't take any more and left the temple. Never to return. I don't know what had a greater effect: the collective madness which I witnessed, or solidarity with Veronica. The following day, Holy Saturday, we went to Filip's Hermitage to tan ourselves. The day was as clear as the tinkle of a bell, the sun was warm, the snow melting, roofs were dripping. There was a smell of young fir trees, sap and spring in the air. And it was so quiet that you could hear the blood running through your veins. After those screams, this silence was so sacred. After that smell of fasting, this forest fragrance was true incense. After that oratory, this world was a chapel.

6

Sitting on the doorstep of *my* Solovky, with my back against the Polar Circle, I recall the words of de Maistre: "I am slowly beginning to disdain this earth — it has barely nine thousand leagues circumference. Pooh! it's an orange."

KANIN NOS
(1995)

On 2 August, 1553, three English frigates passed by the North Cape –
the most northerly cape of Europe – and took a course heading east.
They were the Edward Bonaventura, Bona Speranza *and* Bona
Confidentia. *The frigates belonged to a company of London merchants*
interested in discovering a north-eastern sea route to China. The expe-
dition was led by Hugh Willoughby and Captain Richard Chancellor
– the first sailors to leave traces of their passage along the northern
confines of Russia: maps, accounts, letters, travel logs.

Novgorodians used to go there before them, but they left no evidence,
if you don't count stories told by third parties. Nestor, for example, who
in his Chronicles of Years Gone By, *writes, under 1096, that four years*
previously a certain Novgorodian, a Guryata Rogovich, had told him
about his boy's passage to Pyechora. Nestor's record, full of fantastic
details, is more like a mythical fairytale than an account of a partic-
ular voyage, which, passing from word of mouth, lost more and more
of its reality while gaining in sensationalism and tempo of narration.
The far North, according to Novgorodian accounts, is ". . . the end of
the visible world, the vestibule to hell, where only the hard breathing of
the sea, and weeping and grinding of teeth can be heard . . ." – as
Archbishop Vasily wrote to Bishop Theodor in the 12th century.

So it is foreigners, the 16th-century English sailors, who were the first
to go there and write about their passage, in the first person: "I was
there." The Englishmen's logs are not as colourful as hearsay coming
from a third party; their topographical details, descriptions of the shore,
directions of the winds, often make for boring reading, but the authors
would swear by their lives that what they wrote was true. Sometimes
literally so, as in the case of Willoughby, who never returned from the
expedition. They were still together when they skirted the North Cape.

Then a storm struck, wind dispersed the ships, and they lost sight of each other. Only Chancellor, on the Edward Bonaventura managed to make his way into Port Wardhouse. The remaining frigates drifted on the Arctic Ocean for one and a half months until the ice closed them in not far from Kanin Nos, where the White Sea enters the Arctic Ocean.

"21 September", noted Willoughby in his ship log, "we entered a bay which plunges two miles inland. In the bay swam seals and enormous fish, while on land we saw white bears, reindeer, wild swans and other creatures unknown to us. After a week of storms, seeing that it was late in the year and the weather was bad – nothing but frost, snow and hail – we decided to stay for the winter. So we sent a few of our men southwest to see if they could find any people there. They walked for three days and didn't meet anyone. So we sent our men west, but they also returned with nothing. Then we sent our men in a southeasterly direction, but they, too, returned not having found any people or any traces of man whatsoever . . ."

Hugh Willoughby's log book shows that they were still alive in January. The Saams found them a year later, the following winter. The ships were anchored in ice. There were crests of névé on the stays; the people were dead; and there were vast quantities of provisions.

Meanwhile, Chancellor, giving up hope of ever seeing his comrades, went on, alone, towards unknown lands. And he reached so far, as he himself writes, as to find himself in a place where there was no night at all; only the sun hung continuously over a terrible and mighty sea. Thanks to the uninterrupted light, they made their way without stopping and, after a couple of days, with God's help, they arrived at an enormous bay, a hundred miles long, or even longer. There, they dropped anchor. The local fishermen, terrified by the strange appearance and size of the frigate, took to flight. When Chancellor caught up with them, they were petrified and fell to the ground in front of him, to kiss his feet.

This was Rossya, or Muscovy . . .

Further in Captain Chancellor's accounts, we read about his journey by land to Moscow at the invitation of Tsar Ivan the Terrible: about *prices, merchandise, customs. The Captain draws our attention to the suspiciousness of the Russians, especially as regards foreigners; he is amazed at their attitude to ownership, where the Russian has nothing of his own because everything he owns belongs to the tsar; finally, he is horrified by Russian drunkenness, extreme superstition and bribery.*

"I heard one Russian saying that it is better to live in a prison than in freedom, if only they didn't beat you so hard . . ."

Ivan the Terrible received Chancellor in tsar-like fashion. He was preparing for war with the Teutonic Knights at the time and so was seeking favour with England. The Captain describes the banquet in the Kremlin in detail: the table etiquette, the magnificent outfits of the guests, the dishes, especially swan meat, one of Ivan Vasyalich's favourite dishes.

"They were served in pieces, with berries, each swan on a separate platter . . ."

But when Chancellor returned to England, people did not believe him. Educated as well as simple people doubted the veracity of what he said, referring to what knowledge they had of the North at that time as well as to rumours. Chancellor replied to both in the foreword to his account: "You know these countries from the words of other people, I — from my own experiences; you know them from the books of other people, I — from my own observations; you repeat the general opinion, but I was there."

I

Members of the expedition, who know how to use a pen, are to take notes daily so as to record every day of the voyage; they are to note comments about new lands and the people inhabiting them, about the high and low tides of the sea, about the direction of the winds, about the height of the sun, about the movement of the moon and stars.

> From the Instructions for the expedition of
> Hugh Willoughby and Richard Chancellor, 1553

Solovky

We leave on Saturday, in the evening, after the *banya*. The sun is high, although lateral, like a spotlight above a stage. Its light sparkles on the sea, sometimes a line of brightness, sometimes a billion sparks. During white nights, the White Sea has white eyes. As if on the verge of madness.

We are going to the furthest North: beyond the Arctic Circle. We are "going", because you "go" across the sea, only sh— floats in a barrel according to Vasa. Our goal is Kanin Nos.

Kanin Nos lies at the far end of the White Sea, in the north. Beyond lies the Arctic Ocean. The border is marked by a straight line, which can be drawn on the map, linking two capes: Kanin Nos and Svyatoy Nos. In actual fact, there is no border as there is no way of drawing or writing on the sea. You can only go on the sea and leave a momentary wake in the water – with the keel. In reality, the White Sea does not end but begins in the Arctic Ocean.

Every twelve hours, the Ocean exhales and pours masses of water into the White Sea. First, as if through a funnel (hence Voronka), where the water collects and seethes up to eleven metres; then, it runs down to Gorlo (the throat) – it is narrow there, so it runs down quickly, up to five knots an hour; finally, in the south, it pours out into the Basin in the middle of which lie the Solovetsky Islands, from whence we start. Towards the Arctic Ocean . . .

Zhizhgin

A small island. Sixty versts further north-east. A storm. We hide in a small bay, full of *tyuly*. *Tyuly* is an endearment for: *tyulen'*, a kind of seal. One of them, out of curiosity, has almost emerged from the water, supporting itself with its fins on the step of the *Antur*. In the days of SLON, this was a *zona* and place of deportation. The *zeka*s gathered seaweed. Now it is empty. The last man with the last horse left here a year ago. Only soldiers and the *mayak* (lighthouse) remain. I am making the most of the time that we are waiting for the storm to abate, by introducing *Antur*'s crew:

So, Vasya – Vasily Dimitrov – thirty-six years of age. He constructs yachts with his own hands, from keel to sails. *Antur* is his third boat. His father taught him. They had lived on the shores of Lake Ladoga for generations. Water is in their blood. And the forest. Fishing, hunting. He got his first double-barrel shotgun on his eleventh birthday. He hunts bears on his own. He has eight (yes, yes) to his name. He doesn't count moose because he kills them for winter, like pigs. Marinka makes *tushonka* [conserves] from them. Finger-licking good *tushonka*. I know what I'm writing about, I've licked my fingers.

Marinka brought Vasya down to the White Sea. She ensnared him. They live in Sumsky Posad, not far from the Belomorkanal [White Sea Canal], in a former camp barrack. Vasya works on the railways: they are laying down rail tracks in the forest, repairing them. Vasya's hands are hard, like the rails of the iron road. You can count on them. In addition, Vasya doesn't drink much. And then only rarely. Which is an exception in the North.

Then there is Losha – our deckhand – twenty-three years of age. A young *alkash*, which means alcoholic in slang. Still a boy, he has already fallen off the "wagon" twice; he stopped his detox treatment of his own accord. We have taken him because we feel sorry for the kid. Perhaps the sea will cure him, and anyway, he'll be useful: pulling up the anchor, folding the sails and lowering the keel.

And me – Mariusz, Mar to my friends – aged forty. A foreigner, with no permit. Neither correspondent, nor writer, sometimes learned, sometimes a fool (depending on who asks and why), usually mute, especially when I first meet someone, so as not to draw attention to myself with my foreign accent.

There, the storm has ceased. We can go on . . .

The Strelna

The Kola Peninsula. Tersky Coast. It took us ten hours to cross the Basin, from the south-west to the north-east. We went on mid-summer's night, the shortest night of summer. The sun set slowly, very slowly, and disappeared for a moment, as if it had run behind the horizon to answer nature's call: I didn't even manage to finish my roll-up . . . before it rose. In the same place as it had disappeared – in the north. (Beyond the Arctic Circle, for many days the sun does not disappear from the horizon, it only changes colour from raspberry pink to gold in front of the eyes of a surprised public.) Here, at the edge of the visible world, the sun is the light of life. Even the *olen* follow it as they graze. *Olen* are reindeer with whom the Samoyeds lead a nomadic life: southwards in winter, northwards in summer. Always in the direction of the sun. In Samoyed tales, the first *olen* came down to earth on the sun's rays. *Olen* are children of the sun. And they miss it, as do people in the North. Especially in winter.

We saw Tersky Coast at four in the morning. Against the sun, barely an outline, with the sea dazzling our eyes. We were going alongside the shore, looking for a way into the river. There's one: the water is shimmering, glistening, trembling. The eyes hurt in the brightness. We try to enter. It is shallow. Time after time, we drag along the bottom. Luckily, there is loam and sand. Suddenly, there is a *bar* — an underwater bank of sand at the mouth of the river. We run aground. Losha gets to work with the keel, we with the *koly v zuby*, that is, we try to push ourselves off with the help of long poles. The poles stick in the loam, the current lays us on our side. It's a good thing that Losha managed to lift the keel. We're in the Strelna.

There are a few houses by the river, the remains of an Orthodox church. On the dunes — crosses; a cemetery in the sand. A high, steep shore, barely daubed with greenery although it is already the end of June. Every living soul has turned up on the beach. From a distance, we only see women; how strange! Then it turns out that these are *muzhik*s with scarves on their heads. To protect themselves against mosquitoes. They already wore them like this 100 years ago, according to Sergey Maksimov. They called them *kukol*s, which, in the Orthodox language, means the headgear of a monk in grand *skhima* [monk's habit]. So they appear, and gesticulate, shout something. Several throw themselves into a boat. They approach, ask — one outshouting the other — if we have any *goryucheye*: and if so, do we have a lot.

"*Tolko shilo, muzhiky.*" ["Only *shilo*, lads."]

"*Davaite. Za syomgu.*" ["Give us some. We'll give you some *syomga* for it."]

Syomga! Dear little *syomga*! The tsar's fish, from the salmon family.

Its flesh, the colour of overripe mandarins, with pale flakes of fat, melts on the tongue. It tastes best on white bread and butter. Exquisite ... Delicious ... especially in fresh brine (like *malosol* — lightly salted cucumbers), with a *stopka* of *shilo* early in the morning, after a long journey across the White Sea, on midsummer's night. And that is how we make our way in the North, measuring the rhythm of the sentence with *stopka* of *shilo*, *stopka* by *stopka*, step by step, somewhat unsteady now, as long as we get to the end of the paragraph: *shilo, syomga, syomga, shilo, blakha mukha, syomga, shilo . . . blin*, the *shalonnik* has risen.

You have to be careful sometimes not to get tangled up in your story ... For each writer's world, sooner or later, falls into two: the story and the reader. The tropa, *the path of the pen, should run along the boundary between these worlds, not tending too far either one way or the other. Because it is enough for you to slip a little too deeply into the world of the story, to stop paying attention to your language, to babble away, to mumble in* fenya[*] *and even the most determined of readers who follows carefully, word for word, and walks on your heels, from comma to comma, well, even such a reader will stop understanding the world in which he has found himself, following your* tropa . . .

That is why you have to go back sometimes, apologize if you have crossed the limit. Explain that Russian goryucheye *is fuel, petrol, and that here, in the North, the word has broadened its semantic field and embraced all liquids with an alcoholic content. That* shilo *is what they call denatured industrial spirits, used in the railways to clean rail tracks in the winter, and that you have to be careful not to drink from a dirty barrel which has been used for petrol or diesel crude oil because it leaves a smell in your mouth. Finally, that* syomga *is the only product on which the people of Tersky Coast survive and that the exchange of* shilo *for* syomga *depends on the degree of* pokhmeli, *that is, hangover,*

---

[*] See Glossary: *blatnaya muzika*. Tr.

of the locals: the more booze goes in, the cheaper the fish. For example: in the morning in Strelna, one five-kilo syomga *cost us two bottles of* shilo *but in the evening they brought us three for one bottle, just as long as they could get blind drunk. I should add that* shalonnik *is a south-westerly wind.*

The winds in the North all have a name — *shalonnik, moryana, obyednik, polunoshnik* — and a personality. The *moryana*, for example, a northerly wind, is the heavy breath of the ocean which lashes you in the face as if it were spitting ice. The winds here change frequently and suddenly. It is not so bad if they blow from the direction of the sun; worse when they turn against it. Then a storm is sure to follow, as happened two paragraphs ago, when the *moryana* turned into the *shalonnik* faster than *shilo* goes to your head. The sea water seethed and roared. We barely managed to throw down the second anchor. Soon we were rolling and tossing . . .

We are at a standstill on the Strelna, waiting until the storm abates. Out of boredom, we wander around the shore. First the cemetery on the dunes with the graves dug in the sand. Birds hatch their eggs on the tombstones and, at the sight of us, they raised a cry. A terrible racket. Apparently, insects don't breed in the sand and bodies dry up without rotting. The Coastal people like to lie in death as they do in life: facing the sea. And it is easier to dig, says Vasya; sand doesn't freeze as deep as earth.

Next to the cemetery lie the remains of an Orthodox church: traces of axe marks, of fire. Broken Holy Gates, bird droppings, a stench, the floor full of holes, the remnants of frescoes on the walls, mostly worn away, the eyes as if alive . . .

Higher up, in the thicket of a stunted birch, stands an abandoned camp for rich "Hemingways": uncles from America, who pay dollars to fish for *syomga* with reels. A few camp sites in the Norwegian style, looted down to the bare veneer. Only the signpost remains in the middle of the small square; would this be the parade ground?

There are arrows on it indicating distances: 4,100 versts to Paris, I noticed. The drunken caretaker explained that the company went bankrupt because its shareholders stole from each other and escaped abroad. Tersky Coast is the Klondike for all sorts of traffickers: from the Murmansk mafia down to the local *reket*. They catch *syomga* by the ton here. Up to a hundred tons in one season from one fishery alone. The traffickers have already managed to lay their hands on whichever rivers are richest in fish. The Vazhuga, for example, is protected by OMON [riot police], who have been hired by a Murmansk company exporting the tsar's fish to the Netherlands. Whereas the Strelna does not count as a rich river, which is why the *reket* has not found its way here. Since the end of Soviet rule (that is what they call the militia here!), everyone fishes as they like, uncontrolled: what you draw out is yours. You can drink it away. The kolkhoz went bankrupt, the settlement died out, and the *muzhik*s only come in the summer, as if to a *dacha*: to fish, drink and forget about the whole world . . .

For three days, we *kukuyem* (stand waiting) on the Strelna. Making one's way on the White Sea means waiting for the weather for three quarters of the time and reminds you of mountain expeditions: there, you climb from camp to camp, here, you slip from river to river. Because you can only shelter and bide your time on a river until the bad weather passes. The White Sea is called the "bandit" sea; it is the most overcast place in the entire Soviet Union. There can be four or five storms a day here. Low tides can leave many versts of dry land. Underwater rocks: reefs, shoals, skerries, boulders. Frequent fog, often accompanied by winds. Overall, this does not make sailing any easier. Last year, we barely made it to Konushin and that took us two and a half weeks, yet in fine weather you can cover the distance in three days. On that occasion we went through Gorlo along the Zimny Bereg [Winter Coast]; this year, we're trying – Tersky Coast . . .

The Chapoma

The beginning of Gorlo, twelve versts further north-east. That is as far as our first hop took us before another storm hit us with all its might, as if it wanted to throw us out of the sea in a single blast. We just about managed to reach the Chapoma. It is a difficult river: reefs emerge from the water thickly, like seals' heads, and the sandbar is so high that even the high tides do not cover it.

There is an old fishing settlement on the river, no sign of an Orthodox church, and again a cemetery in the sand. You're immediately struck by the way the village is divided in two. The houses nearer to the sea are wooden and well tended, logs are arranged in high cords and offer protection against the wind; there are gardens next to the houses, *kartoshka*s, greenhouses; the yards are clean, sown with grass, which binds the sand. Further along, on the clay escarpment, are a couple of cement barracks housing five or six families; next to them is an outhouse; the *pomoika* stinks. Marfa, an old woman, curious to see the new arrivals, explained this to me. She came out on to the doorstep of one of the tidy houses and started to chat of her own accord.

"Because you see, young man, the old folk live by the sea, and, there, on the escarpment, are the young ones, for whom the kolkhoz built those *obshchezhitia*. So they live together yet apart. Live and drink non-stop. In the past, *muzhik*s used to drink too, though rarely, just as a celebration. When they'd stacked up the firewood for winter, for instance, *muzhik*s would gather together, women would make *bliny*, with *syomushka-matushka* as a snack, the girls would dance for them and sing, and the *muzhik*s drank, sometimes for three or four days. They only drank *brashka* [home-brewed beer] made from *moroshka* [cloudberries]. But now they devour "Ruska" and wet their pants, losing, in their *delirium tremens*, any shame they may have had. Besides, what traditions are there to talk about, feast days, customs? They can't even make it to the table now; they drink on the road, and fall by the wayside. It's all the fault of the war, when they took the young ones to the front. They took thirty-six of ours. And not one of them returned. Six families were wiped out, six clans which constituted Chapoma. There are only old men and women left. Then outsiders arrived and seduced the Chapoma girls; some stayed on, but it's not the same. Because a *muzhik* who isn't one of ours does not live like one of ours, and that's all there is to it. As long as there was Soviet rule, they were kept in their place. But now they steal whatever they can exchange for vodka, and live from *stopka* to *stopka*. And this year, just so as to make us even happier, they brought *bezprizornye* [homeless] children. They made a summer camp for them in Chapoma. The guards drink with the *muzhik*s, and the children, half-witted from the petrol which they sniff like drugs, loiter in the village and smash the door-locks. Tell me, young man, what's going to happen to us?"

The faded eyes of the old woman were empty. Towards evening, two *bezprizornye* girls came on board *Antur*. Twelve, thirteen years of age. Pretty faces, slim bodies, swarthy. They behaved in a vulgar way, like whores. They wanted some *shilo*. The following day we left Chapoma.

Konushin

Twenty-eight hours further north-east. We've passed the Arctic Circle. Three hundred and thirty versts in the sea. There were two storms on the way, a couple of wind changes, a good deal of salt in our mouths, and the dawn is clear, as clear as only solitude can be. But one thing at a time.

From Chapoma we went along the Tersky Coast. Into the depth of Gorlo. As we moved further north, vegetation disappeared and there was more and more snow. It lay in rifts, in ravines, and sometimes reached the beach in dirty tongues. The coast, too, was changing: instead of loam and sand, there was solid rock. There was no question of approaching any closer, especially as the wind was getting stronger and the surf was rising. The sea was beating the on-shore rocks, beating up a froth, its spume flying in the air. The rivers which we passed did not give us any chance of entry: they were either too shallow, or strewn with nets. Sosnovyets Island, our last hope on the Tersky Coast, proved inaccessible on our approach: stone upon stone, blown by the wind from all sides. In this situation, we took a course towards Zimniy Coast, across Gorlo. Straight into the mouth of the storm. There, on the other side, we know every little river, and the shore is also more accessible, soft. Unfortunately, in the middle of Gorlo, the wind veered by 180° and, before we managed to make it to Zimniy Coast, it had raised the surf so high that here, too, we were helpless. There was nothing left to do other than go on. For when it storms and there is nowhere to hide, you have to ride out the storm as you go.

So we leave Gorlo and cut across Mezen Lagoon. There are 120 versts of open sea in front of us. The most "rotten" part of the White Sea. The swell here heaves with terrible force. Luckily, it suddenly calms down, as if by magic. The sky is a bright, deep blue. In the distance, mirages. At last, we can sleep a bit; after all we have been going for twenty hours already. It's my watch, the lads are taking a nap. I turn off the motor. Silence. The sails flap. There is a light breeze. To the left, in a mist as light as a monk's sleep, is Morzhovets Island. So the Arctic Circle is already behind us. I switch on Jan Garbarek's *Visible World*. I exist. Alone.

In the afternoon, we saw the coast of Konushin. Samoyed land. A closed *zona*, a special missile range. Used elements of missiles from Plisyetsk fall there; from the Far East they fire ballistic missiles there. They practise accuracy of aim. The whole tundra is bristling with fragments of missiles, some huge, visible from a distance. Like in science fiction. Last year, they arrested us in Konushin. They landed from a helicopter: ten *boit*sy [fighters], including a woman, armed to the teeth . . .

II

Everyone, whoever he may be, is forbidden to talk about our religion and persuasion, and questions on these subjects should be answered with silence and pretence that we have the same laws and customs as govern the country in which we find ourselves at a given moment.

From the Instructions for the expedition of Hugh Willoughby and Richard Chancellor, 1553

Konushin

From a distance, Konushin shore looks like a cake. It is as if it were covered with icing: patches of snow, icicles. The sun plays with the light there, sparkles. The sea beats it, spraying it. Black blocks lie on the beach which, from a distance, look like chunks of cake. From close-by, we see it is peat: huge chunks that the sea has bitten out of the coast. Close to, the ice and snow don't sparkle. They are dirty, mixed with clay that is washed down here with every wave. It is only from close-in that the force of the sea is visible. The destructive force. The sea is devouring the coast of Konushin, bit by bit. Like a cake.

Sharapov's house stands on the edge of the landslip. One more year, maybe two, and it will collapse into the surge. I wonder if Sharapov will manage to sober up by then. Not far from the house, a narrow headland of stone and sand juts out, folded like an arm in an insulting gesture. This is Konushinskaya Korga, behind which one can take shelter. Once, not so long ago, since it is noted in *Logbook for the White Sea* of 1964, the house of a small fishermen's artel stood at the end of Korga. Today, the sea seethes there and you have to bypass it at a distance because there once was a case where a boat with eight fishermen was dragged down and only one of them was spewed out. His spine was crushed. Sharapov laughs when I tell him about this because Sharapov has a black sense of humour and says that life is:

"*Suka, blya.*"*

Sharapov's kitchen smells of *bliny* and moonshine. The same as a year ago. We sit at the table, sweating, after a *banya*. We're drinking moonshine spiced with *margantsovka* (potassium permanganate precipitates residue in moonshine!), and we follow up with *bliny* with *pinagor* caviar. The caviar is pink and coarse, and it crunches in our teeth. The moonshine is robust, goes down smoothly, and warms us. Sharapov sets the pace, pours, raises his glass: to our meeting, to the winter gone by, to yesterday's storm. Tanka bustles about, brings us food, serves: cold reindeer meat, elk tongue with wild horseradish, smoked *gorbusha* [hump-backed salmon], salted *golets* [loach]. The wind outside bends the sallows, rustles the grass. The sea seethes again, breaks the waves, bites at the shore. The rain lashes obliquely against the window panes. Korga is shrouded in mist, the kitchen swims, the dog, Lord, is asleep by the door. And it seems as if the past year has not existed. As if that year has fallen under the table.

Sharapov is forty-eight, his wife isn't pretty, and he likes to drink. He is a former commando officer who took part in several Soviet adventures in Africa. Later, as *pompolit* [political superintendent] on trawlers, he went around the whole world in a state of drunkenness. Until they no longer wanted him at sea because of his drinking and sent him to Konushinskaya Korga, as far away from people as possible. This is their sixteenth year here. He and Tanka – the two of them.

---

* "A bitch, a whore." *Tr.*

They man the military meteorological station on the missile range. It is sixty-odd versts, through tundra, to the nearest garrison. All around is emptiness as far as the eye can see. Only polar foxes bark and the sea wails.

Sharapov's life revolves around their barrel, as once did that of Diogenes. The barrel stands in the kitchen, on the stove, and bubbles. It's made of special steel: missile steel, rust proof. A gift from the garrison.

"You pour sugar into the barrel, overripe *moroshka*, cover it with water, and allow to stand for forty days. Then you distil. You get seven litres of pure *spirt* [alcohol], that is, thirty bottles of vodka. You can count for yourself how many days that leaves you to be sober."

Sharapov's eyes are ashen from moonshine, and he talks non-stop as if he were pouring water out of a bucket, hungry for people. This is *govorukha*, according to Maksimov, a disease from which the inhabitants of the Far North who are beset by solitude suffer. Even more terrible is *nemukha*, when man loses his speech and roars. Like a forest beast. After a few *stopka*s, it is difficult to make any sense of Sharapov's garble. He confuses reality with videos and politics with phobias. He loathes people from Moscow, Jews and Shamil Basayev (in that order); professes to patriotism à la Zhirinovsky, is in favour of Volfovich[*] himself, and barbed wire. One moment suspicious, the next expansive, he smells a spy in me, then senses a friend. A moment ago he was brandishing a gun, shouting that I have to show him my permit, then he suddenly turned this into a joke, embarrassed by his own mania. And a moment later, very confusedly, he was telling me stories unfit for printing, repeating like a chorus:

"*Tolko ty tovo ne pishi, Mar, ne pishi, chto Sharapov tebe eto skazal.*" ["Only don't write this, Mar, don't write that it's Sharapov who told you."].

Sometimes it is worth retaining your position as a foreigner in the world

---

[*]A right-wing Russian politician. *Tr.*

about which you write. Thanks to it you can keep a distance, sobriety of judgement, light penmanship. It releases you from loyalties, allows you to move fluently from first person to second or even third, gives you freedom in using names, real or invented. You can introduce several fates into one life or break one life up into a couple of narratives. Of course, misunderstandings, sometimes resentment and grievances might follow . . .

The position of a foreigner in the world about which you write ensures solitude.

Especially if it is happening in Russia, where spymania has not eased off since Chancellor's day, and here, on the confines of the Empire, it has acquired a particularly sharp form. Here, the solitude of the foreign writer is two-fold: it is at once a viewpoint on reality, and full isolation from it. And it is somewhat reminiscent of the predicament of the alien played by David Bowie in the film The Man who Fell to Earth.

Last year, all the border units along the coasts of the White Sea and the Barents Sea were mobilized so as to arrest us. To tell the truth, we walked into them ourselves, like an animal into a hunter's sights. For four days and nights, the storm kept us in Kedy, at the end of Gorlo. We were waiting for favourable weather to cross Mezen Lagoon. Bored, we took ourselves to the mayak, *on Voronov Point. How could we know that operation "Spider web" was under way? Border guards were drinking* shilo *in the* mayak. We saw the vezdekhod *(an armoured vehicle on caterpillars, which, from a distance, looks like a tank without a barrel) a little too late — there was no way we could back away. They noted our details with difficulty; they could barely hold themselves upright. They didn't ask to see our permits; evidently it didn't occur to them that we might not have any. They proposed a drink. We excused ourselves. They gave us some dried reindeer meat and a couple of fresh* nelma *for the road.* Nelma, *otherwise known as North Siberian* belorybitsa, *is a white fish, which is so good that it can be eaten raw. Before the border guards sobered up, we were out at sea. Paying no attention to the storm. We groped our way across Mezen Lagoon. The sea ran wild, merging with the sky. Flashes tore the darkness, sparks flew on the stay. Helicopters didn't stand a chance. They began their chase a day later. For four days, they combed the sea, the coast and air space. The commanding staff of the region took part in the operation. They arrested us in the kitchen, at the Sharapovs'. The* braga *had just matured. We heard the drone of choppers through the hum of the moonshine still. They landed in the sallows, opposite the window . . .*

The following day, I told Tanka what had happened next: about our journey to Arkhangel under the surveillance of two helicopters and one torpedo boat, about our noisy reception in the port, about the many hours that our yacht was searched. About the warnings!

And it is still pouring outside. The tundra is soaked; the ground beneath our feet squelches. There is no question of going out to sea. Sharapov has managed to fall asleep, having first got stone drunk on the dregs of the *margantsovka*. The lads have buried their noses in the video, chasing hard porn. Tanka is bustling about in the kitchen, cooking our dinner, giving me tea. With the tea she has served honey, pale white, like a lump of ice, and with an aftertaste of vanilla. It's Altay honey, spring honey smelling of mountain meadows. Perhaps it is the smell that drew Tanka out of her silence. Suddenly, she began to talk about her life. Dispassionately, quietly, as if she were knitting. I tried to remember the pattern. In rough, in my exercise-book.

Tanka is a Polish woman from Altay. Her maiden name is Baworowska. One of her ancestors had once been deported to Altay country, but who and what for — she doesn't know. She was fifteen, a mere kid who had just finished school when Sharapov came to Katanda. To get married. To her sister. While about it, he also caught Tanka. He found her a course for telegraphists at staff headquarters in Leningrad. Perhaps he was already planning for her to take Irina's place at the station. Irka couldn't put up with life in Korga: the solitude in the tundra, Styopa's drunken rages. She left him. Tanka stayed.

She is his wife and his slave. She looks after the station on her own when Sharapov gets drunk. At times, she also serves as his punchbag. He'll sometimes take aim at her and she doesn't know whether the gun is loaded or not. Tanka often sleeps in the *banya* because she's afraid of sleeping at home. And when Styopa sobers up, because he's run out of moonshine, he cries, apologizes to her, confesses contritely. Then Tanka loves him, because where is she going to go: both she and he? Tanyukha's only entertainment consists of fox traps. She tans the skins to make pelisses. She has already collected enough for a dozen pelisses but she has no way of sewing them. And what for anyway? To strut around the tundra in a pelisse?

A roar suddenly broke into the dark rustling of Tanka's voice. It came from the beach. We threw ourselves at the windows. Below, along the dried-out sand, a *vezdyekhod* was creeping along. In our direction.

Stone Lake

They were soldiers from the garrison, Sharapov's buddies: *komandir* Vitya, son of the vice-admiral of the Northern Fleet, Sergeant Petya from Kazakhstan, the driver of the GT-T (*gusenichny tyazholy tyagach* [heavy caterpillar tractor]) and Private Fedya, half-Samoyed, half-Russian. They had come to hunt swans. And do some drinking on the way. Not having anything to do with the border guards, they didn't even ask how we got here. They took us for their own: poachers. After two *stakhan*s, it was decided that we should go with them. They took a liking to our rifles, especially Vasya's because it fires at long range.

We had to hurry so as to ford the mouth of the River Volosova because the Konushin coast, steep and slushy, does not allow entry everywhere, even with a *vezdekhod*. Clay, with slabs of peat the size of several-storey houses on it, is covered with a "roof" of turf. The earth here slides into the sea by the ton; in places, it hangs undercut by the waves and threatens to collapse at any moment. At high tide, the water comes right up to the landslip, where at low tide it forms a small beach along which we tore with the din of the engine drowning the murmur of the sea.

Following the bed of the Volosov, we made our way into the tundra. Then on we went, a hundred versts through land out of this world. Drenched meadows of blossoming *moroshka*, fields of wild sorrel and sharp grasses, tangled *ivnyak* [osier], clumps of stunted birches, *sopka*s covered in lichen, valleys of dun-coloured mud, lakes like dead mirrors grown black with age, and, everywhere as far as the eye could see, fragments of missiles. The whole tundra strewn with pieces of missile fuselage, some of them large and in glaring colours: metallic orange, virulent yellow, phosphorescent navy blue. On the palette of the calm colours found in the nature of the North, these shades tore at the eyes, confused the brain.

We were looking for elk. And on the way, we were shooting at grouse, geese and ducks. Safari *à la russe*: with the roar of a 200-horse-power engine, in clouds of exhaust fumes. From *sopka* to *sopka*, cutting valleys, ploughing through brooks. Brushwood on the tundra is as delicate as man's epidermis; even the light touch of a foot leaves a mark which immediately seeps with brownish water like a bruise with blood. The caterpillar of our GT-T tore apart the fleece of the tundra, scarring it for forty years. Because that is how long it takes for the gashes left by the *tyagach* to grow over. For the tundra to forget that we were here.

We arrived at Stone Lake towards evening. Since time immemorial, every year towards the end of May, swans have come here to hatch. In June, the birds moult, losing their ability to fly for a couple of weeks. At this point, the Samoyeds would kill them. Just anyhow: letting their dogs strangle them, catching them in nets. Novgorodians took up the Samoyed customs in dealing with swans. Stone Lake lies at the edge of the Kanin-Timan tundra, not far from the old *volok*:[*] on which sailors from Novgorod dragged their boats on the way to the Pyechora. The *volok* joined the Barents Sea with the White Sea at its narrowest point: between Konushin and Chosha Bay. Stalin had planned a canal here, the (Belomorsk–Choesh) White Sea–Chosha Canal,[**] but died and didn't manage to build it. So they made a target range. Today, swans are under protection, which doesn't mean that they are bullet-proof. *Krasnaya kniga* ("The Red Book" of protected species) does not apply to the target range. He who is armed rules the target range.

"Swan song is, in fact, the oppressive silence of swans," I repeat Merrille's words, watching a solitary swan gliding its way across the flat water of Stone Lake. And silence is, after all, solitude.

"Solitude is death," the echo of a shot replied. *Komandir* Vitya had killed the swan.

Then he slit it, salted it, sprinkled some pepper on it and prepared it for roasting. They had modified the grill themselves making it suitable for game; one armful of wood is enough to roast a swan. When

---

[*] A route between two navigable waters. *Tr.*

[**] Sharapov told me about the White Sea–Chosha Canal. His friend's father from Chizha, Dionis Alexeevich Sakharov, took part in an investigative expedition in the 1940s. The aim of this expedition had been to prepare an appraisal for future construction. To tell the truth, I didn't quite believe Sharapov's story, knowing his tendency for invention. The description of the rivers Chizha and Chosha in B.M. Zhitkov's book *Po Kaninskoy Tundrye* (vol.XLI *Zapisok Imperatorskovo Ruskovo Geograficheskovo Obshchestva*, St Petersburg, 1903) – marshy ground, toxic fumes, biting midges and gadflies – seemed to negate any possibility not only of building a canal, but of any kind of work whatsoever there. However, on my return from Kanin, I came across B.G. Ostrovsky's pamphlet *Beloe more* (Arkhangel, 1937), in which I found information (p.86) about the fact that the concept of joining Mezen Lagoon with Chosha Bay by way of a canal had been brought up frequently, even in the days of Captain Kruzenstern (1770–1846), but had never been accepted. Despite this, the author of the 1937 pamphlet had never lost hope: "One should hope that once the lands of Kanin have been brought into cultivation and these territories exploited, the question of constructing the White Sea–Chosha Canal will again be raised."

the meat is almost done, Vitya sprinkles it with *spirt* and adds a handful of mirabelles. They sell *spirt* in litre jars in the garrison canteen. Like fruit in light syrup, with a few plums at the bottom. The label says that the product is for baking purposes, and it costs less than a bottle of vodka. It starts to grow hot in the *izba* [hut]. There is a smell of roast meat. The windows of the hunter's cabin give out on to Stone Lake. The sun is setting red behind the *sopka*, as if it were oozing blood. The *spirt* in the angular *stakan* reflects the colours. Fat drips from the swan's breast, a delicacy of Tsar Ivan IV, Ivan the Terrible. Outlines in the *izba* soften, darkness blurs the faces, shadows dance on the walls: neither boyars, nor warriors, nor *oprichnik*s [Tsar Ivan IV's bodyguards]. Phantoms appear through the fine fabric of the real world . . .

The Shoina

One hundred and twenty versts to the north-east (*v polunoshnuyu storonu* in Coastal dialect). The clouds hung grey, like the bags under Sharapov's eyes when we were saying our goodbyes. Then, it poured. We went along the Kanin Coast, carried by the current of the low tide. It was completely still. The rain was falling silently, continuously. To starboard, the world, like a silent film in slow motion, was slipping past us. Frame after frame, constantly the same − bare, uninhabited land. The only variation were rivers: the Volosova, the Bogaty brook, the Kya. We entered the Shoina surrounded by fog. Luckily, the tide started to come in. The rain stopped, but the wind blew up. We lost sight of the shore. We went with the current, as if following a piece of string. Like blind people, we touched the bottom with our poles, avoiding the sandbanks. It took a couple of hours; time dissolved in the fog. We cast anchor, hoping that with a bit of luck we would not capsize in shallow water. At last − tea and our berths. My sleeping bag was soaked.

The water slapped against the side of the *Antur*, not allowing me to sleep. So I opened *A Year in the North*, about Kanin Coast. Compared to Winter or Mezen Coasts, writes Maksimov, where you can find at least a few human settlements and some bushes, Kanin Coast is completely deserted; covered only in schist no higher than an arshin. In winter, even the Samoyeds would chase the reindeer away from here, in fear of death idols; for, according to their legends, empty expanse tempts the demons of non-existence. In summer, camped on the Stone, they would sometimes hunt sea animals: seals, *tevyak* [a species of seal], and water hare. But only a half-wit from a Samoyed tribe, says Sergey Vasilievich, could be so patient as to lie and wait – in phlegmatic concentration – for whole days and nights, anchored in a boat not far from the shore, for a black head to emerge from the depths in order to shoot it . . .

Suddenly, I was ejected from my dream, and from my berth, by a strong lurch. The air in the cabin grew thick with *mat*. It was Vasya swearing. I jumped on deck. The wind threw sand into my eyes; the keel of the *Antur* was stuck in a sandbar. Because when we were asleep, the water had fallen and the riverbed had turned out to be 100 metres further on. In a word, we had dried out. And all around the yacht, as if in extension of a dream, Inuits – Samoyed adolescents – with brightly painted lips were wading. It looked as if they had been waiting for us to wake up. On the shore, the *posyolok* is buried in sand, only the roofs jut out from hollows, and the wind sweeps the dust. How is it that there's a *posyolok* here? Where do these adolescents with red lips come from? Where does all this sand come from?

This is what had happened. On 15 June, 1929, at a sitting of the WCIK (Central Executive Committee of the Soviet Union), the National Region of Nenets was created, which embraced the Samoyed nomadic lands along the Arctic Ocean: from Kanin Nos to the River Kara. A year earlier, the Northern Committee had decided that the name of "Samoyed" [cannibal] be changed to "Nenets", since they believed the old name to be offensive. In the 1930s, they tried to settle the nomads. Shoina *posyolok* is an example of such an attempt. Unfortunately, the place they chose proved a disaster: it lay on shifting sands. Initially, things did not go badly, the *zvyeroboyny* industry (mass slaughter of marine animals) was developed, as was also fishing for *navaga* [gadid]. Daredevils were attracted by the "long rouble" and the state made sure they earned it. The state also ensured transport, provisions and communications with the world on that side of the Arctic Circle. Then, with *perestroika*, priorities changed and the demand for marine animals fell. Shoina became deserted. Only those "homesick for the North" stayed behind, and those who had nowhere to go back to: Nentsy, those who had grown unaccustomed to *chums* [a sort of wigwam made from reindeer skins], adventurers whose wives had given up waiting for them, failures, and luckless, abandoned women, often with child. Not long ago, they did away with the last border post in Shoina, the last hope of the local girls and the *posyolok*'s sole link with the state. Shoina today, cut off from the world and half buried in sand, looks more like a Samoyed's dream than a real village. The dream of some simpleton from a Samoyed tribe, who, lying around in a boat for whole days and nights, waiting for a seal, *tevyak* or sea hare, has dreamt up this half century, this *posyolok*, these lipsticked adolescents and us with our keel in the sand . . .

"*Yedrit' vashu mat', shto vy zdes' delaete? Zdes' zakritaya zona, nado otmechat'sya!*"* suddenly, as if from beneath the sand, a *muzhik* sprung up. In rubber boots, beside himself, with a *kolun* in his hand. A *kolun* is a special axe used to split huge blocks of wood. The *muzhik* turns out to be the chairman of the *selsovet*, that is, the local community council, to whom the duties of guarding the border fell when the border post was done away with. In an hour's time, we are to report

---

* "What the fuck are you doing here? This is a forbidden zone, you have to register your stay!" *Tr.*

to the *syelsovyet* with our documents. We stumble around Shoina for a long time, up to our knees in drifting sands. The streets are swept by sand-drifts. The houses are scattered among dunes, in deep hollows, and are dug out every day. Here and there, mounds jut out like tombstones, traces of houses where nobody lives. There are neither gardens, nor grass. Only sand, sand, sand. In the *syelsovyet*, the stairs are covered in it — inside the barrack! The sand squeezes its way in here, through every chink and cranny. Even the chairman's office is full of it: it is in glasses, on the table, in the files. The *muzhik*, in the meantime, has lost his resoluteness. Perhaps our story has confused him. (I won't reveal it because it might still come in useful.) Or perhaps it is Vasya's expression. He started to search for *ukases* [edicts], consulted some folders, rummaged through some scraps of paper, raising dust. He explained himself, stuttered and apologized: that this is a border *zona*, that it is a forbidden one, that he doesn't know why himself. And that he has to be aware of who comes here because they could telephone, check it out. And that it's better for us because by reporting our departure we would be continuing our passage legally.

"*Nu-ku, davaote, rebyata, po stakanu, na pososhok, i poka.*"

"*Poka, yedrit'tvoyu mat'.*"*

Tarkhanov

The last 100 versts on the sea going North. Beyond that, we'll go on foot . . .

We left Shoina at dawn, on mid-tide. It barely lifted us off the sandbar. We had to hurry before the *muzhik* saw through our story. We had one and a half tides' time to reach Tarkhanov because you can only get into the *zalud* on high tide. Tarkhanov Zaludye is a

---

* "Come on, boys, a glass for the way and 'bye." "'Bye, you mother fucker!" *Tr.*

narrow space between the coast and the *luda* [a rocky patch], closed off in the north by a headland. According to the *Logbook for the White Sea*, the incoming tide sometimes covers the patch and you can perch on it as if you were on a stake. Whereas at low tide, rocks jut out at the entrance like Swiss guards at a papal gate. So you need more than a fair share of precision and a good deal of luck not to gash the hull as you go in, but there is no other way – this is the last shelter on Kanin Coast. Further, solid rocks grow out of the sea.

They used to hunt for belugas in Tarkhanov until recently, white whales which only live in Arctic waters. They had been killing them on the White Sea for centuries: for their skins, which, a Novgorodian chronicler from the 12th century writes, were being levied as a tribute from the people of the North; for their meat, which, in the 1930s people from the North used to make into pâtés, sausages and preserves; finally, for their fat, blood and bones. After the war, the trade in beluga fell rapidly, although in 1958 some 420 animals were still slaughtered in the region of Tarkhanov. This was the last place on the White Sea where white whales were hunted.

We went under sail, without engine, without words. The sea was white as if light had spilled out to the horizon. I felt as if I were looking the sun straight in the eyes. I had seen the White Sea in various colours: often greyish, like the face of someone who had been frightened, or greenish, like the shadow of the seaweed below; sometimes it took on a shade of pale ochre when the sun was melting in mist, sometimes that of red lead when the sun was setting against the wind. Each season has its own colours of the sea; autumn, for example, has shades of cobalt and bluey-green. The White Sea is sometimes also pink, vermilion, golden; sometimes it plays a whole gamut of radiance, but only he who has seen its whiteness beyond the Arctic Circle can understand those who do not want to return from there. It is not by chance that the motif of the world beyond recurs in their accounts. It is enough to remember Melville's puzzling words from *Moby Dick* about the White Sea's influence on the human soul beyond the grave. Puzzling, because there is no evidence that Melville ever came here.

Land suddenly loomed up in front of us, as if it had just been created. It was Kanin Stone (Kanin Kamen'), a rocky plateau of crystalline schist, falling to the sea in terraces. In gullies there was still snow in places, and, on the rock sills, ice opalized in the sun, but hundreds of rivulets were already running down the slopes; the spring tundra was streaming down. The coast seemed inaccessible: a granite wall, carved into fantastic shapes by the sea. We went alongside, back and forth, like a prisoner in his compound, not able to find the *zalud* [channel]. Then, as sometimes happens in fairytales, we found ourselves on the other side.

Could it be the spell of Samoyed shamans, about whom the Orthodox whisper that they can turn the world inside out?

Kanin Nos

Gorlets zhivorodyashchy, pushitsa golubaya, osoka vodyanaya, myatlik lugovoy . . . no, no, Shalamov was wrong when he wrote that flowers in the North have no fragrance. Their fragrance is stunning; it is enough to bury your face in the tundra's carpet. After the salty smell of the sea, seaweed and wind, the delicate scent of spring tundra goes straight to your head, like *nastoika* — a tincture made from golden root, which also grows here. It's everywhere, on the banks of brooks, on shore escarpments, on *sopkas*. *Rodyola rozovaya* [pink rhodium] — the sacred plant of Samoyed shamans. Its roots smell of roses. Immersed in vodka and left to stand in a dark corner for a lunar quarter, it has been the Coastal people's concoction from the beginning of time. Taken in excess, it can be cruel, like insomnia. There, on earth, as the Samoyeds say, meaning the world as far as the Arctic Circle, it is difficult to find the golden root — those in search of the elixir of life have dug it all up. But here, it grows so thickly that it is impossible to walk without it crunching under your feet. Here, even wild chives flower mysteriously, in tiny violet catkins.

We walked through tundra, diagonally across Kanin Nos to the Arctic Ocean, for twenty hours. First, we climbed the rocky ledges of Stone (*Kamen'*) plateau. Then, we waded along reindeer tracks, through soft, wet mud, bypassing dead lakes with layers of eternal ice on their beds. On the shore of one of these, we found traces of *chum*s, gnawed bones, reindeer antlers. Further along, there are *sopka*s, *sopka*s, more mud, lakes, mud, *sopka*s. The sun has hidden itself behind the clouds; it is difficult to guess what time it is, where the north is, where we are. The ground beneath our feet is soft, gives way, caves in, a swamp; we take a roundabout way, from clump to clump, drenched in sweat. Our muscles seize up; our mouths are dry; short of saliva and water. There is marsh gas in the air, little oxygen, and hallucinations: now trees appear, now the towers of a town, now barracks. We come closer; the barracks don't disappear. They are there! Real, like Vasya, like Losha, like the tundra all around. Decaying with flaking plaster, overgrown with berries. The stoves are in ruins; everywhere are heaps of bricks, broken scrap-iron; here and there, barbed wire lies scattered. Could this be a *zona*? We take a rest. On plank beds. Half asleep, half awake. Our feet are burning, our ears humming. The ocean is humming. The ocean . . . ?

Yes, it was the Arctic Ocean. From the barrack windows, we saw an infinity of leaden colour, with no horizon, no firmament. And in the foreground, at the edge of the earth, a huge red mark. With a hammer and sickle in the upper left-hand corner . . .

III

We should treat every single person that comes to us well. We should feed him until he or she is satisfied, give them clothing and set them ashore, so that he or she might encourage others to come to us and show us the secrets of their country. If one of the arrivals gets drunk on beer or wine, we should take advantage and get to know the secret of his heart.

From the Instructions for the expedition of
Hugh Willoughby and Richard Chancellor, 1553

Kanin Nos

Kanin Peninsula juts out nearly 300 versts beyond the Arctic Circle and reaches a latitude of 68° 40' north, separating the White Sea's Mezen Lagoon from the Barents Sea's Chosha Bay. The peninsula ends in a long headland called Nos. According to ancient myth, Kanin Nos lies at the point where the world meets the beyond. No doubt, physical geography had an influence on the beliefs, since the two seas merge here and the elements seethe: tempests, anticyclones and magnetic storms. On the map, Kanin Peninsula looks like the head of a sea monster from Olaus Magnus's drawings which illustrate his *Carta marina et descriptio septentrionalium terrarum* (*History of the Northern Nations*). Later accounts confirmed the existence of monsters at the polar confines of the earth. Perhaps they were the effect of refraction, that is, optical illusions which sailors often experience in the North, where the smallest thrush can be mistaken for an ostrich, or, perhaps, monsters really did live here. Today, it is the Soviet spirit which lives on Kanin Nos . . .

On the tip of the headland, in peaty mud, stand several wooden houses which look like *saray*s [barns]. Grey beams, eaten into by wind and salt. Between the houses lie footbridges that have rotted. Some sheds, some storehouses. A mess all around, empty crude oil barrels, a rusty tractor without caterpillars, stains of mazut. And, in the foreground, a huge red fence with the emblem of the Soviet Union. It is this fence that we saw from the barrack windows an hour ago. From a distance, you can't see the houses against the monotonous background of the tundra and we could have carried on walking past and gone astray. So thanks to this stain, as vivid as blood on grass, we finally managed to find people. Because people also live on Kanin Nos.

A funny little dog with a mottled coat jumped out to greet us. He wagged his tail and fawned against our legs, happy to see guests. The lens of a telescope glistened in the sun; someone was watching us. We approached nearer. A woman with a bloated face emerged from the first house. She held a rifle in her hand. We stood nailed to the ground. The woman smelt of fish oil. Like an elderly mermaid . . . It was Flora Prokofievna, a medic-Bolshevik, as she introduced herself, and told us to follow her. She led us into a dark hallway where slippery nets hung, further along a corridor, gropingly, then a door, a curtain made of skins, another corridor, another curtain, a kitchen. Nappies hung over the stove in the kitchen; a smell of pee, some people, a mess. They sat us at the table, poured us some moonshine, placed a pan of *omula* [an Arctic salmonoid fish] soup and hot bread in front of us. Friendly, curious about the new arrivals. Somebody new kept popping in all the time as if by chance, casually. We drank a *stakan*, washed it down with fish soup. It warmed us up. Relaxed us. Then Flora Prokofyevna demanded to see our passports so as to note down the details since this was a border *zona*. On seeing my foreigner's documents, she was stupefied. Prokofyevna had never seen a real, live foreigner . . .

"*Kakoy zhe eto inostranets?*" ["What foreigner?"], a *muzhik*, whom I hadn't noticed before, threw in from the corner. "*On zhe svoy, Solovetsky, on na Solovkakh zhivyot.*" ["He's one of us, from Solovky, he lives on Solovky."]

Sometimes it seems I contradict myself. One moment I advise taking a foreigner's position in the world about which one writes, then I reject it, stating that one shouldn't be an observer, a gaping spectator, but a creator and participant of life, not in "the role of a writer" who is always somewhat "beyond" – it doesn't matter whether "above" or "at the side" – but a subject of "the prose which was like a document" (according to Shalamov's description). The antinomy, however, is only apparent because the two points of view essentially complement each other and the writer will always be a foreigner, even in his own country, while, at the same time, he will be at home everywhere – on his own tropa, *his own path. It is worth repeating that this applies to "prose which was like a document" and not documentary literature or pure fiction.*

According to my passport, I remained a foreigner to them, but having lived among them for a fair amount of time, I had become one of them. Because they look at you differently if you live in hotels, have a Udostovyeryenye inostrannovo korrespondenta (*a foreign correspondent's press card), a lot of "bucks" and immunity which accreditation guarantees, and completely differently when you dig your* kartoshka *yourself, can set nets under the ice in winter and survive in the tundra alone. Here, in the North, life is not a joke, the conditions are harsh, nature herself tests man. Others can only confirm – like Yura, the* muzhik *who was sitting in the corner of the kitchen – that you are one of theirs . . .*

Yura and I had once drunk half a bottle of shilo *on our way to Umba. That was my first summer on the White Sea. After a long winter spent*

188

*in Solovky like in a cell, I had set off to wander the White Sea coast as
soon as the ice had started to melt. I didn't know Vasya from Sumskiy
Posad yet so I had to take it as it came – I caught ships as you catch
cars when you hitch-hike. I got a lift from Solovky to Pomorsky Bereg,
where I spent a week by myself roving across the mud, then I saw
Belomorkanal [White Sea Canal], a bit of Karelia, and found myself
in Kem just on time to jump on deck of the GS (gydrograficheskoye
sudno) [hydrographic ship] which was going to Kanin and making a
detour to Umba on the way. They did not even want to hear of taking
me to Kanin because it was a* zona, *there was a target range there, and
it was a state secret, but they did take me to Umba. We had barely left
the port when Yura appeared on deck, carrying* shilo *and smoked burbot
as a snack. He wanted to wash down his luck but didn't have anyone to
do it with because the crew does not drink at sea. Luck? Yes. Yura was
happy because he had signed a contract for the Kanin* mayak. *Up until
now, he had worked in the Donbas mines, and he was beginnning to
feel he had had enough of life. Working in the shafts, constantly underground, like moles. At least they used to earn a decent wage before, but
now there was poverty, strikes, hunger. He had even stopped enjoying
his living quarters; you couldn't open the windows without coal dust settling on the furniture. Departure to Kanin, in such circumstances, was
a stroke of luck. You can make money there, and there is nature in
abundance. You can fish, hunt, see a polar bear. And it is healthier for
the kid, who was wheezing with coal and constantly ill. As if he had
heard us talking about him, Piet'ka, Yura's son, appeared on deck. Mum's
still crying, he said, and doesn't want to see the world. Kat'ka, a champion at gymnastics on the apparatus, couldn't envisage life in the Far
North. There were no sports palaces there, no friends or television. There
weren't even any shops! That's women for you. But Yura was optimistic.
She would get used to it, he kept on repeating, she would get used to it.
Then he fell silent. Perhaps he had started to doubt, perhaps his thoughts
were already roving around Kanin Nos, or perhaps the* shilo *had struck
him dumb. There was a light breeze coming from Kandalaksha, Reindeer*

Islands were suspended in a mirage, in the distance loomed the coast. Not until we were in Umba, when they had lowered the gangway, did Yura suddenly come to. We had a drink na pososhok *(literally — for the pilgrim's staff, or, as we say — for the road), we embraced Russian-style, kissed each other . . .*

We embraced Russian-style, kissed each other. Well, well, who would have thought that we'd ever meet again? And where? On Kanin Nos! We have to drink to that. Yura ran to wake Kat'ka up; there was a commotion in the kitchen. They were running here and there, carrying this and that, speaking all at once, one over the other, rejoicing. Only Prokofyevna didn't soften her tone and, learning that I was collecting material for a book about the White Sea, kept questioning: what was I writing? Any bias? And wasn't it by any chance against the Russians? My stories, it appears, satisfied her because she explained, somewhat more gently, that they were living here in a collective of nine people (not counting Piet'ka and little Varvarka); together they were looking after the *mayak* and meteorological station, and together they were suffering poverty after the collapse of the Soviet rule. Before, they had lived in comfort; provisions and the post would arrive regularly, the hospital helicopter would come whenever it was summoned, the wages, too, weren't so bad, but now . . . Huh, better left unsaid. If it weren't for the game and fish that they caught themselves, they would, no doubt, starve to death. They had recently run out of cigarettes and for one and a half months the *muzhik*s had smoked grass. That's why they are all going to vote unanimously for Zyuganov, although, to be honest, they don't trust him either because "he who has been wearing out the chairs in Moscow for a long time, has got a soft backside". Here, on the confines of the former Soviet Union, life does not stroke backsides. Here, you can see the drivel of reform, the chaos of *perestroika* and the cunning mugs of the democrats more clearly for what they are. You can't deceive Prokofyevna; she has survived Stalin and will outlast Yeltsin. She was sixty-two yesterday but doesn't feel her age and still likes to play the hooligan. It is she who, during the August coup d'état, painted the Soviet flag on the fence so that, from the sea, from a distance, people could see that the Soviet spirit has not died . . .

During this banquet of surveillance and ideology, Prokofyevna did not stop ordering the collective about. The table was abundantly laid. What wasn't there? Sterlet in cranberry jelly, and *pelmeny* with *nelma*, and *pelmeny* with *shokhur*, and marinated snipe, and grouse pâté and, as hot dishes, the rest of yesterday's wood grouse, and reindeer lungs in home-made wine, and, finally, in the middle of the table, a bucket of cloudberry moonshine. Prokofyevna, with both pride and bitterness, emphasized that, apart from flour for the *pelmeny*, they had caught everything themselves with rifle and rod. We started raising toasts, sniffing our glasses, drinking and eating. I don't know whether it was the strong moonshine or tiredness, but it seemed to me that everyone was telling the story of their life all at once. A polyphony of fates from which I fished out the plots, barely the scraps of plots. Take Flora, a medic who had spent her entire life in the North: in camps, special *zona*s, polar stations. Or the mechanic Dyma, an "Afghan" who went on and on about the war to the point of laughter, tears, and hiccups. Or Uncle Kola who did fifteen years for the murder of his wife, was released, had married again, and run away to Kanin so as not to kill his second wife. Or Kat'ka, medallist for vaulting in gymnastics, now fat, alcoholic and suffering terrible migraines. And Pasha-*bich*, that is, "a former intellectual" as he himself interprets the term, once a poet, bard, dissident, and now completely indifferent. The plots weaved in and out, got into a tangle, merged into one fate, one sculpture. As if I were constantly looking at the same stone, slowly turning, and chiselled to the point of pain. How much time could have elapsed? I don't know. A lot, if I were to go by the moonshine: half a bucket. Suddenly, a grinding, the stone stopped, came to a halt . . . It was a guitar. Silence fell. Complete silence. The guitar began to grind again. I didn't immediately understand what Pasha, drawing a rouble across the strings, was singing because he started in a whisper, as if to himself. A bluish semi-darkness seeped through the window, enveloping both the dishes and the faces of the banqueters with a shade of wax, which gave both food and people the appearance of still life. It was Tyutchev, Pasha was singing his poem *Silentium*:

> *Kak serdtsu vyskazat' sebya?*
> *Drugomu kak ponyat' tebya?*
> *Poimyot li on, chem ty zhivyosh?*
> *Mysl izrechonnaya yest' lozh';*
> *Vzryvaya, vozmutish kluchy, —*
> *Pitaisya imy — i molchi.**

Tarkhanov

We left Kanin the following day, in fog. The tundra was exuding milky smoke. The sun, like a slice of lemon, was shining through the mist. Yura and Kat'ka led us to the old Samoyed nomad track called *letnik*, because, in the summer [*leto*], you can follow it on *narty*, a kind of sleigh used in the North. *Letnik* runs through the middle of the tundra, climbs up to Stone (Kamen') plateau, crosses the Great Bugryanitsa, the Shoina, the Kya and reaches the Chizha. Yura explained that we should keep to it until we reached the first *sopka* and then follow the stream down to the sea, then follow the coast to the *zalud* [channel] where we had left the *Antur*. The mists were thinning, the sun grew hot, and the day promised to be exhausting. I slowed down after a couple of versts; I wanted to be alone. I arranged

---

*How is a heart to show itself? / How can another know you? / How will he grasp by what you live? / A thought expressed is but a lie; / By stirring up the springs, you will trouble them: drink of them, and remain silent. *Tr.*

with Vasya that he and Losha would wait for me by the stream at which we were to turn towards the sea, and I waited a while until they disappeared over the horizon. Until their voices could no longer be heard. The primitive world spread out all around me. There were no traces of civilization, culture or history. No past. No ruins, no monuments. Complete emptiness, both in space and in time. Perhaps this is where that particular feeling comes from, that feeling experienced by wanderers in the Far North of being on the edge of the world and of life. The edge of reality.

Further on, the old Samoyed track led through rusty mud, weaving in and out. At times, it disappeared altogether, in quagmires, in the grass; at others, it unfolded as a streak on small thickets of cloudberries, like a shadow. Once, I even had the impression that it was drawing a figure of eight because the clumps I was passing seemed familiar, and then I remembered Samoyed Vylka's "parable about a *tropa*". Tiko Vylka (1882–1960), hunter, tale-teller, and shaman according to some, natural painter (he received a Winchester sporting rifle and 1,000 bullets from Tsar Nicolas II for his album of drawings!), Polar expedition guide, and Soviet president of Novaya Zyemlya, received in the Kremlin by Kalinin, that same Vylka was wont to repeat that everyone in the tundra has their own *tropa* which has been destined only for them: a *tropa* which it is not easy to find and which you might walk past and miss all your life. It often happens that you cross it a couple of times a day, going for water or firewood; or it happens that you track a reindeer along it and then deviate, following the reindeer's trail into a thicket of sallows. But if you listened to your *tropa*, Tiko Vylka taught, it would lead you, like a song and would, itself, turn inside out, without you even noticing when. And on you'd go, into the depths of that same tundra because neither *tropa* nor tundra end here . . .

Here? There? For Vylka, they are two sides of one and the same path, which he tried to catch on canvas and in songs. In his paintings, you can see the concentration, so characteristic of nature in the

North, converging within a small number of forms, a few tones, above all in the light. It is thanks to the light that Vylka's landscapes are transparent – the peace of eternity shines through them. Even in what you would think are trivial scenes of Samoyed life – *Hunting* or *By the Campfire* – you can see the reality of everyday life frozen in the light as in an amber, but Vylka's true art can only be appreciated in his northern landscapes – in *An Unknown Bay*, in *The Ice of Karsk Sea*, in *Bear Sopka*s – which not so much illustrate that world as expose it on canvas. That? This? In Vylka's art (and life), they are different sides of one and the same reality, just as the ribbon of reflections in the dark sky of *Northern Lights* is barely a reflection (like a negative) of *Tropa in the Tundra*, and the traces of the brush – the artist's *tropa* . . .

Somewhere far away, Vasya's rifle resounded. I replied with a shot. Only now did I realize that the sun had traced a semi-circle in the sky, meaning that half a day and night had passed from the moment I had been left alone. The fumes from the marshes must have dulled my sense of time because I would have bet that only an hour had passed. We managed to reach the *Antur* in the middle of the night. In the meantime, the wind turned against the sun, which was hanging over Tarkhanov Point like a blister of blood.

The Great Bugryanitsa

The *shalonnik* struck in the morning when we had barely left the channel. The sky became overcast in the wink of an eye. Water was coming from everywhere. The sea reared up and was covered in foam. Yellow-white tufts of it fell on deck. To return behind the bar was out of the question. In the circumstances, we risked entering the Great Bugryanitsa twenty versts lower down. According to the *Logbook*, this is the most suitable river for shelter in the vicinity of Kanin Nos. We

managed to make it out in the wall of foam and water with difficulty. Through binoculars, the coast merged with the sea, into one
homogeneous leaden surge. Only in one place did the water seethe
with dirty dun-coloured eddies. This was the mouth of the
Bugryanitsa, its current was whirling on the *koshky*. *Koshky* are
underwater sandbanks, which dry out at low tide but are dangerous
at high tide. Especially so during storms, when there is no question
of checking out the bed with poles. So, as was usual at such moments,
all that remained were Vasya's intuition and a stroke of luck: Losha
at the keel, I at the engine, Vasya at the helm. We slipped into the
Great Bugryanitsa on the edge of the keel.

The *shalonnik* intensified. This is the second day that it's blowing.
We are standing on a meander of the river, sheltered from the sea
by only a series of *baklishs*, that is, rocks submerged by incoming tide.
It is a poor shelter, but rocky sills prevent us from going higher up.
The banks of the Bugryanitsa are steep, gullied by streams, covered
with wet moss. In 1877, the hunter Foma Uvakin found the dying
Nikolay Zograf, the leader of one of the first scientific expeditions
to Kanin, here. When the Samoyeds who had accompanied Zograf
found out that the scientist was preserving samples of collected fauna
in alcohol, they stole and drank the collection and abandoned the professor in the tundra. A rotten boat held down by a couple of anchors
corroded with rust juts out from the *nyasha* (miry, black loam); a bit
higher up, overgrown with enormous leaves similar to burdock, stands
a semi-decayed cabin. It is the remains of a fishing *stanovishche* [post]
that until recently belonged to the Shoina kolkhoz. Today, pieces of
net are scattered around the cabin, a jagged axe, a bucket with a hole
in it, a kettle, black with soot. Inside are traces left by animals, empty
bottles. On one of the bottles there is a well-remembered Polish label,
like an echo of my homeland: "Wodka Wyborowa".

The *shalonnik* does not abate. This is the third day that it is howling.
There is an incessant whistling in the stays, in the head, to the point
of nausea. The waves are leaping over the *baklish*s and thundering

furiously against the boat. The wind throws us on our side. We lower the mast, no mean feat in such rolling. The anchors flounder in the silty bottom; they don't hold. Every twelve hours, at low tide, we move them (four anchors, each weighing 100 kilos), up to our groins in sludge. The stench of decay stops the breath. Hydrogen sulphur, the smell of the devil.

The *shalonnik*. This is the fourth day and no end in sight. The cold is penetrating. The hours drag on, like years "in the nick". We eat, sleep, play cards. At odd moments, I try to read, note something down, but my thoughts are scattered. So I kill the time with *blatnye* [thieves' slang] words, which Vasya whispers to me. Here, for example, is an interesting *polonicum: a polyak* (a *mar* like myself) is, in slang, a *vor odinochka na fyeny*, that is, a thief who works alone.

"*Ty, Mar, kak nastoyashchy polyak, voruyesh nashu russkuyu dyeistvitelnost' i prodayosh yeyo v Parizhe, kak svoyu . . .*"*

Morzhovets

Is it an evil spell or a lesson in humility, this charmed Arctic Circle which it is impossible to cross? We had to wait another two days and nights in the Bugryanitsa for the White Sea to calm down and the rolling to subside. We intended crossing the Voronka in one go: 220 versts of open water. When we finally did leave, the sea was smooth, the *moryana* was blowing, the sails were full and Miles Davis was blowing on his trumpet. Above Konushin, a small cloud appeared. Then a second one and a third. The *moryana* suddenly died out, the sails dropped, *Sketches of Spain* had finished. And in the Mezen Lagoon, the weather finally did change for the worse — *skurvilas' i v*

---

* "You, Mar, like a true *polyak*, are stealing our Russian reality and selling it in Paris as if it were your own . . ." *Tr.*

*kharyu zadulo*ⁱin Vasya's language. Nevertheless, we went on while visibility permitted. Halfway into the lagoon, the fog drifted out. Fog with wind on the White Sea is fatal. You may as well say your prayers. Even a compass is useless because the Voronka is famous for its magnetic anomalies. Vasya puts it in a word: *hana*. The end. We were saved by a polar owl. A huge white bird. It emerged from the fog without a sound, cut across our path and disappeared in the fog. Like an hallucination. We turned to follow it. After a moment, land loomed up in front of us. It was Morzhovets. If it weren't for the owl, we would have gone into the Gorlo, on to the *Kedovskye Koshky* [Kedy Sandbanks] . . .

Morzhovets lies at the mouth of the Gorlo, on the very line of the Arctic Circle, twenty-eight versts from Zimny Bereg [Winter Coast]. It is a large, flat island of granite, oval in shape (about forty versts in circumference), covered in slabs of ice and earth. The approach is difficult because its coast changes every year, gradually sinking into the sea and forming dangerous shoals around it, like the Brigand Shoals on which we almost ran aground, hiding from the radar. Because making one's way on the White Sea isn't just a struggle with the elements; it is also the art of avoiding military binoculars and radars. Especially if you're going around without a permit. It is easier to hide in fog, and easier to perish. Because of its location, Morzhovets is an excellent observation point both for the surveillance of undesirable people and for hunting water beasts. The island's name even contains a trace of the sea horse (*morzha*), now totally extinct in the White Sea. Until recently, Morzhovets was still one enormous slaughterhouse – the main place for the slaughter of *belukh*s, meaning baby seals.

With the beginning of winter, huge pods of Greenland *tyulen'* [seals] would migrate to the White Sea and here, on the floating ice, the females would pup. In February and March, the ice with the

---

*Literally: "became a whore and began blowing in our faces." *Tr.*

animals on it would be carried northwards, along Zimny Bereg [Winter Coast] to Mezen Lagoon where the young would gather strength and take to the water. At the beginning of May, the pods would swim away to the Arctic Ocean. And during all this time, the hunt for *kozha* (skins), as they called the seals here, would take place in the White Sea. Especially for *belukh*s whose white, fluffy fur fetched the highest price. They hunted in artels made up of ten to fifteen boats, with five to seven *muzhik*s to each boat. The *muzhik*s would approach the seal *zalyoshek* [breeding ground] – where up to 5,000 "skins" covering a square kilometre were basking – in their boats, jump out on to the ice and smash the seals over the head with truncheons. Neither the *belukh*s, nor their mothers would slip away, for the *belukh*s didn't know how to move yet and the mothers, well, they would stay by their little ones. The *muzhik*s would skin them on the spot and despatch the skins together with the fat to the shore, leaving the bare carcasses on the ice, covered with a thick layer of frozen blood. The expansion of the fur hunting industry was at its peak at the beginning of the 20th century. In the winter of 1901, there were 440 *muzhik*s in seventy-five cabins on Morzhovets. Later, brigades of kolkhoz members took the place of the *muzhik*s and helicopters started being used to slaughter the animals. Only the truncheons remained from the old days, and the seals continued to be smashed over the head with them in the same way. With the development of technology, the population of Greenland seals rapidly decreased and, with the collapse of the Soviet Union, the interest in "skins" declined. Today, the cold storage plants of the fur hunting kolkhozes are loaded with goods which no-one is collecting . . .

Finally, the wind dispersed the fog. Morzhovets loomed up in front of us in all its splendour. Here and there, shreds of mist still drifted, the dew on the *yagel* [an Arctic lichen] glistened in the sun and the Zolotukha, one of the two small rivers on the island, was steaming all colours of the rainbow. Morzhovets was deserted, unforested and uninhabited, apart from the military. The hunters' cabins had rotted long ago and turned to dust. As if time had turned back on itself and ran backwards. In 1856, Maksimov noted in his travel notebook that there were no houses on Morzhovets and that nobody lived here apart from an observer and some *mayak* [lighthouse] attendants.

Kedy

We continued our passage against the wind, with the engine on. We were too exposed on bare Morzhovets: we could have been given a rough time both by the storm and by border guards. It is best not to tempt the devil, especially as the Gorlo is not far and the coast there is open to navigation. Which does not mean that from now on we would be travelling legally; here, what is open to navigation is not so for everyone, especially foreigners. Here, you have to report where you're going and what for, prepare your itinerary beforehand so that the appropriate organs can approve it, and acquire consent on paper . . . To be without consent on paper is like being without a blessing in a monastery; every action is considered unlawful, a disregard for administration, power, authority. Nevertheless and despite everything, the difference between the open coast, to which we were making our way against the wind, and closed *zona*s, which we were, at the same time, leaving, heartened us since it seemed that our worst problems were over. In other words, we were returning to earth, as the Samoyeds call this side of the Arctic Circle . . .

A couple of versts beyond Voronov Point, the Great Kedovka, which we knew from the previous year, flows into the sea. The bed is sandy here and you can dry out and rest. On the right bank of the river, somewhat above the mouth, stands Kedy, a typical fishing *stanovishche*: a house, a warehouse, a couple of sheds, a *banya*. A *stanovishche* is a seasonal settlement to which *muzhik*s come every year for the fishing period, leaving their women and children in the village, often for many months on end. The White Sea has been pol-ishing Coastal life for ages, just as the waves eat away the coast, and it has given it a form in tune with the austerity of nature. The basis of this life was the male community, whose roots reach way back into the distant past when the North was colonized, and the fundamental form – the fishing artel – was conceived during Murmansk cod fishing seasons. The community embraced all ages from teenagers to old men; it had its own hierarchy, division of roles, customs, language. For boys, it was both a school of the trade and of life, with a whole arsenal of trials leading to higher levels of initiation. A strict code of behaviour ruled in the community, which was defined by the merciless law of the sea, and the greatest punishment was exclusion from the artel because, alone, man had no hope of surviving in the North. Such col-lectivism, imposed by nature, acquired a religious grounding in the Orthodox concepts of *sobornost'* (community) and *poslushaniye* (obe-dience) and spread not only on monastic property, of which there was an abundance everywhere here, but also within the *skit*s of old believers, of which there were even more. On the other hand, one should remember that the people who were predominant among the Pomor ancestors were restless, often evaders of the corvee, schismatics and adventurers, so that the communities which they formed were free and based on a respect of authority and laws set by the sea. The Bolshevik collectivization programme, without apparently changing much in traditional coastal life (the community was called a kolkhoz, the artels – brigades), did, in essence, kill off the spirit of traditional collectivism, replacing it with *shilo* and a plan.

In the past, Kedy and Morzhovets were a centre for the fur hunting industry on the White Sea. Artels from Mezen, Koyda, Syomzha and the Zimniy Bereg would gather here for the season. There would sometimes be up to 500 *muzhik*s. About sixty cabins. With the fall in demand for seal skins, Kedy declined. Today a six-man brigade is enough: a chief, a mechanic, two fish scourers and two tractor drivers. They attend to the fisheries from Moyda to Koyda, over fifty versts

of coast. On every fishery, every ten to twelve versts, two, three, sometimes four fishermen live, who, twice a day, at low tide, gather the
nets. The brigade's duties include visiting all the fisheries, collecting
the catch, cleaning, salting and despatching it to the kolkhoz in Moyda.
When we got to them, the entire brigade was cleaning a *pinagor*. Its
pink caviar, like a bloody foam, covered their hands. They salt only
the caviar from the *pinagor* and feed the rest to the cattle. On the
whole, they look down on the *pinagor*, and wait for schools of *syomga*
to arrive. *Syomga* and *pinagor* don't come together. The chief recog-
nized us, invited us into the cabin, promised a *banya*. Before we had
chopped the firewood, the brigade had finished work. They washed
their hands and we sat down at the table. Fried flounder, slightly
salted caviar, dark bread and a *stakan* of *spirt*. The *spirt* is provided
by the kolkhoz, two *stakans* per head a day. At the table, tongues loosened and the men subjected the whole world – the source of their
misery – from Yeltsin to Kola, to their baroque *mat*. Kola is the
chairman of the kolkhoz. They used to be "heroes of work" and held
second place in the Soviet Union but, today, they are a billion in debt
and have no prospect of getting out of this hole. It's impossible to
leave here because an aeroplane ticket costs three times their wages,
which they don't receive for months on end. In summer, you can get
by somehow, on fish and berries, but in winter . . . It's better not to
think about winter. Reforms, privatization, capitalism – they are all
one and the same *blin*. May the Gaydars roll in it themselves! They
are already handing over the fisheries on Tersky Bereg (Tersky Coast)
to lease. The dealers pay, hire out any old scoundrels for the season
and the local *muzhik*s go short. That's how it is. What the Communists
haven't managed to destroy, the Democrats are finishing off. Here,
on the Coast, they have lived together since the dawn of time: they
have fished together on communal fishing waters, they have helped
each other out at sea, and shared the catch out evenly, irrespective of
luck, and if a *muzhik* went missing at sea, they would take in his
family. And now? Everyone scowls and looks out for himself. Free

market, competition, commerce? What competition are we talking about if the mafia from town has control over the cold storage ships, the *blat* [c.f. *po blatu*] and bank credits, and our man has a leaking tub and old net? Free market – the very idea, one shop in the middle of the tundra, they fly the goods in and however much they decide to add for transportation, they squeeze out of us. Those who came before so as to earn a "long rouble", to make money, lined their pockets and fled, but the locals, where can we go? Drop dead, that's what . . .

The faces at the table fluttered like fish and grew still. They became silent. We finished our *spirt*. Time to check the *lovushka*s. Losha stays behind to keep an eye on the *banya*, and we go down to the shore with the brigade. *Lovushka*s are ingeniously constructed nets, sort of enormous drag-nets, stretched on to strong poles, driven into the sea-bed. The whole forms a barrier, four metres high, set up perpendicularly to the shore escarpment and reaching half a kilometre out into the sea. The net is sewn together, in several places, into a poke-net the size of a disco floor in an average bar. The incoming tide covers the *lovushka* and the fish, swimming alongside the shore, catch their noses in the mesh, search for a way through and find themselves in the poke-net. Later, the water level drops, people drive up in a tractor and gather the fish in the sand, like potatoes in a field. Sometimes a ton, sometimes a ton and a half. There weren't many *pinagor*s this time, a sign that *syomga* is coming soon. I approached nearer. The fish, like children's rubber bath toys, lay half-buried in the sand as if they wanted to bury themselves with their fins.

Winter Zolotitsa

At three in the morning, we went to the *banya*. We flogged ourselves, took a good steam bath, sweated. Oh, a little Russian *banya* in the middle of the tundra! Then barefoot into *moroshka,* naked into the lake, some strong tea, and on our way. We made the Gorlo slowly, like unhurried passers-by, along Zimny Bereg, surveying the land through binoculars. The day was rising: the fishing waters were full of movement, the tractor had come, smoke was drifting from the cabins, they were hanging out the nets, pulling firewood from the sea, draining water from boats, sorting out the fish and watching us, shielding their eyes from the sun with their hands. Moida, Megra, Ruchy. The barometer was falling. Intsy Point, the narrowest place in the Gorlo. The Cape of Bears, the beginning of a forest, the first trees. At the level of Little Tova, the *zakat* – a westerly wind – arose. The swell grew. We stepped up the gas. Tatarikha. Tova. The sea grew dark in front of our eyes. Beyond Sharp Point, all hell broke loose. There were six versts left to Winter Zolotitsa. The *zakat* went mad. We dropped our sails. Upper Okat was getting closer and closer . . . the river mouth . . . the fairway . . . on the left, a barge . . . the buoys are dancing . . . at our side, a sandbar . . . Vasya roars . . . a bar . . . we're through!

We drop anchor opposite the kolkhoz warehouses in Nizhnyaya (Lower) Zolotitsa. This is the oldest settlement on Zimny Bereg, its beginnings reaching back to the end of the 16th century. Here, you can see the traditional Coastal "star" plan of the village, which came about when small hamlets joined up, as well as the typical alignment of buildings along the shore. Here and there, old, pre-revolutionary wooden houses with richly carved façades and enormous, fancy porches – half-obliterated traces of a rich past – have still survived. But mediocrity and kolkhoz elegance predominates: corrugated iron, tar paper, slate, air-bricks. And everywhere the eye can see, scattered scrap-iron, refuse and rubbish. Above all, barrels, thousands of rusty crude oil, petrol and oil barrels, with which the coast of the White Sea is literally strewn, especially close to where people live. There are a lot of full ones among the empty barrels; there is no shortage of free fuel. But what are barrels and fuel when you can find whole tractors here, abandoned in the mud and sand by drunken men. They stand on the beach like the remains of prehistoric animals, gnawed by corrosion and sea salt. At each stop, the anchor barely lowered, Vasya and Losha meticulously inspect the local dumps, often bringing in booty. They have gathered about half a verst of copper wire alone and, with the parts they've found on the way, they could put together a new engine. They call their expeditions *zakhvat* [seizure] and their spoils *privatizatsya*; I detect in this the influence of television, which has recently been impressing viewers with plunder from Chechenya and Russian reforms . . .

But we came across plunder on such a scale in Winter Zolotitsa that the lads, forgetting about the dump, just stood and stared. On the sandbar at the mouth of the river, a barge, which the swell had thrown up from the sea, stood high and dry. As later became clear, the Captain was so drunk that he didn't manage to get into the fairway. The barge was carrying goods for the kolkhoz, some of which were already intended for the following winter: sugar, flour, oil, tinned foods and vodka! Information about the vodka spread through the village like wildfire. The *muzhik*s jumped into their boats, paying no attention to the storm. They were obviously not all going on a rescue operation, but to tear into the spoils like vultures. In the meantime, the barge capsized and water began to flood the hatches. There was little time, the swell was growing. The *muzhik*s climbed on deck, flinging their fists around. Sacks of sugar, sacks of flour, some cartons, boxes, all went flying into the sea, just so that they could get to the vodka. Someone fell into the water, someone else got crushed. A fat woman was running along the shore, wringing her hands. She was the shop manager who oversaw the kolkhoz stores. Finally, they found the booze. A row broke out. Everyone wanted to drag a crate out, but the hatches were small, allowing only one at a time. They dropped a couple of crates in the sea and smashed several faces to blood before they gathered their wits and finished their plundering in turn. After which, they dispersed in their boats like phantoms and, if it weren't for what was left of the cardboard floating around the barge, you would think this to be fiction and not life.

Later, they drank themselves to a stupor, squealing like piglets. Zolotitsa went wild. In the night, the storm ceased, a fog lifted from the sea, entered the river, and spread over the village. A sticky, grey slush full of whining and squealing which carried over the water. Towards morning, the fog dissipated, laying bare a hungover reality. Empty bottles floated on the river, scraps of crates, a partially burnt mattress, pieces of polystyrene, a wooden boat turned upside down, completely new nets, a soggy packet of Bialomor cigarettes, plastic sunglasses, a torn, quilted jacket, a red buoy, the front page of *Pravda Severa*, a dog's corpse, patches of oil . . . We raised anchor.

Anzer

We took a south-westerly course, intending to cut across Dvinskaya Guba [Dvina Lagoon] to arrive at Zhizhgin, which is a stone's throw from Solovky. We broke away from Zimny Bereg at the level of Vyeprevsky Point. Gorlo was behind us. We went under sail, taking turns to catch up on our sleep. While I was on watch, a pod of *belukh*s came up to *Antur*. They swam behind us for a couple of versts, looking like snow-white pillowcases billowing in the wash. Boards from broken rafts used on the Dvina to transport timber drifted from the opposite direction. Five seagulls were sitting on one, like on a tram. From time to time, the shapely little head of a curious seal would emerge, or the blunt head of a sea hare chasing a school of herring. Now and again, just above the water, flew wild ducks or, high up, barely visible against the sun, a flock of cranes. But as far as the horizon, there was no trace of human beings. Before we reached Zhizhgin, we turned westwards. There, on the horizon, in a glowing mirage, shimmered Anzer . . .

So this was Solovky! Anzer is the second largest island of the Solovetsky Archipelago and lies at its north-easterly extremity. From a distance, you can see Golgotha, multiplied by refraction: the white stamp of the church at its summit gathers the sunlight, the rays break up in the damp air, playing with the colours of the rainbow . . . Suddenly, what is this? We come closer, not believing our eyes: Anzer is upside down, Golgotha at the bottom, looking like an atomic mushroom. It's an optical illusion, of course, but it's so clear that it is disconcerting. From nearby, everything returns to normal. Then Kalguev Point obstructs the view of Golgotha, we go along the coast to Trinity Bay, cross the rocky sills on high water and throw down our anchors near the hermitage of St Eleazar. All around, the forest is rustling, the air is filled with the smell of *ivan-chay* [willow-herb]. It is deserted; there is not a living soul, only somewhere, in the distance, a woodpecker is hammering. We decide to spend the night here, although there is barely half a tide before we reach home. We want to say farewell to our voyage, wash away the dust . . .

Vasya has kept something special for the occasion: *shilo* made with golden root and a jar of elk meat *tushonka* [conserves]. Losha gathered some wild chives and caught a couple of fat *kumzha* [salmon trout] which went straight into the frying pan. The *kumzha* simmered in its own sauce, melted in the mouth. We drank to celebrate our voyage. The *shilo* stabbed like a knife and blasted the head with brightness. The sun, in the meantime, was setting behind Golgotha. Against the light, the chapel looked like a hole in the sky. In 1710, *starets* Jesus saw the Virgin Mary there, who told him that a stone church would stand in this place — the Temple of the Lord's Crucifixion — and that this hill would be a second Golgotha flowing with blood. Losha asked me whether this was the same Jesus whom the Orthodox say is their God? No, Losha, I replied, this was the monk Job, Peter the Great's confessor. And it seems he knew too much about the tsar because he ended up on Solovky under strict surveillance. He lived here for a long time, keeping silent and fasting in solitude until he attained *skhima*, meaning the dignity of a great penitent, and took the name of Jesus. In the place where he saw the Virgin, he built a hermitage and erected a wooden temple. In the 19th century, a stone church was built there. In the days of SLON, it was a *zona* for women, where drug addicts, prostitutes and *blatnyachky* [members of the criminal underworld] with syphilis were held, as were, according to accounts, some Catholic clergy, too. Today, ruins rise up there, covered in vulgar graffiti and buried in a heap of rubble. There is a belief among the Orthodox that Russia will not be reborn until it rebuilds the temple on Anzer's Golgotha . . .*

Pssst! Vasya gave us a sign to be quiet. A white reindeer appeared from the forest on the shore of the bay. A lone bull. He stood by the water for a while, then bowed his head as if he were looking in a mirror. He was within shooting range.

Solovky, mid-March; there is a blizzard outside, you can't see the world. I finish writing "Kanin Nos" while waiting for the aeroplane on which I want to despatch my text to Kultura. It is snowing heavily today, the moryana *is blowing so that the lower curb-plates of the house creak, and it is hard to believe that a paragraph ago we were sitting on Anzer, eating* kumzha *and elk* tushonka. *The following day, it was sunny, there was a favourable breeze, the day was crystal clear and we covered the last verts at a leisurely pace. We entered the Bay of Good Fortune, now ice-bound, under sail, with music. Fanfares, welcomes, joy, a taste of success, and behind us 1,500 verts. Then a couple of weeks passed, a few guests, a few books, and I started to miss the sea, the tundra. The other side of the Arctic Circle. Sometimes images would return, faces. Sharapov, Tanka, Flora Prokofyevna. Sometimes I would still wake up on Kanin Tropa but, slowly, that other world began to fade, to stop existing. Because the world, in effect, has not been given to us once and*

---

*A year later, a company from Arkhangel allocated a considerable sum for the rebuilding of the temple of the Lord's Resurrection at the foot of Golgotha. Rumours started to circulate around Solovky: some people mutter that this is the beginning of Russia's rebirth, while others whisper that "dirty" money is being laundered . . .

for all, but is constantly, uninterruptedly, being created in our presence. The past, with the passage of time, dies, as does our memory of it, or sooner, and the place we visited the day before yesterday ceases to exist for us, just as the places which we will never visit do not exist. There, a crow has flown past, framing itself in my window. I was just following the trajectory of its flight when the crow disappeared. The snow is falling and the trajectory . . . where was it? It is the same with a *tropa* in the tundra, or the wake left by a keel in the sea. They exist, they are real solely here and now. That is why I resolved to repeat the journey to Kanin Nos and back — this time on paper. While I was writing, I noticed that the world of the Far North is twisted, chaotic, and that reality here is devoid of shape, which, in temperate latitudes is created by culture. The rudimentary forms of civilization which came into existence here were destroyed by Sovietism, and nature is dominated by water, ice and mud, elements, therefore, without a form. In such a situation, repeating the journey lost its sense — it was like looking for tracks in a quagmire — while the writing itself ran along its own *tropa*, finding in language a firmer ground than the undergrowth of the tundra. I mean to say that the text is more real than the world which is, for the text, a "pre-text" . . .

Glossary

Alkash: an alcoholic. Diminutive: *alik*. Can be "on a torpedo", that is, have a temporary detox patch sewn in, or "*v zapoyu*", that is, be on a prolonged drinking bout.

Banya: Russian baths. An essential element of Russian existence, especially in *glubinka* (the depths of the country), where civilization in the form of hot water has not penetrated. There are two kinds of *banya*: "black", where there is no chimney and the smoke streams insides, blackens the interior which has to be aired before you wash, and yet still manages to burn your eyes, and you can get dirty while you wash; and "white", which is with a chimney and similar to a Finnish sauna. The very construction of the *banya* has something of the "Russian idea" in it: most important are its upper beams and the degree to which they are air-tight — they must not allow any steam to escape; the lower logs can be rotten as long as they hold up the upper ones. Numerous *inostranyetstsy* visiting Russia have written about the Russian *banya* and one could put together an interesting anthology called *The Russian Banya Seen Through the Eyes of Foreigners*. More about the *banya* on pp. 60–63

Bezmolviye: silence. Isolation, quiet. Father Pavel Florensky wrote the following to his wife on the subject of *bezmolvie*: "One of my acquaintances is asking me why I don't mention sounds, only colours and shapes when I speak about Solovky. Because it is noiseless here, like in a dream. It is the kingdom of *bezmolviye*. Not literally, of course. Because the din here is annoying, too, and one would like to shelter somewhere in deep silence. But you can't hear either the internal voices of nature here or the internal human word. Everything here slips, as in a shadow theatre, and sounds come to you only from the outside. It is difficult to explain why there is no music of objects or of life here and I can't understand it myself. Only the surge of the sea and the whistling of the wind, these are the silence of Solovky." See also *hesychasm*.

Bich (abbreviation for: *bivshy intelligentny chelovek*): a former member of the intelligentsia. For example, a doctor of science working in a boiler room, a poet deported to a kolkhoz, etc. Just after the Revolution, clergy, aristocrats, officers, rich merchants, etc. were called *bivshye*. I found the following paragraph in Father Florensky of Solovky's letters: "These people should rather be called *bivshye intyeresnye* (formerly interesting) because they have grown grey and nondescript here, so that it is difficult to believe that they are the same people who used to be so important." Today, the name *bich* is given here to all sorts of riff-raff — poets, painters, philosophers and other jesters who work as seasonal gatherers of sea-grass or *skit* guards, and so on. See also *bomzh*.

Blatnaya muzika (or *fenya*): the slang of the criminal underworld. Likhachov, the last Mohican of the Solovetsky Geographic Society and today an eminent expert in Ancient Russian literature, researched *blatnaya muzika*. Likhachov landed up in SLON for his humorous paper entitled *Meditations on Ancient, Traditional, Consecrated, Historical Russian Orthography, Violated and Distorted by the Enemy of Christ's Church and of the Russian Nation.* Dmitry Sergeyevich became serious in SLON and undertook philological research in earnest, and his *Offenders' Card Games*, published in *Solovetskaya Ostrova* in 1930, is taken to be the scientific debut of the future academician. In the *zona*s of Solovky and the Belomorkanal, Likhachov collected excellent material for his work — today considered a classic — on the subject of *blatny* slang: *Characteristics of Original Primitivism in the Language of Thieves*, in which he tried, as a philologist, to find the traits of the *blatnaya* world. "Extraordinary expansiveness characterizes the words of a thief's language," he wrote, "and the words extend far beyond the offender's reality. And with them spreads the poison of a thief's ideology." In his *Solovky Notes*, published half a century later, Likhachov mentions two key-words both in the Soviet and the post-Soviet world, words first heard in SLON used by thieves: *blat* and *tufta*. *Blat* entered Russian prison slang from the Yiddish of the Odessa underworld where it was the equivalent of "palm", or our "deals", while *tufta*, meaning "sham", described work done for show. Dimitry Sergeyevich had his first lessons in *tufta* on the construction site of the Solovetsky narrow gauge rail track where the frozen earth had to be broken up with crowbars, and *zeka*s would lean against the bars pretending to smash the ice while, in fact, they were resting. In the 1930s, both words, together with the *zeka*s, filtered through to Belomorkanal and further, to all the labour camps in the Soviet Union, and finally came into everyday use in the free world.

Blyad': in today's Russian, the word fulfils the same role as "whore" in English. Variations of this include: the endearing *blya* or *blyakha*, and *blin*, which is used by youngsters. In ancient Slavonic − from which the Russian form derived − *blyad'* had two meanings which complemented each other. "*Ditya, ali ne razumeesh,*" Archpriest Avvakum taught in the 17th century, "*yako vsya siya vneshnaya blyad' nichto zhe sut', no tokmo prelest' i tlya, i poguba?*"* For the Archpriest, reality was, at one and the same time, both a whore and a lie, for the external world, he claimed, was in essence an enchantment (and deception, too), vanity and ruin. Sometimes, looking at boats reflected in the water or at stone paths leading to nowhere, I think that maybe Avvakum was right and my effort to describe Solovetskian reality is just another (verbal) labyrinth or empty mirror. To put it another way, I have the impression that I'm leading the reader on a wild goose chase and offering those who are curious about this world . . . *blyad'*.

---

* "Child, don't you understand that all this external *blyad'* matters nothing; it is only charm, decay and ruin." *Tr.*

Bomzh (abbreviation for: *bez opredyelonnovo myesta zhityelstva*) : a person without a fixed address, a vagabond, in the past called a *strannik*. The Russian *bomzh* is what remains of the "free man" in the sense of *voli volnoy*, that is ". . . freedom linked with space", according to Likhachov, "which is not limited by anything. In the past, just as today, a vagabond lost all status and didn't belong to any human community, but to "another world".

Dengi: money. The word *dengi* came to the Russian language from Tartaria, together with other financial terms, and is a vestige of the Mongolian tax system which, according to Heller, had no equivalent in feudal Europe. Today, *dengi* are like the icons of the new faith: capitalism *à la russe*. Indeed, just as unbelief could be turned, in Russia, into a religion and the leader of atheism could be embalmed and his remains, like *moshchy* (relics), idolized, so, after the loss of faith in socialism, it was in the natural order of things for the post-Soviet *khlyst*s to bow to the Antichrist — capitalism — and take to idolizing *dengi*. Note, too, that *dengi* is like a miracle: everybody talks about it but few ever see it . . . It is not by chance that Brat [Brother] is reading *Diary of a Writer* by Dostoevsky, who remonstrated against the new faith: "The people have begun to distort the ideal as never before and there is a widespread cult of materialism. I call materialism bowing one's head to the rouble, to the power of golden coins. As if the idea that the coin is everything, that it is all-powerful and that everything that had been said about it and taught by the fathers was nonsense, had suddenly got through to the people." And somewhat further on: ". . . the worship of free profit, pleasure without effort, has come about; every kind of swindle, every kind of crime is committed in cold blood; they kill just to grab a rouble from a pocket."

Der'mokratiya: instead of *demokratiya*, meaning: democracy. From the word *dyer'mo* — shit. This is how the Russian language adapts the concepts of the western world to Russian reality. See also *prikhvati-zatsiya*.

Glubinka: distant regions. Trains don't go that far, planes don't fly there, correspondents, whether Russian or *inostrantsy*, don't go there. Bearing in mind the immensity of Russia, one could say that its *glubinki* cover eighty-five per cent of the country. The lack of knowledge about what happens there has been the cause of many erroneous political prognoses made by experts on Russia from Harvard or Warsaw, who – one would have thought – knew Russia. Even the Russians themselves who live in Moscow have no idea how their kinsmen in Shoina, Moida or Taivenga live.

Gulyat': to revel. *Gulyat'*, in Russian, is to loaf about, and to have fun, to drink, and to prowl about the village, and to have it off with whores, and to get into fights. As early as the 12th century, the Bishop of Belgorod thundered from the pulpit at the Orthodox people: ". . . and they only consider a feast day to be a success when they are lying like dead, completely drunk, true imbeciles: agape but mute, eyes open but blind, and legs totally paralysed." N. Witsen, accompanying the ambassador of the Netherlands during his trip to Russia (1664–1665), wrote that they were not permitted to visit Moscow for a long time because "From Christmas to Epiphany, the Russians drink heavily and don't want to be disturbed."

Inok: a monk; from the ancient Slav *in'* meaning one, ". . . because night and day he talks to God in isolation," as Nikon Charnogorets describes the concept of *inok*. While the Archpriest Dyachenko, in his *Comprehensive Dictionary of Orthodox Church-Slavonic*, derives the word *inok* from *inoy* meaning other, different, ". . . because he ought to conduct his life in another way, differently from the people of this world".

Inostranets: foreigner. In Russia, as probably nowhere else, the *inostranets* feels an "outsider". The theme of Russian suspiciousness, spymania and a barely hidden aggression towards arrivals from foreign countries is repeated like a chorus in the memoirs, notes and travel journals of foreigners. I have frequently experienced it myself, especially in the so-called "Russian" *glubinka*, where it is enough for you to behave differently or have a different accent in order to arouse suspicion. No doubt the spirit of collectivism cannot bear anything that does not belong to its mass. It is worth noting that it is not so much your nationality, faith or language which determine whether you belong to the collective, as a common fate (cell, *zona*) and the same lord (lord-State). There are many nations and cultures in Russia, various languages, and more atheism than there are cults or sects, so it is not your nationality that arouses aversion here but the fact that you can leave here at any moment, and it is not your convictions or faith that are being judged, but the fact that you live according to your whims and observe life here from the side. One has to look into the etymology of the word *inostranets* in order to fully grasp its meaning. In fact, *strana* in ancient Slav, from which it made its way into Russian, means "side", and only later took on the meaning of country, while the word *inoy*, or "other", derived from the ancient Slav word *in'*, meaning "one" or "alone" (whence *inok*). And so *inostranets* is not only a foreigner, but someone from the other side – not ours! – someone who is singular, not like everybody else. An outsider.

Hesychasm: a Christian and mystical vision of the world combining religious and philosophical elements with spiritual and ascetic practice. It is being much spoken and written about here at present, especially in Orthodox circles. Here is an example: my notes from a conversation with Brat.

19 August

The Lord's Transfiguration – one of the most important Orthodox feast days, celebrated with particular care on the Islands, especially at the Spaso-Preobrazhensky monastery. The bells have been ringing since morning, their sound carrying far across the water. Brat came this afternoon, bringing with him a bottle of Moldavian Kagora wine and some dried bream. We discussed *hesychasm*, the mystical Orthodox doctrine which emerged on Mount Athos, in Greece, in the 14th century, although its roots reach back to the Egyptian wilderness of the 4th century AD. Grigory Palama, Grigory Sinayta, Nil Kabasilas . . . they all taught that it is not matter but energy which is the warp of life. Christ on the mountain of Tabor — according to the *hesychasts* — showed us the way: like a lens, He focused Light within Himself. Thanks to the practice of *bezmolviye* and specific techniques of prayer and meditation, the *hesychasts* achieved enlightenment, of which *Notes from a Cell* — a sort of spiritual journal kept in the cell by a precursor of the movement, Simeon the New Theologian — are a fascinating record. Later, the Orthodox faith often departed from *hesychasm*, believing it to be a heresy and considering it no more than "a contemplation of one's own navel and an art of withholding one's breath". Not so long ago even, Bulgakov wrote: "the nonsensical fantasies of the *hesychasts* about the possibility of achieving the incredible light will soon fall into oblivion." Meanwhile, *hesychasm* has not only not fallen into oblivion but is beginning to awaken an ever greater interest in the circles of an Orthodox faith which is enjoying a rebirth in Russia, of which recent publications on the subject give evidence. Here Brat gave me some titles . . .

". . . but don't you think it's just a fashion," I interrupted Brat, "like post-modernism in other intellectual circles. When I was in Moscow, I visited Sergey Khoruzhy, philosopher, mathematician and translator of Joyce. The reason for my visit was *Diptikh bezmolviye* / [Diptych of Silence], his book on *hesychasm*. Sergey Sergeyevich had just returned from St Petersburg, where there had been a scientific symposium on *bezmolviye*. For three days, they rattled on about silence! And the *Diptych* itself . . . is also nonsense. On the one hand, Khoruzhy writes about the necessity of returning to the source of Russian thought, that is the writings of the Holy Fathers, stating that 19th- and 20th-century Russian philosophy has been dominated by German idealism which is alien to the Orthodox spirit, while, on the other hand, he uses Martin Heidegger's terminology in order to interpret Palama's arguments. Palama warned: "He who discusses *bezmolviye* without experiencing sacred silence succumbs to madness."

"The problem is," said Brat, "that the elders of old, like Nil Sorsky, for example, who was one of the great Russian *hesychasts*, never inquired into *bezmolviye* by using words but only through practice, that is, through silence and prayer. Their brief remarks, which remind you of aphorisms, are only pointers, nothing more. Indications how to practise. In other words, they outlined with words the contours of that which cannot be expressed in words, like in some psychological test where the profile of one figure – shaded – marks the shape of another – empty. While the philosophers of today construct post-modernist puzzles, sinning by verbosity or trying to say something about . . . that which can't be put into words. And as long as they amuse themselves with gossip from the West, they will stew in their own sauce, but when they start to ramble on about *bezmolviye* they become both pitiable and laughable. As early as the 14th century, a certain monk from Calabria, Varlaam, tried to ridicule the practices of the *hesychasts* through speculative debates. In the West, the Calabrian monk was considered the father of the Renaissance, and in the East, a heretic and fraud. From Varlaam, speculative European thinking arrived at Kant and started to penetrate Russia. Philosophers of the so-called 'silver age', Merezhkovsky, Ivanov, Berdyaev, tried to grasp the Orthodox experience through a system of concepts borrowed from the Germans. Khoruzhy, on the other hand, while apparently rejecting their approach, in fact followed the same path. And, as a result, he drowned the essence of *bezmolviye* in empty prattle."

"I think," I interrupted, "that Wittgenstein would be far closer to the *hesychasts* although he was every inch a man of the West. Listen to what he wrote to his publisher, von Ficker, in 1914:

'. . . my work is made up of two parts: one you find here, and the other in all that I *haven't* written. And it's precisely that second part which is important.' Meaning that what is written should mark the boundaries of that which remains unspoken — that which is truly important. Wittgenstein's main argument goes: 'By stating clearly that which is expressible, you can indicate that which is inexpressible.' Isn't that close to *bezmolviye*?"

Silence falls. We take small sips of wine. Outside, a lapwing screams and the sea roars, and Brat nibbles on the bream and chews over the thought that someone from the West, and a philosopher-logician at that, can come close to Orthodox truths. Finally, he spoke.

"You see, Mar, *filo-sofia*, in Greek, is the love of wisdom. Meaning, obviously, the human reason. Which is basically fallible, short-lived and empty. While Orthodox asceticism, of which *hesychasm* is the most mature fruit, is *filo-kalos*, translated into Russian as *dobroto-lubye* meaning the love of beauty. (*Dobrota*, Beauty, is one of the names given to the Lord in ancient Slav.) Maybe that is why in Russia it is not philosophers but artists who more frequently touch upon the essence of being, starting with Andrey Rublyov and Theofan the Greek, great Russian *bezmolvnik*s of the 14th century, right up to Pushkin, Tyutchev, Tolstoy . . . In other words, silence is a higher form of art, a sort of creativity for which man himself is the raw material. Silence is the practice which the Orthodox East set against the theorizing of the West. Not *cogito ergo sum* but rather *sum* first and only then, and not necessarily at that, *cogito*. The scope of *cogito* is barely a fragment of reality, although it often claims to be the whole of it. *Bezmolviye* does away with the shell of discursive thought and allows one to go beyond the boundary which separates this rational fragment of our existence from Reality. Wittgenstein tried to mark this boundary with words, but the Orthodox monk crosses it in silence, leaving the chattering world behind."

"Well, as a philologist I can't accept such a radical rejection of the gift of language. The point lies in how to use it. Some people chat, others mumble, still others blab, and the world swells with gossip: they gabble on television, they gabble in newspapers and on the internet . . . There's a flood of words, mud, we're getting stuck! And here I agree with you – it's better to remain silent in isolation. Wittgenstein retired to Skolden, a fishing village in the north of Norway. Because language requires silence. This isn't a paradox, it's . . . experience. Sometimes I think that language is the best proof of the Creator's existence because everything exists in it: a blade of grass, a shade of the sky and the rustle of the forest, and a comma which can give life, and a full stop which closes the eyes for ever."

The bells for evening Mass rang out in the monastery. We finished our wine.

Kabak: a drinking-house. The word passed into the Russian language from Tatar in the 16th century. (Vodka appeared in Russia at the same time.) Ivan Pryzhov, the author of *History of Drinking-Houses in Russia*, writes that ". . . it's enough to follow, day by day, the emergence and development of national institutions, as we are trying to do with *kabak*, in order to discover that the Tatar world has left a mark on us not only by certain borrowed words, but also by the acceptance of the Tatar spirit itself, and that these words express the bestial characteristics of the wild hordes which have ousted our national customs". According to Pryzhov, the *kabak*, where vodka was drunk, replaced the Slav *korchma* [inn], where mead, wine and beer were drunk. Hence the translation of Esenin's *Moskva kabatskaya* as *The Moscow of Inns* is incorrect . . .

Kartoshka: potatoes. The example of *kartoshka* is the best illustration of why I introduce Russian words into the Polish text. A foreigner writing about Russia "translates" Russian reality into his own language. (I use the word "translate" in the Latin sense of *interpretor* – I clarify, understand, resolve.) But that reality exists within the Russian language – was taking form within it over centuries. In the past, the word *yazyk* used to mean both "tongue/language" and "the people" because it is in the language more than anywhere that the people are apparent – their spirit, existence, life. It took me two whole years of living in Russia to realize that a foreigner cannot understand this country if he thinks about it and judges it in his own tongue/language. Until, finally, I understood that Russian reality has to be learnt through the Russian language and only then, having lived here for some time so as to experience the words within myself, could I attempt to translate that experience into my own language. I was already in the process of writing when I noticed that certain Russian words, although having a Polish equivalent, speak of a different experience, a different world. The longer I live here, the more I trust key-words, sign-words, myth-words, which mean far more than can be gleaned from the word. *Kartoshka*, for example . . . For us, in Poland, it means a potato, something you serve up to accompany meat, and people say that it's fattening and it is being eaten less and less. While here, *kartoshka* is the mainstay food, a ritual and a way of life. In spring, *kartoshka* is planted, in summer dug up, in autumn gathered, and in winter one lives on . . . *kartoshka*. To translate *kartoshka* by potatoes is to take away its magical and life-giving sense, it is to translate/transfer reality itself (in the Latin sense *transfero*), or . . . to lose it in the process of translating.

Kelya: the Russian language differentiates between *kelya* in a monastery and *kamera* in a prison. Polish, like English, embraces this in one word: "cell". On Solovky, both Russian meanings merged to become a symbol of the Island which, until recently – until the invention of the aeroplane – was cut off from the world for eight months of the year. The history of Solovky is the history of the cell in both its meanings – they are intertwined as one thread in this multi-dimensional story. Obviously, the story of the Islands goes beyond the Russian cell, just as the history of Russia is barely an episode in the history of Solovky, although certainly the best-written episode. As did the history of Russia, that of Solovky arose in the cells of scribes.

Kormushka: ever since I arrived in Russia I have been hearing this word used in all sorts of situations, which allows one to assume various meanings. It is difficult to know what is what. The dictionary gives *kormushka* as a cattle manager or a bird tray. Colloquially, as in Polish, it is also used as "trough", meaning the source of considerable income, usually from public funds. In Russian history, on the other hand, it has an extremely rich tradition, it has grown into an entire system: the system of *kormleniye*. Kluchevsky writes: "In Rus, the word *kormleniye* was used for legal and administrative positions which gave the employees an income collected directly from the subjects. This income was called *korma*, which is the equivalent of present wages, hence the official position was called *kormleniya*." Already at the end of the 16th century, foreigners writing about Rus, like Fletcher for example, noted: ". . . that the Russian people hated administrators in the provinces, since their interests were fundamentally alien to them. These administrators, who changed every year, would arrive in the provinces fresh and hungry and would strip the people without any scruples so as to grab as much as they could for themselves and as gifts for their superiors, who closed their eyes to what was being done. The Russian people have long ago come to understand that administrators come to the provinces not so as to maintain order, but so as to strip them of their fleece – and not once a year, as owners fleece their sheep, but all the year round."

Ladan: church incense. In *Khozhdyenii igumena Danila* [*The Pilgrimages of Igumen Danil*] from the 12th century, the oldest Russian travel journal to the Holy Land, a description of how *ladan* is produced on the Greek island of Rhodes can be found: "Sap oozes from a tree called the hornbeam, which looks like an alder. This is taken off with a sharp iron. In another tree, which looks like an aspen, an insect as large as a caterpillar lies under the bark. The insect bores into the wood and wood-dust pours like wheat bran and falls to the ground as wild cherry glue. People gather this wood-dust, mix it with the sap of the first tree and boil it in pots, after which they pack it into sacks and sell it to merchants as ready incense."

Mat, matershchina: vulgar words, swearing. Russian *mat*, expressive and extremely rich, is a sort of language within a language, where one word can express . . . everything. I will never forget the most beautiful dawn on Troitsya Bay [Trinity Bay] on Anzer, where we arrived by yacht in the night. Everything was quiet, mute even, and there was a scent of fir trees, the sea glistened silver in the sun, an eagle was circling over Golgotha . . . suddenly Losha emerged from the hatch, stretched himself, squinted and exclaimed with rapture in his voice:

"*Yebat' moi ushi*!" [literally, "Fuck my ears!"]

Muzhik: a peasant. The word is more frequently used, especially in the provinces, to denote "one of ours" [lad], as opposed to outsiders, that is, all sorts of *chinovnik*s [state officials], visiting intellectuals, tourists, people from Moscow, etc. It also takes the place of our "sir" in phrases such as: "Hello, sir/*muzhik*, what's the time?" We read, in Heller's *History of the Russian Empire*: "Just as *obshchina*, both for Slavophiles as for lovers of the West, was a treasury of specific characteristics of the Russian people, so in the *muzhik* they saw the incarnation of the god-fearing people." Yury Chirkov, a former *zeka*, and author of a book about SLON called *And Everything Was So*, recalls his conversations with Sivov, a country priest who used to like discussing the subject of abolishing serfdom: "Freedom for the *muzhik*s has many aspects, everyone understands it in his own way. For one, freedom means sleeping day in day out by the stove, for another, it means taking care of his farm, for a third, it means stealing and drinking. So that liberation of the *muzhik*s from serfdom was the beginning of terrible drunkenness, banditry and disorder: if you want

— work, if you don't want to — don't. Nobody can be forced — freedom has been granted. There is only drinking and *gulyat'* left."

Obshchezhitie: literally: communal life, cohabitation; living together. Pavel Florensky saw the origins of the <u>precept</u> of *obshchezhitiye* in the Orthodox <u>concept</u> of the Holy Trinity, formulated by Sergey Radonyezhsky and Andrey Rublyov in the 14th century. "*Obshchezhityelstvo*," he wrote in 1918, "always marked a spiritual renewal, like at the beginning of Christianity. And the beginnings of Kiev Rus, just after the adoption of Christianity, were marked by *obshchezhitiya* whose centre was the Kiev-Pecherska Lavra (Monastery), and the beginning of Muscovite Rus, with its return to spiritual contemplation, was characterized by the introduction of *obshchezhityia* in the centre of the country, following the advice and with the blessing of declining Byzantium. The concept of *obshchezhityia* as cohabitation in complete love, likemindedness and economic community, whether it be called *koinonia* in Greek or *communio* in Latin (originally: *communism*), was always close to the Russian soul . . ."

Obshchina: community, commune. A collective form of Russian life in the country: the land belonged to *obshchina* and not to the individual farmer, and was worked by turns so that good and bad plots fell to everyone fairly. The main aim of the *obshchina*, according to Heller, was to safeguard perfect equality. Slavophiles saw, in the *obshchina*, a characteristic specific to Russia, an expression of its collectivistic spirit and of its love of equality.

Osolovely: dejected, morose or . . . not him/herself. Here, on the Islands, the word has taken on a new meaning (from the name of the Islands) and denotes a person who cannot live without Solovky. *Osolovely* — in the local language — means mad about Solovky, "Solovkysized", in other words: a Solovetsky madman. Not everybody, of course, goes crazy. Many come here (tourists, for example) in order to roam around, snap some photos, take films of the landscape, and disappear without trace. People like that don't get much from here: a couple of rolls of film, a video cassette, sometimes the clap. But there are also those who, having once visited, return over and over again, and dream about Solovky, and ramble on about Solovky, and finally remain on Solovky for good. These are said to be completely *osolovely* and even if they do tear themselves away from the Islands for a while, they have the White Sea in their eyes. And wherever else they may be, they will always be . . . *osolovely* (dejected). Not themselves.

Po blatu: "on the crook", between friends. See *blatnaya muzika*.

Podryasnika: a monastic garment, usually black, worn by novices until their ordination. Many wrongly take them to be *ryasa* – a monk's habit – from which it differs in that it has narrow sleeves.

Pomoika: rubbish dump, a hole for swill/dishwater. Here, in the North, it is difficult to know where to draw the line between *pomoika* and non-*pomoika*. This applies not only to ordinary refuse – bottles, tins, discarded bits of food and all sorts of rubbish, which is strewn wherever man can reach, but also industrial waste – used engine oil which is poured from boats straight on to the sandy beach, shipwrecks abandoned at sea, elements of rockets which have fallen after lift-off and lie scattered in the tundra, rusty tractors, unfinished constructions, etc. Nature in the North is too frail to neutralize all this on its own. There are people who say that the Solovetsky Islands themselves are a vestige of the Great Rubbish Bin. Pavel Florensky, in his letters from Solovky, often repeats that everything here is accidental: people thrown here by the wind of history, and stones carried down by a glacier, and plants transplanted from a different climate . . .

Poslushnik: a novice in a monastery. Derived from *poslushaniye*, meaning "obedience", the first quality of one aspiring to monkhood. In the lives of saints, you frequently come across absurd tasks which the *starets*es set *poslushnik*s such as, for example, carrying water from a pond to a river and back again or planting plants with their roots facing upwards. All this was in order to break the spirit of pride (and faith in one's own reason!) – which was Lucifer's sin. Yury Chirkov recalls similar jobs during the days of SLON, for example, one *zeka* was ordered to dig a hole, then another to fill it in, ". . . so that they got to understand more quickly that they hadn't come here to visit their auntie and eat *bliny*". Or they forced *zeka*s to pour water from one hole cut in ice into another, then measured the level of the water and cut food rations because the norm hadn't been met. The fashion on the Islands today is *poslushaniye* of lay people who live outside of the monastery yet remain in close contact with their spiritual father. Such *poslushaniye* often brings specific material gains. You can, for example, ask your dear father for a "blessing" on your journey in the form of money for a ticket.

Prikhvatizatsiya: instead of *privatizatsiya*, from the word *prikhvatit'* – to gather, steal, take what doesn't belong to anyone. *Prikhvatizatsiya* is an example of how the Russian language, flexible and vivid, with the help of one or two consonants changes concepts belonging to the western world and bestows them with its own Russian meaning. See also *der'mokratsya*.

Pustyn': hermitage. A place of isolated prayer, often in a forest, in the marshes, far from human settlement. A particular type of Russian anchoritism which in a way was created as a reaction to the rich monasteries, usually entangled in lay intrigues and political dealings. Frequently, monks would gather around a particularly pious *pustynnik*, attracted by his fame, and with the passage of time the silent *pustyn'* would be transformed into a swarming monastic *obshchezhitoye*. The history of the Solovetsky monastery, which was created at the place where the *pustynnik* Savvaty prayed, is an example of such a meta-morphosis. The painter, Nesterov, visiting the Islands in 1901, wrote to a friend: "I'm sending you these few sentences from the Solovetsky monastery. I found interesting and peculiar things here and I have the impression that I have already seen this in a dream and put it across in my first paintings, in certain sketches. The type of monk here is new, to be sure, but I intuited the landscape in *The Hermit*."

Reket: a new Russian word, created from the English "rake" / "to rake", and used to denote the old Russian practice of . . . pillage.

Severnoye siyanie: the aurora borealis, the Northern Lights. An extraordinary luminous phenomenon which appears in the Northern skies, generally in autumn or in winter. Of the descriptions which I have read, the best is that of Father Florensky in his letters from Solovky. On 7 January, 1937, the day before his fifty-fifth (and last) birthday, Pavel Alexandrovich wrote to his son, Vasya: "Today was a special day – the sky grew bright, it was freezing. Towards evening, the Northern Lights played out. At about seven in the evening, in the northern part of the sky, there appeared a bluish luminous segment which reminded you of the radiance of a rising moon, only it was brighter and more clearly defined. This segment rose above the horizon, ever more brilliant in the north-easterly part of the heavens. Suddenly, concentric arcs, the same bluish colour, started to fall away from it, across the entire breadth of the sky. Or, to be more precise, the segment itself was as if made up of arcs and now, in front of my eyes, was falling apart. Then it grew darker, became blacker than the rest of the sky and a brilliant halo of light encircled it. On the side of the segment, the halo was clear cut, on the outside it gradually merged into the sky. Incidentally, the sky is not black during the Northern Lights, but shines like a spilt Milky Way. After a certain time, these arcs, pulsating in the sky, started to break up at the zenith creating a sort of luminous tent and one could see, demonstratively and convincingly, that its columns were nothing other than torrents of energy tearing away into the atmosphere – streams of corpuscles, which were lighting up the rarefied gas. The columns shimmered with the intensity of light and changed places in the sky. Then in the north-east, next to the bluish bands, a vast and intensive light the colour of raspberries, as if a weightless and transparent cloud, appeared. The lights began to shimmer and change places even quicker, like lightning, until they fell apart into flat, luminous clouds, raised at the edges, which stretched to the ground as if they were curtains of light, and draped into picturesque folds, rippling whimsically. Their tubular structure made one think of pleated material; its green glow gradually disappeared upwards, but grew thicker downwards, to be suddenly cut off. The curtains rose and fell as if swaying in the wind, ripples ran through them again and again and the whole picture kept changing. All at once, at the very edge of the green brilliance, an orange hem appeared — a red-orange like the halo of a fire. The ripples came even faster. Some ripples swelled, others vanished . . . and the upper part of the curtain disappeared while the lower part writhed like a luminous snake. This whole spectacle was played out on the northern part of the heavens up to the zenith, and from the west to the east, although it was stronger and brighter in the east. It lasted about two hours. Then it began to die down. The curtains fell apart in shreds, the light paled. At half past one in the morning, I went out to have a look at the sky one last time. In the north, masses of brilliance swirled, similar to clouds around the moon, but they were lit up from within. And because the sky had already grown darker, their brilliance was particularly distinct."

Shilo: (literally: awl) industrial spirit/alcohol, used to clean engines, rails, etc. Drunk in one draught, it stabs the brain like an awl — hence the name. Then it pours white light through the veins and stupefies for some time, holding the drinker in mute rapture like cocaine.

Skit: a sort of isolated hermitage where a small number of monks live in prayer and work. It is something between anchoritism and monastic life. The father of the Russian *skit* was Nil Sorsky (1433–1508), ordained a monk at the Kirillo-Belozersky monastery, one of the more famous scribes of his time and author of *The Rule of the Skit*. He lived on Mount Athos for a number of years and from there brought *hesychasm* to Rus. He was the chief advocate of the so-called "*starets*es from beyond the Volga" who opposed the opulence of monasteries. In his *Testament*, he asked that his body be left to wild animals to eat. See also *pustyn'*.

Stakan: a glass; a measure of vodka drunk in one draught.

Stopka: a small glass; a measure of vodka drunk in one gulp.

Tropa: path. The Russian *tropa* brings together the wolf's[*] tracks and metaphor — the tracks with the trope. Or, to put it another way, the singularity of one's path in life with one's style of writing. Varlam Shalamov best grasped this in his story entitled *Tropa* [The Path], which I quote here in its entirety.

Varlam Shalamov
TROPA

In the taiga, I had my own wonderful path. I trod it down myself, in the summer, when I collected firewood for winter. There was a fair amount of deadwood around the cabin — cone-shaped larches, grey like *papier mâché*, were embedded, like stakes, in the marsh. The cabin stood on a hill, surrounded by low bushes with bushes of green needles. In autumn, the cones would swell with nuts and bend the branches to the ground. My path ran through this brushwood towards the marshes. Once, before the marshes became marshes, a forest grew there, then the roots rotted in the water and the trees died — a long, long time ago. The route taken by cars and people followed the other side of the mountain.

For the first few days, I felt it a pity to tread the fleshy red lilies-of-the valley, and the irises like great butterflies both in their petals and in their pattern, and the huge snowdrops crunched unpleasantly under-foot. Flowers in the Far North have no fragrance. At first, I used to catch myself automatically picking a bunch and bringing it up to my nose. Then, I stopped. Every morning, I would look to see what had happened along the path during the night. There, a lily-of-the-valley, crushed by my boot the previous day, had risen, crooked to be sure, but alive while another lay squashed for ever, like a toppled telegraph pole

---

[*]An allusion to the author's name, Wilk, which, in Polish, means "wolf". *Tr.*

with porcelain insulators, and the tangled fibres hung like torn cables.

Then the path became beaten down and I stopped paying attention to the tree's branches which grew across my path; I broke away those that swiped me across the face. On each side, stood young larches, a hundred years old at the most. They turned green in my presence and, in my presence, lost their needles. The path grew darker with each day until it became an ordinary mountain path. Nobody, apart from me, used it. Only grey squirrels jumped around; sometimes I would find the Egyptian hieroglyphics of partridges or the triangular traces of a hare. But birds and animals don't count.

I followed this path for three years. It was a good place to write poems. I would return from a journey, follow the path and unfailingly walk away with a verse. I grew used to my path, to my forest study-workshop. Usually frost caught the mud before winter and it appeared to shrink, like sugar-crystallized jam. On two consecutive autumns, I would arrive before the snow so as to leave deep tracks which would harden in front of my eyes for the entire winter. And in the spring, when the snow melted, I would find the previous year's footprints, I would put my feet in the old tracks and the poems would again come to me easily. In the winter, obviously, my study would be empty: cold does not permit thought, one can only write in the warmth. In the summer, on the other hand, everything became colourful; I knew every detail of my magical path by heart – the low spreading bush, the larches, the bushes of wild roses reminded me of someone else's poems, and if there weren't enough of these verses, I would mumble my own. Then, returning to my cabin, I would write them down.

The third year, somebody followed my path. I wasn't around then, so I don't know: maybe a roaming geologist, maybe a postman on foot, maybe a hunter. The person left heavy boot prints. From that time, poems stopped coming to me along the path. The stranger's prints appeared in spring, and throughout the entire summer I did not write a single line there. I was transferred elsewhere in winter and I did not regret it because the path was irretrievably spoiled anyway.

I have often tried to write a poem about that path but I have never managed it.

Vor v zakone: literally: a thief within the law. A crook who abides by the laws of the criminal underworld.

Zeka: (an abbreviation: *zaklyuchonny, z/k*) – a prisoner. The forms: *zek,'zeki* . . ., which Shalamov, in his letter to Solzhenitsyn (November, 1962), considers as incorrect, often appear in literature.

Zona: a zone; enclosure. In Dal's *Dictionary*: "a strip of land, a belt of the globe along the equator". It is the labour camps which gave the word *zona* its sinister meaning. Rossi distinguishes between several kinds of *zona*s, depending on their purpose (for example, the female *zona*, the working *zona* . . .), the kind of fencing, etc. With time, the concept of the *zona* passed from the world of the labour camp into general use and today it establishes the living space of obedient citizens here. Or, more accurately, it divides this space into *zona*s of different forms and types: *opasnaya zona* (dangerous zone), *pogranzona zona* (border zone), *zakritaya zona* (forbidden zone), *zona osobovo naznachenia* (special purpose zone), *zona osobovo rezhima* (special regime zone), etc. Tarkovsky, in his film *Stalker*, gave us a philosophical commentary on the *zona*.